TAIL OF THE STORM

TAIL OF THE STORM

Alan Cockrell

With Illustrations by
MSgt Walter E. Sistrunk, Jr., ANG

THE UNIVERSITY OF ALABAMA PRESS
TUSCALOOSA AND LONDON

Library of Congress Cataloging-in-Publication Data

Cockrell, Alan, 1949–
     Tail of the storm / Alan Cockrell ; with illustrations by Walter E. Sistrunk, Jr.
     p.   cm.
     ISBN 0-8173-0772-9 (alk. paper)
     1. Persian Gulf War, 1991—Personal narratives.   2. Persian Gulf War, 1991—Aerial
operations, American.   3.   Cockrell, Alan, 1949–
     I. Title.
DS79.74.C62   1995
956.704'4248'092—dc20
     [B]
                                                                                    94-26404
          British Library Cataloguing-in-Publication Data available

For Eleanor,
She Who Deserves Better.

Dedicated to
those who flew or served
in the Tail of the Storm.
Finally, their story is told.

A pilot's business is with the wind,
with the stars,
with the night,
with the sand,
with the sea.
He strives to outwit the forces of nature.
He stares in expectancy of the dawn
the way a gardener awaits the coming of spring.
He looks forward to port as a promised land,
and truth for him is what lives in the stars.

Antoine de Saint-Exupéry,
Wind, Sand, and Stars (1939)

CONTENTS

Acknowledgments ♦ xi

Prologue ♦ xiii

1. The White Snakes ♦ 1

2. The Talon's Spell ♦ 19

3. The TJ Blues ♦ 37

4. Downrange ♦ 48

5. Troubled Skies ♦ 63

6. Zaragoza ♦ 85

7. Pain of a Different Death ♦ 94

8. The Probable Cause ♦ 106

9. Bernoulli Baptism ♦ 113

10. Maiden Flight ♦ 122

11. My Kind of Fliers ♦ 128

12. Herculean Dreams ♦ 137

13. Eye of the Storm ♦ 151

14. Dawn Patrol ♦ 164

15. Face of the Bear ♦ 174

16. Crew Unrest ♦ 180

17. Master Caution (Push to Reset) ♦ 192

18. In Lindbergh's Prop Wash ♦ 203

Epilogue ♦ 224

Glossary ♦ 227

ACKNOWLEDGMENTS

Thanks to Mary Cockrell, my beloved sister-in-law and dispassionate counselor, whose help in putting the manuscript in final form was invaluable. I also thank Walter Sistrunk, Jr., for preparing the illustrations.

Quotations of Antoine de Saint-Exupéry that appear on page vii and at the beginning of chapter 7 are taken from *Wind, Sand, and Stars* (New York: Reynal & Hitchcock, 1939), pp. 43 and 227.

In chapter 18, Charles Lindbergh is quoted from *Spirit of St. Louis* (New York: Charles Scribner's Sons, 1953), pp. 301, 289, 296, and 302.

PROLOGUE

Some walls in the house were bare and in dire need of decoration, so we went out on a rare spending spree. But before going we made an agreement. I would pick out a painting that suited my fancy, and she would choose one to her liking. We would not judge one another's selections. Mine would hang in the study, hers in the bedroom.

Almost immediately I spotted mine from a distance. It was a bold painting of a magnificent three-masted bark running before the wind, sails billowing, seas breaking across her decks. Just standing there, staring at it, made you smell salt spray and hear the wind howling through the rigging. Yes, that was for me. The painting glowed with visions of adventure, challenge, and discovery.

She continued to browse while my painting was matted and framed. Then she made her selection. It was done almost entirely in subtly contrasting shades of her favorite color, lavender. A lady, dressed in a flowing, wind-blown gown stood at the shore, her back to the viewer, and in the distance—sails. "This is me," she proclaimed, with her characteristic lopsided smile and a subtle sigh. "I'm she who waits."

I had voyaged in and out of her life for seventeen years on vessels borne not by sails but by wings. The first time I had departed for the west and an odious, petering war. Not long after we hung the paintings, I left her on the shore again and flew east toward a gathering storm.

ONE

THE WHITE SNAKES

Our birth is but a sleep and a forgetting:
The soul that rises with us, our life's star. . . .
But trailing clouds of glory do we come.
—William Wordsworth,
Intimations of Immortality

Something bizarre is being born out there. An embryonic gray-ish white snake, gnarled and pulsating, twists and grows in the stratospheric hurricanes, then billows into an enormous caterpillar. A long, pointed snout emerges and approaches, imperceptibly at first but then gathers momentum and rockets inexo-rably toward us, its grotesque body billowing and boiling behind it.

A small arrowhead shape materializes at the point of the tentacle. Growing vestiges of wings, tail, and engines, it flashes underneath us at a closure speed equal to that of the turning Earth. And we fly on-ward above the wisps and boils of the dying snake, watching as the bluish gray expanse ahead gives birth to yet another white serpent.

On the cloud deck far below is the stain of a long comet on the satin surface. It's the shadow of our own tentacle. At the point is a nucleus—which is us—crowned with a rainbowlike halo cast by the refraction of the sun's rays around the aircraft. I've noticed at times, when the shadow is nearer, that the center of the halo is the plane's cockpit. I stare at it like a child spellbound before an aquarium.

And I chew absentmindedly at the hole. I'm one of the few heavy jet pilots who still wear gloves—a habit, I suppose, from my fighter pilot

days. My right nomex flight glove has a hole in it on the index finger, where I fiddle incessantly with the sharp-edged autopilot controller. I need a new pair, but I like the feel of my old ones. This cockpit fits me like the gloves. It's old but warm and familiar. The seats and upholstery are frayed, like my gloves. The instrument panels and consoles are caked with the paint of countless brushes. I'm surrounded by the switchology and instrumentation of a twenty-five-year-old technology.

Yet, strangely, I sometimes feel like a nineteenth-century citizen cast in a futuristic dream, like a sojourner from the past living out a fantasy. I must have plowed up a magic bottle in a Pickens County cornfield and asked the genie inside to give me wings; to send me to some future world of adventure and excitement. And the genie said I had much to learn if I thought such things were the keys to contentment. Nevertheless, he would make it so.

I clearly remember Dave "Pink" Floyd's sobering remark that morning nine months ago. He was signing a hand receipt and holstering a .38 caliber revolver. The subject of a nearby conversation—one of many in the buzzing operations room—was the latest news release. Iraqi forces were steadily flowing south into Kuwait. The Saudi oil fields were in dire jeopardy, and the president had announced additional call-ups from the Air Reserve forces. The bell had tolled for us less than twenty-four hours ago.

Pocketing his twelve rounds of ball ammunition (the Geneva Convention had outlawed hollow points), he interrupted the conversation.

"This sounds like . . ." The talk stopped. Heads turned toward him. "Like . . . Armageddon."

There weren't many biblical scholars in the room, but there were a lot of believers. A couple of people uttered affirmations.

I was still having trouble believing it was happening. Peace was supposed to be "breaking out all over," right? That was the fashionable phrase of the time. I had foolishly said as much myself to a large audience at Calloway High School just a few weeks ago, while awarding an Air Force Academy appointment to a graduate. Now I was hoping no one there remembered the faddish remark.

The call-up was no surprise—we had known for about two weeks that it would be coming. The Pentagon had planned to deploy several divisions of troops to the Persian Gulf area, and we knew, given the current level of airlift capacity, it would take thirty days to move just one division. Obviously, we were indispensable to the unfolding events 7,000 miles away. We all began to tie up the loose ends in our personal lives before the official word came. I had just returned home from a four-day trip with my airline job and called the Guard base right away. "What's going on?" I asked the flight scheduler. "Do you think we'll be called up?" His answer was immediate and business-like.

"You were next on my list to call. We're activated. Be here at 0900 tomorrow morning."

It was five minutes before nine, and the crowd of crew members and support personnel began to flow toward the large theater-style briefing room next door. I walked down the aisle, found the row with my name taped to it, and slipped in beside the men who would be my crew for the next six weeks. I sat down beside First Lieutenant Robert "Bones" Maloney. He had recently graduated from the University of Southern Mississippi and for the time being was Guard bumming until he could build enough hours to get an airline job. I hardly knew Bones and had never flown with him before.

Next to him was Master Sergeant Brian Wigonton from Haleyville, Alabama. Brian was a veteran jet mechanic from the active Air Force and had checked out as a flight engineer since joining the Guard. I reached across Brian and greeted the other engineer, Technical Sergeant Walt Chapman, the avid hunter from Meridian. Brian was older than Walt, but they complemented each other well and preferred flying together. I was tremendously glad to see them on my crew. Two good engineers would be a great asset and would make life much easier and would maybe even greatly prolong it. Sitting beyond Walt were Sergeants Jack Brown and Mike Gandy, the loadmasters.

In a few minutes Captain Jeff Carter, the first pilot, squeezed by and sat down, completing our crew. He worked hard managing his laundry business in Jackson and was worried about how an extended absence would affect it. There was no one else who could effectively take over.

Being in the Guard had always been a risk to Jeff. If something like this ever happened, he could lose the business that had been handed down in his family for generations. This crisis had to end quickly or he was in trouble.

After some opening remarks in which Lieutenant Colonel Bill Lutz, a lawyer until today, welcomed us to the "longest UTA in history," we began our inprocessing. They checked our emergency notification files for currency. They issued us green cards to replace our red identification cards, so that we were indistinguishable from regular Air Force personnel. We filled out forms, registering our families in government military medical programs. They checked our immunization records and medical files. We ragged and bantered with a few unlucky ones who, grimacing, were found delinquent and were pulled aside for shots.

The intell people made us review and initial our SAR cards. The cards were made primarily for fighter pilots, but just in case we crash-landed our behemoth jet in enemy territory and survived, the rescuers needed some way to establish our true identity via radio before coming for us. Bitter lessons were learned in Viet Nam when English-speaking enemy soldiers seized the survival radios of downed airmen and lay in wait for the rescue helicopters. According to plan, the cards would contain questions that the rescuers would ask of us. They were personal questions that we each had listed and would answer by way of survival radio. I don't remember all of the ones I listed. One was "what color was your first car?" I had listed fire engine red, but that was unacceptable. They said that I would probably not remember it under stressful conditions. I shortened it to just red, and they accepted it.

Then they checked our dog tags. "Is this all current?" the clerk asked. I looked at them.

> Alan H. Cockrell
> 523-70-3180
> 20 July 49
> B-Positive
> Southern Baptist

"Hey, man, what could have changed?" I asked.

"Well, you could have converted to Islam, maybe. . . . Get outta here."

At the next table a military lawyer offered to write up a will on the spot, but I told him I had one. I did sign a power of attorney, though.

The chaplain told us he was available for counseling and offered Bibles, but I had one of those already, too.

Finally, we filed into the big briefing room again for the chemical warfare briefing. When it began, the huge room fell quiet. We had sleepily sat through countless routine training classes over the years, but this was different. This time our attention was riveted on the briefer. Saddam had chemicals and had used them against some of his own people. He could use missiles, aircraft, or artillery to deliver the sinister gasses. Now, for the first time since chemical warfare training had been introduced years ago, we paid attention.

Plastic zip-lock bags were passed out to each of us. I knew what they contained, and a ripple of foreboding swept through me. I thought of my kids. I wanted to drop the bag with its repulsive contents on the floor and kick it away. But I opened it and pulled out each item as the briefer instructed.

First was a packet of twenty-one pyridostigmine bromine tablets. Under the label was the note "Nerve Agent Pretreatment Tablets." The written directions were ominous.

Directions for use:
1. Commence taking only when instructed by your commander.
2. Take only every 8 hours.
3. *It is dangerous to exceed the stated dose.*

Next was the nerve agent antidote. The briefer continued. "You have been issued three injectors of atropine and three injectors of 2-PAM chloride. You will self-administer this only [he emphasized "only"] after exposure to nerve agents to counter their deadly effects. Injections are made through your clothes into a large muscle in the outer thigh or in the upper buttock." He simulated giving himself an injection. The situation in the Middle East had caused an abrupt attitude adjustment among us. No longer did the thought of giving ourselves these shots seem so repulsive. Nerve gas causes an ugly death.

The victim's mouth foams, his body convulses, and he jerks and quivers, like a fish out of water, until sweet death intervenes.

The green injectors read "ATROPINE INJECTION, 2 mg. For use in nerve gas poisoning only." The second, fatter syringe read "PRALIDOXIME CHLORIDE INJECTION, 300 mg, for use in nerve agent poisoning only." I wanted to ask what would happen to us if we injected the stuff prematurely or by mistake, but I thought the better of it.

All the while, as I listened, questions fell through the cracks in the floor of logic and reality somewhere high above my head. This scene had to be a bad dream. The things this guy was saying didn't happen to real folks, let alone me. Why was I really there anyway? I blew off the standard old answers. Duty is as inherent in me as a bodily organ, and patriotism is the fuel that sustains it, but the real reason I was there was categorically selfish: I'm driven by a passion to fly airplanes. But was this the price? The atropine became a symbol of all the absurdity and wickedness in the world, and yet without it I probably would never have been able to pursue and capture this dream of jet flight.

Next was the protective suit demonstration. Our suits were at that moment being loaded on the aircraft. The suits, known in military jargon as the "aircrew ensemble," consisted of numerous items each of which had to be put on, or donned, as they more often said, in a specific sequence. It was important to protect the whole body if possible because chemicals could come in the form of liquid droplets as well as gas. One drop on the skin could be fatal.

First you put on one of two pairs of cotton long johns, followed by a pair of cotton gloves and tube socks. Next you put on plastic bags over your socks. Then you stepped into one of two pairs of the charcoal fiber coveralls. They feel like coarse, fibrous wool, with a texture that makes your skin crawl, and they cook you in heat, both absorbed and retained. They were good for fifty hours wear time, after which they lost their impermeability and had to be discarded. The gloves and plastic bags were then taped to the coveralls with masking tape to make an airtight seal. Next you donned the standard issue USAF nomex flight suit over the charcoal suit, followed by the usual flight boots. After that, you pulled on rubber gloves over

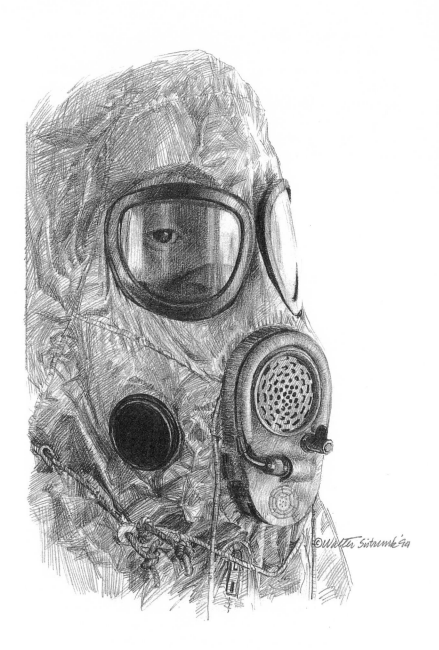

the cotton ones and standard issue USAF nomex flight gloves over those. By then your hand was so stiff that it was almost useless. Next you strapped an air filter pack to your side and adjusted it. It had an outlet that plugged into the aircraft's oxygen system and another that plugged into your mask.

Finally the brain bucket came on. We each had a custom-fitted USAF helmet to which was attached a chemical warfare protective mask. The mask was not specifically designed to be worn independently of the helmet, nor was it intended to be worn alone, for example when we were outside the aircraft. No one ever expected us to need it for that. A totally different kind of mask was available to soldiers and ground service personnel but was not issued to us. Our masks, unlike the ground masks, were awkward because you couldn't make yourself heard from them by shouting. Unless you were plugged into an aircraft interphone system, communication was almost impossible.

Once the helmet was on, a large plastic hood spread over the helmet and shoulders with an opening around the mask. Last we wore two ghastly large transparent plastic bags that covered our entire bodies. I had worn the complete suit in an exercise the previous year and did not relish the thought of putting it on again.

The suits were very impractical. A practiced person needed about twenty minutes to put on the whole outfit with the help of a buddy. The whole concept was designed for use in flying in a known chemical environment where you had plenty of advance warning. But it was almost useless for no-notice alerts. The gear, already sized and customized to fit each individual, was packed into huge, cumbersome rubber bags weighing about forty pounds each that were tied at the top. To be carried they had to be toted the way a drifter bore all his belongings in a gunny sack, slung over the shoulder or heaved with a fisted hand. We suspected the sack was about to become our constant but loathed companion, yet few of us realized that it foretold perilous times ahead.

Finally, Day One ended and we went home to a last night with our families.

The Charles Sullivan Air National Base, located among the tall pines on the north side of the Jackson, Mississippi, International Airport, was a madhouse on the morning of Day Two. Under the watchful and wet eyes of our loved ones, we made ready for bag drag number one.

Our chemical sacks were loaded for us on the aircraft by the unit's Aerial Port personnel. This was the last time anything would be carried for us. We picked up our chemical gear and revolvers and bullets and were told to be discreet about having them. The roving newsmen and cameras might get wind of our defensive gear—and we didn't want to alarm the American public, now did we?

Joining our chem sacks was a host of other bags and containers which we had to carry. We each had a main bag, usually a government issue B-4 bag weighing fifty to eighty pounds packed with personal gear. Our helmet bag contained not a helmet but a communications headset, checklists, gloves, a flashlight, and various other trappings of long-range fliers. Some of them weighed ten or twenty pounds.

Then there were the individual flight kits, fat briefcases into which was stuffed the literature of military flight: The "Dash-1," which was everything you ever wanted to know about the C-141 and more, much more; the "Dash-1/Dash-1," which contained the C-141 performance charts and test data; Air Force Regulation 55-141, which described down to a gnat's hair the science of flying C-141s the Air Force way; Air Force Regulation 60-16, the science of flying anything the Air Force way; Air Force Manual 51-37, the instrument flying handbook; Air Force Manual 51-12, the weather manual.

Along with the flight kit each crewman had a personal bag, which I called a survival kit. It could be placed beside his seat for easy reach. Everyone's kit was different, built to suit individual tastes, but the kits were necessary for the maintenance of our sanity. Mine was a blue fabric bag with an abundance of zippered compartments containing some essential trappings: binoculars; a camera; a Sony Walkman with microspeakers that would fit neatly inside my headset; extra batteries; a collection of tapes with the music of Phil Collins, Tinita Tikeram, the Moody Blues, Alabama, and songs of the Civil War; three books—the Bible and *Major British Poets,* both mainstays, and a techno-thriller of some sort; a plastic bottle of distilled water to stave off dehydration in the plane's super-dry atmosphere; and an assortment of munchables.

Then there were the communal bags. Each crew carried a "trip kit," another fat briefcase containing various regulations and reams of forms and paperwork: per diem vouchers; noncontract fuel purchase, forms 1801 and 175 for filing flight plans; aircraft commander's reports on facilities and crew members; forms, forms, and more forms—and requisition forms for forms.

And then there was that most essential of burdensome items, the crew cooler, cumbersome though it was. It was not an official item; it was the personal property of some member of the crew and would be stocked with ice and various foods and liquids. The cooler's owner would normally be responsible for keeping it stocked, for which he would assess fees, but it usually stayed in his room on crew rests.

The "black bag" was one that got special care, for it held our duty orders, mission itinerary, and flight-planning documents such as the C-141 fuel-planning manual, plus various plotting charts and devices. We also carried in it secret material that was issued. The bag bulged with mission paperwork when we flew. It was not an issued item—we bought ours in a base exchange store—but it served its organizational purpose well and caught on among the crews. I appointed Bones to carry it and guard it with his life.

Finally there was the gun box. It was a large ammunition container in which we stowed our pistols and bullets when we were not flying. The loadmaster toted the box and saw that it was registered and stored with the security police at our rest stops.

We were to move this mountain of material about 500 times in the coming year: rooms to bus, bus to plane, plane to bus, bus to rooms. The cycle repeated itself again and again. In the burning desert heat we heaved and lugged. In the gray English drizzle we lifted and shuttled. In the New Jersey snow we tossed and caught. In the wee hours of a Spanish morning we formed conveyer lines and moved the bags from bus to ramp, then from ramp to plane. All hands pitched in, officers and airmen alike. There was no special status or privileges here. Everyone's bags belonged to all of us.

Occasionally, through the years of Guard flying, new lieutenants not yet wise to crew life and swelled with the pomp of shiny new wings and bars would carry only their own belongings or worse yet would expect the enlisted crew to carry their gear for them. Such expectations were quickly banished. One dapper young officer began to wonder after a few days why his B-4 bag seemed so heavy. His crewmates elbowed each other and snickered as they watched him heave, grunt, and grimace for several days—until at last he opened a zippered side compartment and dug down, discovering a 10,000-pound-test-strength tie-down chain coiled beneath his dirty underwear. Message received.

Any bag would eventually be ignored if it proved excessively heavy. Jeff had brought along what became known as the Bag from Hell. It was back-cracking heavy, and after a while most of us wouldn't pick it up. Jeff got the message and downloaded it at the first opportunity.

Traveling light had become a priority and an art for us, but it was to become even more so in the coming months. And after the bags were loaded, there was always the "laying on of the hands" ceremony—we had practiced this for years. You were foolhardy if you didn't at least see, or better yet touch, your belongings to make sure they had come on board. In the not-too-distant future, Pink Floyd, getting his jet ready to fly, would be in too much of a hurry to observe the laying-on ceremony. His 141 would thunder away for a ten-day mission with his B-4 bag containing all of his personal gear sitting on a New Jersey ramp. And there it would sit like a lonely sentinel—a symbol of Pink's impending misery, pointed to and guffawed at by heartless mechanics.

Bags quickly became a great drag on our morale, for whenever we moved them we were reminded that we were perpetual itinerants, and every time we heaved, not a one of us would cease to wonder how long this wandering would go on. Even after hours of crew rest, the bag drag depleted our energy and sucked our spirit. Five hundred times we did it, give or take a few: 100,000 pounds' worth of bag drags.

It was big coverage for the press. We and a Reserve C-141 outfit in Maryland were the first to be activated. Reporters stuck microphones and cameras in our faces and asked ridiculous questions. "How long do you think you will be gone?" "Did you ever think this could happen?" "What does your wife think about your going?" The governor said some words, and a few generals from headquarters shook our hands. We kissed our wives, performed bag drag number one, and roared away, seventy or eighty of us, all on one plane—the other planes were gone already. We were headed for Charleston Air Force Base, South Carolina, where we would be split into crews and would be given different orders. The two pilots at the controls had been a stockbroker and an accountant until today. We trusted them completely as they sucked up the gear, accelerated out over the Pearl River, and rolled into the eastern skies. We plugged our ears, leaned back in the red webbed bench seats, and dozed off, confident that this thing would blow over and we'd be home by Thanksgiving.

The Desert Storm airlift was such a monumental operation that someone decided to ask a computer to explain the immense magnitude of it in terms a carbon-based unit could comprehend. It told us that we airlifted the equivalent of the entire population of Oklahoma City (450,000 carbon-based units) plus all of its vehicles and all its household goods—every pot, pan, pillow, television, refrigerator, everything—one-third of the way around the world in less than 180 days. The Berlin airlift—valiant though it was—paled in comparison.

The air route to the desert resembled a great wishbone. The upper stem of the wishbone took Slim Lindbergh's old course from North America up across Newfoundland, near the southern tip of Greenland, and ran south of Iceland and across Great Britain into the German staging bases. From Germany it snaked down through France, carefully avoiding overflight of neutral Switzerland, and moved on to the boot of Italy.

The lower stem of the bone took a more southerly route across the Atlantic. It went just north of Bermuda and the Azores and across Portugal into the staging bases of central Spain. From there it crossed Barcelona and Sardinia, joining the upper stem in southern Italy.

From the boot, where the two stems joined, the route ran east by southeast just below Greece and took a right turn over the island of Crete. It "coasted in" to the African mainland at a place called El Daba on the Egyptian coast, just west of Alexandria. The Egyptians insisted that all of the immense volume of air traffic converging on the Persian Gulf enter and depart across El Daba. We didn't know why. It was to become a tremendous problem as the Persian Gulf heated up. Later, flights from Germany were routed across the Eastern Bloc countries to relieve the Mediterranean routes, but still all traffic bunched up at the great choke point of El Daba.

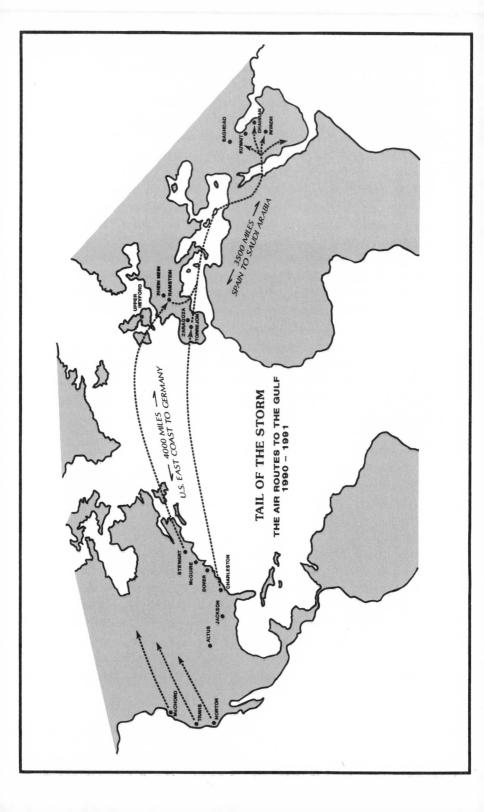

TAIL OF THE STORM

THE AIR ROUTES TO THE GULF
1990 – 1991

3500 MILES
SPAIN TO SAUDI ARABIA

4000 MILES
U.S. EAST COAST TO GERMANY

BAGHDAD
KUWAIT
DHAHRAN
RIYADH

UPPER HEYFORD
RHEIN MEIN
RAMSTEIN
ZARAGOZA
TORREJON

STEWART
McGUIRE
DOVER
CHARLESTON
JACKSON
ALTUS
NORTON
TRAVIS
McCHORD

The route ran southeast from there to the pyramids at Luxor, twisted eastward over the Red Sea, and fanned out to various points in what the Air Force called the area of responsibility, or AOR. The AOR stretched from east Africa to India. But I wondered what the term "AOR" really meant. Who was responsible? For what? To whom?

All along the route there was a constant flow of air traffic. Air Force C-5s and C-141s were joined by civil DC-8s, DC-10s, L-1011s, and Boeing 747s from a variety of airline and air freight companies. The civilian planes were a part of the Civil Reserve Air Fleet. And Uncle Sam had called them, like us, into wartime duty. The flow of hundreds of these great jets continued day in, day out for months. All along the route we were constantly flying in the contrails of the guy ahead, always being assaulted by the white snakes. Some celestial giant looking down at us would have seen an interminable line of ants meeting and passing one another in pursuit of some desperate cause. It was a line that military strategists called the "logistical tail." This was becoming the mother of all such tails.

I believed in the "Free Kuwait" cause and, like most all of those with whom I had been mobilized, was willing to do what was necessary to bring the aggression to an end. But it was obvious that although the goal in this game might be freedom, oil was the football. That didn't bother me. Oil seemed to be a factor at every turn in my life.

I had been an exploration geologist a few years back. Finding oil then had been the challenge and the objective. But the oil industry crumbled, and I dusted off my wings and turned to a career in the airlines. There I again found oil to be a commodity crucial to the health of an industry that consumed billions of gallons of refined products a day. And now it was the undisputed star player in the events breaking in the Middle East, which had swiftly sucked me in.

I had gotten to Viet Nam late. I was sent to Korat Air Base in northern Thailand to cover the retreat. I could have gone sooner, but I needed to finish college first. I wanted to avoid the draft because I wanted to fly, and to do that I needed a commission, for which a college degree was required.

Since I couldn't major in jets at the University of Alabama, I had to pick something else to study. Aerospace engineering should have been a natural, but I never cared for equations and slide rules. Business would have been easier, but I wasn't interested in abstract studies, and I had a great fear of being bored in school. Boredom would have been an enemy. It could cause failure, which would deny me my ultimate goal. So—motivated by the great field trips I'd heard about—I decided to try geology. I took to it like a hawk to a thermal. I loved it and excelled at it. I enjoyed it so much that occasionally disturbing thoughts began to creep in: maybe I'd like to do this for a living. Still, the dominant passion thrived. The big scare didn't come until my senior year.

It was noon on Thursday, the biggest day of the week in ROTC. The building had almost emptied. The Corps was forming on the quad in the shadow of Denny Chimes for the big military parade. But I had no interest. I was standing alone, staring out the window in the cadet lounge, when Dennis Utley started to pass by on his way out, stopped, and looked in on me. He knew something was wrong.

We had been friends since junior high—had learned to fly together as Civil Air Patrol cadets. But Dennis's pursuit of flight had stopped with the private pilot's license. He was headed for medical school on an Air Force scholarship. And he was well aware of where I wanted to go. We were entering our senior year of college and were on the final stretch toward becoming second lieutenants in the Air Force. The results of our precommissioning physical examinations had just been distributed.

He walked to the window and stood beside me silently for a moment, then asked what was bothering me.

"No pilot training, Den. They disqualified me." I took a hand out of my pocket and motioned. "Eyes."

I swallowed hard and resumed the stare out the window. Dennis knew what it meant to me. He knew how I sweated the advanced ROTC physical we took in our sophomore year. I had passed that one, but now my worst fears had materialized.

He just stood there with me a minute, not saying anything, just being there. That was the only proper consolation. Then he gave me a quick shoulder squeeze and said he had to go. But he stopped at the door, turned, and offered a suggestion.

"Maybe there's still hope," he encouraged. "Why don't you go down to Admin and talk to Sergeant Johnson?"

I nodded and stood there by the window, feeling that I was at that very second at a turning point in my life. I had come to a crossroads, and the path I had been certain that destiny wanted me to take was barred. The other directions led to existences that seemed dim and unfulfilling. But I was surprised at how I felt. I wasn't as devastated as I thought I should be. I loved earth science; I had made many friends in it and had already anticipated a bit of a letdown when I left it behind for a flying career. That would not be a bad alternative. But then despair set in again when I realized that I still owed Uncle Sam four years even if I couldn't fly. And geological engineering was not among the career tracks available to air force officers. I didn't feel like making the pass-in-review parade that afternoon. I just slipped away.

But maybe there was something to Dennis's suggestion. It would be a miracle if I could somehow cut through the military red tape and get back on flying status. More pilots were needed to feed the Viet Nam meat grinder, and not everyone was raising a hand all at once to volunteer. There might be an opportunity.

I visited with Sergeant Mike Johnson, who was very sympathetic but broke the news that there were no waivers for substandard eyesight, no matter how close I was to the exalted 20/20. I thanked him and started to leave, but I'm certain he somehow read how deep the disappointment was in me. He stopped me.

"Wait," he ordered, while reaching for a voluminous regulation manual. I sat curiously for several minutes while he flipped pages, read, and flipped more. Then he held his finger at some appropriate place on a page and with the other hand flipped through a correspondence file of some sort. I was growing more discouraged by the minute. It seemed as if his mind had forgotten me and wandered away into some administrative duty that he had suddenly remembered. But then he finally spoke while scribbling on a memo pad.

"I've never tried this before, so I can't promise you anything. Why don't you take this to an ophthalmologist and have him examine you?

You'll have to pay for it, but it's worth a try. Have him write a letter to the detachment commander, and bring it back here to me. If he finds your eyes OK, I'll talk with a friend of mine at Maxwell. But no promises, understand?"

Scribbled on the paper was the gibberish of diopters, accommodation powers, and other such eye quality standards that the Air Force required of its fliers. I assured him that I understood, thanked him, and turned to leave, but then I thought about how this man was going beyond his job. Here was an administrative sergeant—a clerk—who wanted to make a difference, wanted to create a pilot for his Air Force. I returned to his desk.

"Sergeant Johnson. If you pull this off, I'll saw my wings in two and send you half."

He laughed, proclaimed it a deal, and returned to his paperwork.

A few days later I returned with the letter. The civilian doctor, who had also read the deep desire to fly in my eyes, decided to find them perfect, and Sergeant Johnson set to work, calling upon the favor that a buddy at higher headquarters owed him.

In a month, I was back on flying status. It was the most wonderful feeling that had ever possessed me. And from that point onward, I felt a great respect for those senior noncommissioned officers who are truly the rivets that hold the Force together. Because one man who worked at a desk in a mundane basement cared, another man's life dream was launched skyward. And so it began.

TWO

THE TALON'S SPELL

The long awaited day came—the one Sergeant Johnson had made possible. I dropped Grandma off at her sister's in Tchula, Mississippi, on my way out into the world. She rambled on about gardening and recipes and such during the three-hour drive over to Tchula, but I don't remember much of what she said. I was too excited about the orders in my briefcase. I was to report to the Seventy-first Flying Training Wing, Vance Air Force Base, Oklahoma, for course number 442-DV, class 73–06, undergraduate pilot training (UPT). It was the last time I ever had meaningful conversation with my grandmother. "I hope you find a nice girl there," she whispered as she gave me a parting hug.

I blew it off. Much was at stake. I intended to commit 100 percent to the task ahead, and I doubted there would be much time for chasing females.

The long drive west itself symbolized the great changes coming for me. Gradually, the forest died away, and as I passed Tulsa, half the world became sky—a vast dome of burning blue from one horizon to another. "What a place to fly," I thought as I unloaded my modest belongings and carried them up to the room. Again and again I tripped, as I constantly looked up at the screaming T-37 jets pitching out in tight turns over the base, and each time I returned to the parking lot I paused to watch the T-38s take off, way out in the distance. Their thunder portended a much different kind of flying from that of the little screamers flying overhead.

I thought I must have died. This had to be Heaven. The sound of the jets, the smell of the burnt fuel rolling in from the flight line on the prairie winds, flight-suited student pilots driving around in sporty cars—I was beside myself with excitement. It was exactly the way I had envisioned it, the way I had dreamed.

I was awed at my roommate, Dan, who was an advanced T-37 student and had soloed three or four times. I immediately regarded him as a squire would his knight, and Dan, delighted, instantly became my mentor.

I strolled over to the officer's club that first night and looked around for another new face—someone with wide, searching eyes, like mine; someone who stood to the side, and wore civvies instead of flight suits because he had not gotten his yet. And immediately I found one. His name was Steve Hart, and yes! He also was in 73-06, the new class starting tomorrow. I had found a classmate. Tall and stout, he was from an Oregon timber family, and we were instant friends. We left the club that night drunk not with alcohol but with exhilaration. The dream was to begin tomorrow.

"Gentlemen, welcome to Vance Air Force Base, and to Enid, Oklahoma. Let me first tell you a few things about Enid. It has four bars and forty-four churches, so don't expect much in the way of nightlife."

The base commander paused for the obligatory laughter.

"Now, if you decide to go into one of the drinking establishments here, you should fit in fairly well as long as you don't bad-mouth wheat, cows, or oil."

I didn't intend to bad-mouth anything or anyone. I was just glad to be there. We looked around and sized one another up. After all, the year ahead would be a race to see who could finish at the top of the class for the choicest of follow-on assignments. A few of the guys had been in the Air Force for a while. One was a captain already. Word spread like wildfire that another guy already had logged 500 civilian hours. He would likely do well. Yet solid friendships began to form immediately.

The first few weeks were a breeze. They bused us out each morning to Woodring Airport on the east side of town (Ringworm Field, we called it) and began screening us in the USAF's smallest trainer, the T-41. It was nothing more than a beefed-up Cessna 172. Having over 200 hours in my logbook—mostly from lifting the University of Alabama Skydiving Club—I sailed through the program but not without some trepidation. My instructor's impatience with my undisciplined civilian flying habits began to show on the fourth flight.

"Lieutenant Cockrell, you're gonna learn to fly this thing the Air Force way, or go back to whatever the hell barnstorming act you came from!"

I didn't want to go back. I learned it his way.

But my stick partner—the other student with whom I shared an instructor—wasn't so fortunate. He was the academic type who knew all the book answers. He reminded us of an eager grade schooler who was constantly raising his hand in class, waving it back and forth, and begging to answer the question, while the rest of us cut eyes toward one another and suppressed snickers. "Right, OK," was his standard transition to a follow-up argument with the classroom instructors, but the poor guy pinked every single ride. (Back then we referred to a failed flight lesson as a "pink" because it was documented on pink paperwork. These days UPT students use the term "hook" to signify the same thing. "Hook" alludes to the "U" for unsatisfactory.) After three straight pinks, they gave you an "88" ride with a senior flight examiner. If you pinked that one, you then took a "99" ride with the chief of standardization/evaluation. If you hooked that one, you were history.

By the end of week number two, I was the lone student at the table. Then they moved an eager young guy from Ohio named Pete Lee over to my table. He became my friend and brother in Christ forever.

T-37 Tweet   ©Walter Sistrunk

The T-41 program ended after about fifteen hours of flying, and those of us who were left were fitted for helmets and masks. Our time had come. The academic portion of our training had begun in earnest, and those who had majored in nontechnical studies in college began to feel pressure. In the mornings they threw heavy doses of aerodynamics, weather, propulsion, navigation, and aviation physiology at us. In the afternoons we ambled out with our instructors to the pudgy little Tweets to put our newfound wisdom to use.

The name "Tweet" evolved not because the plane appeared birdlike or flew with the grace of an eagle—God knows it didn't—but because it screeched with a shrill that set teeth on edge and made ears quiver. The Tweet was a preposterous six-thousand-pound dog whistle. It was a machine from hell that happily carried out the devil's mandate of converting fuel into insane noise.

But it was easy to fly and was an especially good trainer because of its side-by-side seats. Your instructor—his helmet, visor, and oxygen mask giving him the appearance of a frightful monster—could spy your every move, with a godlike eminence.

I took to the Tweet well and had a good instructor. Steve and Pete weren't so lucky. Their IPs were screamers—impatient hotheads who wished they were somewhere else, flying "real" airplanes. Still, Steve and Pete hung tight. But Dan, my roommate, was beginning to have problems with his advanced instrument maneuvers.

Shortly before my first solo in the Tweet, I came back to the room, and found Dan in a near stupor. The living room of our small apartment smelled like a distillery. His head hung low and he looked up at me when I walked in. His face was smeared with tears. Dan had had his 99 ride that morning. The whiskey and tears testified to its results. I tried in my feeble way to console him, but he just slipped away into his bedroom and shut the door. When I returned from flying the next afternoon, his room was cleaned out.

UPT Class 73-06 plodded along through a hot summer of T-37 flying, and most of us soloed. Those who couldn't turned in their gear and cleared the base. While Steve and Pete struggled with ornery instructors, I continued in good fortune with levelheaded IPs who treated me well. Still, I lived in fear that I would be assigned one of the screamers.

I marveled at how UPT could be so stressful and yet so enjoyable at the same time. I was having the time of my life, but occasionally I needed to get away from the base. I took therapeutic drives down Enid's tranquil streets, watching children playing and people mowing lawns. I dined with the farmers at the Wagon Wheel Cafe and paused to watch combines harvest the golden wheat in the shadows of the giant grain elevators north of town.

Enid seemed the all-American town to me. It was a family town where the work ethic was a respected way of life, where beef and bread and energy were produced to feed the impersonal metropolises that seemed so far away (and good riddance). I liked it there. It just seemed rich. And it got a great deal richer when my grandmother's wishes for me proved prophetic.

I tested the limited nightlife around town and didn't care much for it. I met Eleanor at a picnic held by one of the forty-four churches. She was tall and beautiful, and within a couple of weeks the T-37 had to move over and make room for her in the hangar of my affections.

Pete and I seemed to be the only two bachelors of 73-06 who found quality female companionship in Enid. Eleanor became the focal point of my life, and many Sunday afternoons found us in Meadow Lake Park, in the shade, where she quizzed me from study guides. Four months into UPT and still I was pinching myself. Here I was, lying with my head in the lap of this angel, pretending to be studying, and tomorrow I would be flying jets again. Yes, yes! There was a God.

Still, the long hours in academia and the intense flying took its toll on our vitality, and we devised various ways to vent. Poker was the most expedient escape, and consequently a couple of times a week someone would write an announcement on the scheduling board to the effect that a seminar in combinations and permutations was to be held in so-and-so's room at 1800 hours. The session usually began after a surprise hit-and-run attack on the o-club bar and was almost invariably held in the on-base apartment of one of the bachelors. We sat around the tables in sweat-soaked flight suits, throwing down quarters and cards, begging the married guys, who fidgeted and glanced at their watches, to stay a little longer.

It was at such a game that the most profound statement ever made about my character was proffered. Although I had pretty good hands for flying airplanes, I couldn't shuffle cards worth a fiddle. On every other attempt the cards exploded and scattered, to the dismay of my impatient classmates, prompting Steve Randle to remark, "Al, the trouble with you is, you ain't got no friggin' class."

Willy Mays, our resident scholar, clown, and dreamer howled. Willy was one of the best fliers in our class and the most charismatic individual. We became good friends, although we differed on some fundamental beliefs about life. I watched his progress closely, knowing that he would be one of my main rivals for a good "pick."

The competitive atmosphere impressed itself upon us from day one. Our academic test scores and our periodic checkride marks combined to establish class standing, on the basis of which our ultimate duty assignments would be made. As we approached graduation, the Air Force would send the base a number of assignments, corresponding to the expected number of graduates. Each assignment specified a type of aircraft and a base. The list would be published, and each student would submit his preferences in numerical order. The top-ranked student would be awarded his first choice, and subsequently ranked students would get their highest available choice; the bottom guy took what was left. In such a scheme the fighter jobs usually went high on the list, as well as the C-141 assignments, because of their strong airline quality experience. The instructor, C-130, and tanker assignments usually went about the middle of the class, and the bomber jobs went toward the bottom. And because of this, our class had become somewhat of a test case. The Strategic Air Command was so tired of getting pilots from the bottom of the classes that they demanded that some of their bomber assignments be earmarked for the middle of the class. Thus, some of our good fliers were bound for bombers, whether they wanted to go or not. I preferred a C-141 slot because I wanted to travel the world and build flying time quickly. But that aspiration was to be snuffed out when I lit the afterburners on my first T-38 flight.

About the time the weather began to cool, we finished the T-37 phase and were fitted with G-suits—those of us who remained. The T-38 Talon was the second of the UPT jets, but it contrasted vividly with the first one, the venerable T-37. Where the Tweet was flounderlike and round nosed, the '38 was supremely streamlined and beautiful. Where the Tweet was slow, the '38, with its powerful afterburners, was canned speed. While the Tweet screeched, the '38 thundered. It was long and sleek—years ahead of its time. Its flowing aerodynamic lines radiated visions of flight, fast flight, and nothing else. A stranger to the ground, it appeared oddly out of place, there on the flight line. Heaven-sent, it was the stuff of young men's dreams and old men's treasured memories. It was love from the first millisecond—the most beautiful, graceful creature God had ever begotten.

When the throttles were shoved into the afterburner range on that first demonstration ride, you sank back into the seat under the tremendous acceleration. Your lungs seized and the name of your Savior escaped your lips as the runway stripes raced at you with a blur. Within seconds you were cutting through the air like a knife on stubby blades that somehow passed for wings, while Garfield County angled back and shrank into yesterday. You sat out on the long needle point nose and gawked at a new stratospheric world that was bigger, higher, clearer, and faster changing than any altitude the Tweet could ever aspire to. Feeling like a rookie jockey clinging to a blind racehorse, you burned white contrails against the blue heavens over the Oklahoma panhandle and left sonic booms cascading across the prairies. You worked to develop that delicate touch on the sensitive control stick but sometimes blundered into roll rates of over 360 degrees per second. Or maybe you dished out and let your nose get buried in

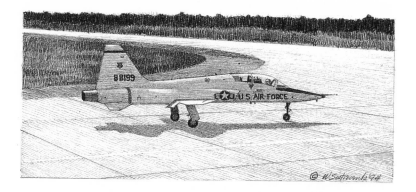

T-38 Talon

the brown and green of the beneath world, and your guts knotted up while your instructor cursed and took over the controls, slamming the throttles to idle, gingerly pulling the nose back into the realm of blue. Gradually, you learned to keep your mind well out in front of a creature that gobbled 800 feet of airspace per second. You developed an uncommon sense of awareness, unparalleled in any other human endeavor.

And within a few short weeks, your solo was at hand. But now the event was much different. In the world of the Tweets, the first solo was a big deal. Your instructor rode with you on the appointed day and got out of the little jet after a few satisfactory landings. He then entered the runway supervisory unit, the RSU, and watched you carefully, microphone in hand, as you nervously flew a few patterns around the field. Afterward, you were locked into a seventeenth-century-style wooden stock while your classmates happily hosed you down. But come time for you to go it alone in a T-38, it was all business.

You walked in one morning and saw the S-word beside your name, and when the time came, you grabbed your gear and went out to your assigned jet alone. And you secured the straps in the empty rear cockpit, mounted up on that magnificent white steed and mated yourself to it, and rocketed out to the "tubes," where you were supposed to practice the basic maneuvers in a special piece of airspace assigned you. You didn't practice much of anything. You just held on, trying to keep it pointed in some relatively safe direction while your senses buzzed, and you marveled at the tightrope you were walking—mishap was only a slip away, yet you were riding the pinnacle of life. Then you found your way back to Vance Air Patch before the fuel got too low, set that puppy down on one seven right, and taxied it back into the same hole you came out of—you hoped. You stopcocked the throttles and listened to the engines spool down and rode the bus back in, and your IP said "How'd it go?" without even looking up at you, and you knew that at last your epiphany was at hand.

But for some of us bitterness—and worse—awaited still.

We were about halfway through the '38 program when the wing commander met with us in the officer's club for a rendition of his safety philosophy. Midway through his presentation, his portable radio squealed, and he spoke into it. We all sat horrified at the hissing message that came back to him. A T-37 had crashed near the town of Nash. One fatality was suspected. Later that day we learned his identity. I didn't know his name, but his face burned through my memory. It was the red-haired kid who was a couple of classes behind us. I had shot the breeze with him in the break room. He was the quintessential kid next door—always smiling, always talking of home. And now he was dead. The Tweet, spinning out of control, had slammed into a wheat field. The red-haired kid had stayed with it too long. He had ejected too late. His body was found still strapped to the ejection seat.

For the next few days our mood was somber, and then the pressures of the program compelled us to look ahead and concentrate on the task at hand. But violent death would strike our band eventually—we knew it. We just didn't talk about it.

By T-38 midphase I was reaching my stride. On my first formation flight I discovered one of flying's greatest joys—to waltz the sky inches from another aircraft. I reveled in the challenge of absolute concentration and was truly at home on the wing. I dreamed of becoming a Thunderbird, flying one of the beautifully painted jets in the famous diamond formation, thundering across an azure sky; crowds looking up, shading their eyes in unbelieving awe. I don't know what it is that makes pilots want to impress surface dwellers with their thundering prowess—just ego, I guess. But I know that any pilot who doesn't have such a desire is probably minimally skilled anyway. And this "shine-ass" tendency, as it's known, is the torment of commanders, who work hard to suppress it and to make examples of those who succumb to it. Yet a chosen few have both the means and the license to bathe crowds in thunder, to wash them with waves of wild delight and wonder. I should have been one of them. But Willy Mays was the one destined for Thunderbird blue.

We took our formation flight checkride together, he with a check pilot in his jet, me with an examiner in mine. I knew he was good, and I set about to bring it out. We were flying a standard USAF formation. I was leading and Willy was on my left side, or left wing. No matter what I did—whether I climbed, descended, or turned—he stayed in his position, which was slightly low and slightly behind. From his vantage point, my left wing tip was superimposed on the circle-and-star symbol painted on my air intake. Keeping the wing tip on that star was his sole objective.

And there he sat, as if glued to some invisible bar between us, making us one instead of two, his wing tip only three feet out and behind mine. He was doing well, and I decided to challenge him. The signal for directing the wingman to change positions to the other side of the leader is a quick wing dip by the leader to the opposite side. To do this, the wingman reduces power very slightly and gently slips under and across to the opposite wing. But we had never been taught to do this except in level flight. We were in a 45 degree left bank when I swallowed hard and gave him the signal. I watched as Willy first hesitated, then slowly dropped low and crossed to the high side of the formation, resuming a perfect position on the right side. I rolled into a steep right bank and signaled him again to cross back to the left side. He was good, damn good. I challenged him again later, after signaling him to fall back into extended trail, by immediately starting a four-G loop. As soon as he had radioed that he was in his position 2,000 feet behind me, I jerked the stick back, pulled the T-38's long nose straight up, and continued the pull over the top into a giant 600-mile-per-hour loop. It was standard practice to give the wingman a little breather before starting such maneuvering, but again, I knew Willy could hack it.

Then it was his turn to lead, and I reaped what I had sown. I hung tight on the wing and stayed solid through the maneuvers. Then he signaled me back to extended trail. I took the spacing and settled back to follow him through the enormous loops. At one point during an almost vertical climb his jet entered a supercooled layer of air and began to "conn." It was as if a great white tentacle were reaching out from his tailpipes and racing toward me. I had the wild feeling that Willy had impossibly and instantly reversed his course and was screaming straight at me. I flinched when the vapors hit. No drug could ever duplicate the euphoria of the spectacle. It was no trivial expression that the words "naturally high," a slogan concocted by Willy Mays, were embroidered on our class patches.

We finished the ride and climbed onto the crew bus, soaked with sweat in midwinter, as our check pilots wondered aloud why we hated each other. But it wasn't so. We grinned at one another. And we both passed with high marks.

My celebration of the aced formation checkride was short-lived. For the first time since we started, Steve Hart was having trouble. He just couldn't seem to hold the wing tip on the star. He began to sweat each ride, and we all helped and encouraged him as best we could, but his instructor would not recommend him for his checkride. Soon the 88 came, then the 99. Within weeks of graduation—almost a year since a glorious beginning—Steve washed out. He said his goodbyes and was gone. It was as if our friend had crashed somewhere out there on the prairie. We mourned his departure as if he were dead. It wasn't fair, we lamented. Steve was a good flier. Maybe he wasn't cut out for formation flight, but he could have been a valuable asset to the Air Force as a bomber or transport pilot. It just wasn't fair.

Eventually the Air Force would wise up and discard the idea of training all pilots in a fighter preparation format. In 1993, UPT began to implement changes that divided students into fighter or transport tracks at the end of the T-37 phase. Those destined for fighter-type jobs would continue in the T-38, and those chosen for the "heavies" would continue their training in a transport-type trainer. But the change was twenty years too late for Steve.

In the last days the much-heralded assignment block arrived. The flight commander handed the list to me and asked me to write it on the training board. As I did so, my classmates stood behind me, examining each entry, murmuring and buzzing with excited speculation. Seven of the twenty-seven assignments were fighter jobs.

I had already picked mine out, an RF-4 to Shaw AFB, South Carolina. That was my dream assignment—to fly fast, low, and alone, with only a navigator for company, photographing hostile positions. The RF-4 was armed only with a camera. I wasn't keenly interested in dropping bombs. And I also reasoned that since the Alabama Air Guard flew RF-4s, I could build good credentials for an eventual job there. I listed the two single-seat fighters, the A-7 and F-106, as second and third, then the F-4s. The T-38 had made me completely forget about my original desire to fly the C-141.

The next day the picks were announced. The RF-4 had been taken by someone who ranked above me. I was going to Tucson to fly A-7s.

Willy got an F-4, Pete a C-130. But never again would I have such an enviable choice. It wasn't just a once-in-a-lifetime choice; it was a once-in-a-million-lives choice.

Eleanor took leave of her senses and consented to take up with an Air Force bum and follow him God knew where. We were married the day after graduation. But before we left for Arizona, I borrowed a hacksaw and sawed my new wings in two. I had a promise to keep.

While the year of UPT was one of the finest of my life, the one that followed ranked as one of the worst. The instructors in A-7 school were combat veterans, fresh from a war that frustrated them and thwarted their will to fight and win. They loathed a government that had mandated not just defeat but disaster. And as usual with military instructors, they did not relish coming home to teach.

It was not the happiest of environments in which to learn the fighter pilot's trade. At times I felt that the instructors were taking their frustrations out on me, and I suppose I invited such treatment. I wasn't tremendously interested in bombing and strafing, and I guess it showed.

A few weeks after we had settled in at Davis-Monthan, the phone rang; it was Willy calling from F-4 school up at Luke AFB in Phoenix. "Have you heard about Phil Molina?" he asked. I knew from his tone that Phil was dead. A member of our UPT class, Phil had gone home to fly C-130s in the Air Guard. He had been flying copilot when it happened. A blade from one of the early electric propellers had separated and sliced through the fuselage, cutting hydraulic lines and control cables. The craft had plummeted to the ground. Visions of Phil's grinning face immediately flashed across my memory. I wondered how many times I would have to endure this experience. But the worst was yet to come.

I made it through A-7 school and was assigned to the 358th Tactical Fighter Squadron, the Lobo Wolves, a proud unit with a great heritage of honor and courage. In the years that followed, I flew the A-7 across the southwestern deserts and the jungles of Thailand, bombing and strafing until I had had enough. I wasn't cut out to be a career fighter pilot. At my zenith I made the squadron Top Gun board one month, but finally I had to admit it. I had the right stuff, or else I wouldn't have been there. What I didn't have was the right heart. I put in my papers, and Ellie and I packed up and headed for a new life of which we knew little.

Within two years, after a couple of interim jobs and some graduate school, destiny led me to Jackson, Mississippi, for what appeared to be a long and thrilling career as a petroleum geologist. The hunt for oil had its own brand of excitement. And what's more, the Mississippi Air Guard had invited me to join them flying C-130s. Scott and Brad were born, and Ellie and I thought we had finally found our place in the sun.

On January 19, 1982, I sat down and opened the evening newspaper. I stared in horror and disbelief at the photographs of the four Thunderbird pilots who had crashed while performing a practice air show maneuver in the Nevada desert. The entire diamond formation had slammed into the ground, following the leader whose flight controls, it was later determined, had malfunctioned. The four dead included Captain Willy Mays, Thunderbird Two, from Ripley, Tennessee.

For days I was cast into that vaporous domain where cries of "why?" and "what if?" continually strafe and dive-bomb you. It's a feeling painfully familiar to fliers when they lose one of their own. I sat idly at my desk in the office, staring out the window, useless to anyone. And still it was not to be the last time I would have to deal with such a loss.

The time I spent flying C-130s was some of the best years of my flying career. I truly had the best of both worlds: an interesting, challenging, well-paying job and an open opportunity to fly almost whenever I wished. But in the mid-1980s the oil business fell on hard times, and I took on the title of consulting geologist, which was a smoke screen for unemployed geologist. I jumped from retainer to retainer, never having more than a year or two of security, and supplemented my income by flying heavily with the Guard.

I began to take all the training courses and extra duty the Guard and Air Force could offer. During one such period while I was TDY at Maxwell Air Force Base, Montgomery, Alabama, I suddenly confronted my past in an incredible encounter. I was walking down a sidewalk near the Air University when a sergeant saluted me and stopped.

"Wait," he said, closely examining my name tag. "Do you remember me, sir?" I didn't. He extended his hand. "I'm Mike Johnson—the guy you sent half your wings to!"

I was awestruck. It had been years since I sawed the wings. I hadn't thought of him in a long time. We talked and caught up with one another's lives. It was a warm feeling—almost like a family reunion. This man had never been able even to approach the fulfillment of the wing, yet he had understood what it meant to me. He had received the half wings; they had been forwarded to him in Viet Nam. And to that day, they were proudly mounted in a display case in his den.

I'll never forget this man who had made such a profound difference in my life. I've saluted him many times with a snappy aileron roll, up high where almost no one notices.

We all loved the C-130 beyond comprehension. We flew the "Hercs" down low over the catfish and cotton farms, in formation. On Tuesday and Thursday evenings motorists on Interstate 20 would marvel at the sight of our three-ship formations crossing at what must have seemed treetop level, giving birth to billowing parachutes on Bull Run Drop Zone near Edwards. We practiced landings on short runways, and flew to places all over the country—and a few out of the country—in support of other active and reserve units. It was the ultimate flying club.

Then, in 1986, an old dream was suddenly resurrected. On a Saturday UTA, Colonel Bailey asked for a show of hands from all of us who wanted to switch to C-141s. Mine was one of the few that went up. But despite the lack of enthusiasm from the crews, the announcement was made public. Senator Stennis, seeking more jobs for his constituents, threw some heavy political weight around and made us give up our almost new C-130s to become the first Air Guard unit to be equipped with the C-141B Starlifter. I had come full circle at last.

The '141 was a big four-engine jet transport with a worldwide strategic airlift mission. Suddenly there was no more low-level flying, no air drops, no formation flying, no short runways, and very few nice weekend cross-country trips. Bull Run DZ was shut down.

Although the jets were beautiful and sported a modern, streamlined appearance, they were old—older than some of those who were flying them. They were maintenance headaches, and the transition to our new global mission was not easy for the crews. Suddenly it wasn't a very suitable part-time pursuit anymore. An operational trip to Europe and back took a minimum of four days. It was tough for most guys to get off from their jobs for that amount of time. Great changes began to develop among us. Those who couldn't do it dropped out. Those who took their place had jobs that were more flexible. Our ranks began to swell with airline pilots and self-employed people. Some didn't have jobs—Guard bums, we called them. They volunteered for all the flying that the scheduler would give them and made a decent living at it.

Again I went back on active duty, this time for six weeks to check out in the Starlifter. It was an opportune time, as I was again between retainers. The course was designed as a refresher for people who had previously been qualified in the Starlifter but who had been in a desk job or some other pursuit that had taken them out of the cockpit. The "short course" wasn't intended to check out pilots who had never flown the C-141—there was a twelve-week course for that purpose— but the Guard had persuaded the Air Force that we could hack it. After all, the C-130, to which we were so accustomed, was, like the C-141, a Lockheed product. There shouldn't be too much difference. But in fact there were tremendous differences, we would discover.

My stick partner and longtime friend Hugh Stevens was the argumentative sort. A computer programmer by trade, he always kept one eye scrutinizing detail, and when I displayed disrespect for certain minutiae, Hugh mounted an intensive campaign to educate me. It was not uncommon for Hugh to burst into my room, through the connecting kitchenette, armed with a "Dash-1," gleefully documenting some minute fact that had been in dispute and about which I had ceased to care. During the long debriefings after our simulator flights, Hugh invariably engaged the instructors in protracted discourses over some morsel of flying knowledge, while I sat back and yawned, fidgeted, and tried unsuccessfully to subvert the debates. For six weeks he dogged and niggled me unmercifully, but finally we graduated and happily returned to Jackson to become the pioneers of a new concept of strategic airlift in the militia. And as the oil business grew steadily worse, I found myself increasingly plying the world's skyscapes in the big jets to make ends meet.

In 1989, I gave up on the oil business and joined United Airlines, commuting to Chicago to fly Boeing 727s. My life was completely dominated by airplanes at that point—maybe too many. I had to keep up with, and devote time to, three aircraft: the C-141, the 727, and my own Grumman AA-5.

By then I had spent fifteen years "flying the line" for Uncle Sam. Had I still been on active duty, maybe as much as half of that time would have been spent flying a desk. Young Air Force pilots often complained of the incessant pressure to "broaden" one's career. Most of them wanted nothing else but to fly, to be the best they possibly could, maybe to command a squadron and pass their knowledge on to the next generation. It seemed rational, but the Air Force continued to insist that all pilots become managers, bean counters, and upward-moving professional administrators.

It has been changing more in favor of pilots recently, but I remember when a visiting general was speaking at Officer's Call at Altus Air Force Base while I was in C-141 school. He was asked why the Air Force couldn't establish a career track for those who wanted exclusively to fly for twenty years.

"Oh, but we have" was his response. "That career track you speak of is called the Air Force Reserve and Air National Guard."

I'm exceedingly glad that reserve component funding came from Capitol Hill and not from the Pentagon. Otherwise the militia would have been neglected stepchildren. As it was, pork barrel politics worked in our favor. The politicians whom we sent to Washington were big on the Guard. "Nothin's too good for my boys down thea. I want 'em to have the best tanks and arrowplanes money c'n buy." And for the most part, we got them. Life was good.

Our unit, in particular, had done well. We were the 172nd Military Airlift Group, Mississippi Air Guard—"The Wings of the Deep South" we'd called ourselves. We had been the first militia unit back in the early 1980s to get brand new "H" model C-130s; the first such unit to respond to the Hurricane Hugo devastation; the first into earthquake-ravaged Soviet Armenia; the first of any Guard or Reserve unit to plunge into Operation Just Cause—the liberation of Panama; and the first unit in the entire history of American airpower to log twenty-five years of accident-free flying. Our unit drew its strength from a vast population of Mississippians to whom the slogan "Duty, Honor, Country" was much more than just poetic words uttered from the lips of a fading old soldier. Mississippians had never heard that "patriotism" was supposed to be an outdated and unfashionable thing. And it was no secret that the Mississippi Air Guard was a proud, shining star over a state that abounded in problems both real and imagined. Mississippians had invested their trust and pride in us, and we carried the banner of the Magnolia Militia the world over. Even foreign radar controllers recognized the call sign "Ruler." One thickly accented German controller had once asked me on a congested frequency, "Rula Eight Fife, are you from Mizzizzippi?"

"Citizen Airmen" the recruiting pitches called us. It meant that you held a regular job (maybe), or you were a student, using the Guard to work your way through college (a smart idea), or maybe your wife worked while you bummed it at the Guard Base. Whatever you did, at least once a week you had about an hour after work to make the transition from whatever job you normally toiled at, to the cockpit of a military jet. You had to give Uncle Sam twelve of your weekends and at least fifteen additional days each year. But to stay reasonably proficient in the jet, everyone put in three or four times as many days. You'd take a couple of days off from work, pair them with a weekend, and cross continents and oceans as routinely as your neighbor drove to his Warren County deer camp.

It was uncanny to me how people from such different backgrounds could join together for such a specialized and demanding task—and do it with relative harmony. The other pilot across the cockpit from you might be a stockbroker or lawyer. The flight engineers and loadmasters could be accountants, truck drivers, or students. But no matter what you did outside the gates, your heart was always sprouting wings, yearning for the smell of burnt JP-4 fuel (which you joked about) and the whine of the big turbines. Being a macho crewdog, you rarely spoke of yearnings of the heart. But they were there. Yes, it was a great job—flying, getting paid for it, and serving your country.

By all accounts, I had enjoyed a flying career that spanned the spectrum of military aviation. I had known the thrill, the joy, and the excitement of the fighters. The heavies had matured me as a flier, had shown me the world, and had taught me the satisfaction of job accomplishment. Along the way, I found the kind of friendship and brotherhood that rarely existed in other enclaves of life. I had good reason to be content, to feel immensely blessed. Time and again, over the years I felt indebted to someone, or something.

And now, a wretched despot, empowered with the world's fourth largest army, had invaded our ally and threatened our vital interests. It didn't matter whether I was enthusiastic or not about rushing to Kuwait's aid. The account had come due. I had to settle it.

THREE

THE TJ BLUES

We have begun our letdown into Madrid. The flight across the Atlantic from Charleston has been typically long and abundantly dark, and we are feeling the first ripples of the soaking fatigue that will intensify and linger for months.

The Spanish controller orders us to a surprisingly low altitude across this vast city. I guess noise pollution isn't a big concern here. Now I see why. Dawn is only a couple of hours away, yet the long strings of bright little pairs of eyes inching past yellow streetlights reveal a city alive. Madrid's not up early; it hasn't gone to bed yet.

We skim across the living plasma of light and humanity, marveling at the vitality of life below and its indifference to our ephemeral passage. After the hours of dark empty ocean, we become infused with it. The amber glow permeates our souls and preps us for the rejoin with society at the place called Torrejon, five minutes ahead.

We've all seen Torrejon before in less tumultuous times. We call it TJ, which is the identifier painted on the tails of its wing of F-16 fighters. We contact the tower and are cleared for a visual approach to runway two three. After landing we are instructed to turn off onto a connecting taxi way and wait.

The vast ramp is packed with airlifters. In the dawning light, we see the gargantuan beehive of activity that TJ has become. Enormous dark hulks are parked on almost every available space, their red and green wing tip lights piercing the darkness. Here and there the stomachs of

the leviathans are exposed, their huge clamshell doors swung open, the interiors bathed in light. The hulks are being serviced by hosts of vehicles with sweeping headlights, scurrying about like frightened rodents. Towering tails move back and forth above the jumble like prowling sharks, gracefully swinging and turning as they maneuver. The magnitude of the spectacle is the first indication that we are caught up in something big beyond our wildest expectations.

After what seems a long wait, we are cleared to taxi to a parking space that has just been vacated. The engines spool down, and we download our burden of bags and equipment and wait for the promised crew bus. And wait. And wait. "The two biggest lies in the world," Walt mutters. "'Check's in the mail' and 'crew bus is on the way.'" A frustration that we will come to know and loathe begins to set in.

Finally the bus arrives, and we are driven the two miles along the vast flight line, passing row after row of behemoth jets with blinking lights and laughably small figures of people hurrying about them. Farther still, we pass racks of inert bombs, missiles, and other sinister munitions. Fuel trucks, cargo loaders, strange tractors of several varieties, and other buses filled with flight crews jam the roadway. Rows of fighters are being pored over by mechanics under portable floodlight units, tweaking them up for their departure to the killing fields.

We are delivered, finally, to the MAC command post—the CP— and wait for our turn at the debriefing window. The hallway is alive with crewdogs. Some, like us, are inbound, as we can see from their ruffled hair, stubbled faces, and fatigued eyes. The "outbound" crews are a bit fresher, are pumping the inbounds with the latest rumors, and, with a hint of pleasure, are informing us of the ordeal ahead that is to be our "crew rest."

Finally the CP controller logs us in and, with a bit of a smirk, asks if we prefer eastbound or westbound on our next assignment. Of course we want to go east, or "downrange," as it is now dubbed. We're eager to get into the action. It could be over soon. We don't want history to pass us up. He dutifully notes our preference and sends us off to crew rest.

We arrive at the military hotel and step off the crew bus into Dodge City circa 1880. The lobby and walkways connecting the hotel with the officer's club are alive with shouting crewdogs, many toting bags, sucking San Miguel beer, and cavorting with one another, pistols strapped to their sides and shoulders. Weary pilots lean against the check-in counter, running fingers through sweaty hair. Someone has posted a large map of the Middle East regions, which is rapidly collecting graffiti and other scribbled gems of crewdog wisdom. The area is abuzz with activity. The atmosphere of crisis and the uncertainty of the coming days spawn excitement rather than foreboding. The place seems almost festive, as old acquaintances are rekindled and the stress of many hours in the air is released. But I have a hunch the festivities will be short-lived.

I look around for a familiar face but see none other than those of my own crew. We get our room assignments, two rooms for six of us with a single bath, and are told we're lucky; an hour earlier or later, and it could have been a cot in the recreation center ballroom. We drag our bags down the long hallway and up two flights of stairs, past housekeepers shouting at one another in rapid-fire Spanish, and find that the frenzied activity extends throughout the building. It seems impossible that anyone could sleep here. Crewdogs are their own worst enemy. Coming in from a mission, they are often loud and boisterous, buoyed by the San Miguel and the relief that the mission is behind them.

Bones, Jeff, and I crowd into the small, two-bed, one-cot room. We don't care much for rank, privileges, and the like in the Guard, but Bones, the junior officer, insists on taking the cot, and I choose not to spoil his wishes. We strew our vast array of gear and personal bags in the only space available, and proceed to stumble over them constantly. We soon discover that the air conditioning is out of commission, and we throw open the windows in a futile plea for relief. But then we reel at the roar of a C-5 engine test, the din pouring in as if the nozzle were backed up to the window, though the plane is a mile away. The mechanic at the throttle powers the engine up to takeoff-rated thrust, then back to idle, again and again, as if on some mission of vengeance against us.

One of our loadmasters stops by the door and says that Tom Clayton's crew is out on the dayroom balcony. Eager to see familiar faces, we proceed to the balcony and find Tom and his crew, sitting beside a cooler of San Miguel and judging the landing patterns of the arriving C-5s and C-141s.

"You weak wick!" cries Tom as a Starlizzard flies a wide downwind leg. "What a bomber pattern. Close it up!"

As I arrive, a sergeant dressed in a pressed blue uniform steps up and informs us that alcoholic beverages are not allowed on the balcony. I sense the reluctance in his eyes and voice, as he explains that the policy is not his but that of the base services officer. I shake his hand and usher him away from the snarling crewdogs, assuring him that I will take care of the matter, that he is absolved of responsibility, though I have no intention of taking action. He probably knows it.

As the sun rises over the prominent plateau east of the base, I leave the balcony crowd and start back to the room. On the way I notice a familiar face approaching from a connecting hallway. The man has a watermelon under one arm and a leather attaché case in the other hand. My heart soars: it's my old friend George Fondren. But the gleam that I expected from him is absent, replaced by concern in his eyes. There was a time when he would have relished such an operation as this. He would have seen it as a great challenge, a job to do in his uniquely rebellious way, which bypassed the bureaucracy. For him there was opportunity in confusion. He got satisfaction from seeking ways to defeat the blundercrats at their own game, which he did with delightful cunning. But his bulging briefcase shows that he is trying to tend to his businesses, which are languishing in his absence.

George is a true son of the South. Descended from a family in which the torch of military service has been proudly passed down through the generations, he is the very essence of a military flier. Handsome, well groomed, and square-jawed, he could equally well have stepped from a Hollywood movie set or from the pages of Faulkner. He is southern to the core, a deep respecter of ancestry and heritage, and a fierce individualist.

George is sometimes regarded as arrogant by those who envy his human skills but not by his crews. He's famous for taking care of his crews, especially the enlisted members. He will use the fresh Mississippi melon and his persuasive southern charm to gain favor with the next crew scheduler. He will secure the best missions, the best quarters, the best crew rest hours, and the best of any amenities that can be had.

A standup comic in small trusted crowds but timid in larger ones, George is a supreme master craftsman in the art of bovine scatology, as General Schwarzkopf would say. We—his selected friends—are his "clients," he the sponsor ever seeking to impart street wisdom from the other side of his awareness "membrane." He has invited me over to the edge of the membrane a few times for a glimpse through, but I'm unqualified to accompany him across.

It is with few people that I've ever enjoyed such a candid relationship. We can be brutally critical of one another without reprisal. The most damage that's ever done is a slightly miffed ego. We point out perceived flaws in one another's character, sometimes with uncanny accuracy. Of course such accusations always bring vehement denial. I've noticed that he reads me a little better than I read him. We sometimes use the other squadron members as a medium to communicate with one another; they are jealously aware of our unique comradeship. They constantly ask me how he is faring. They ask him about me. I tell someone that he is a sneaky schemer, knowing that my assertion will reach him through the grapevine. He spreads stories that I am a fanciful dreamer who climbs to mountaintops to ponder the schemes of life. To that I plead guilty.

Some people take George too seriously. I think they envy his power and talent to motivate people. Like no other officer I've ever seen, George can simply stick his head into an office or workshop and instantly cause a wave of delight to spread among the enlisted people. And I am closer to him than most. He is a caring man who understands the permanency of true friendship.

George's crew has been alerted for a mission, and I regret that there is no time to spend with him. I'd like to hear some old yarns and catch up on the news of mutual friends. But we speak only briefly, and he vanishes into the sea of airmen, leaving me with a touch of isolation and loneliness.

I roll over at the sound of the knock and watch Jeff rise to open the door. A slit of light sears the darkness, and a barely audible, almost apologetic voice informs us that we are alerted. I stumble over the jumble of bags, cots, and equipment, searching for my sweats while Bones mutters something into his pillow. The combined effects of jet lag, hallway noise, and oppressive heat have left us ragged. Rubbing eyes that feel like sandpaper, I stagger down the hallway like a drunk.

The lobby area is active as usual, and after a few minutes' wait for the phone, I call the CP. We are to deadhead to Dhahran to pick up a broken C-141, an engine problem of some sort, but it has been temporarily repaired and is airworthy, I'm assured. This is doubly bad news. Not only am I unenthusiastic over the prospect of flying a plane that has been "temporarily" field repaired (why didn't the original crew fly it back? might they have refused?), but the deadhead time going down will not count toward our eventual time off at home.

We have a revolving flying time account. Our maximum limits are 150 hours in the last thirty days, 275 hours in the last sixty days; or 330 hours in the last ninety days. When any of the limits are approached, we are routed home to "burn down" to a usable level, which normally takes about a week. Thus we seek to "max-out" as quickly as we can. But duty time doesn't count. Only actual flight time is used. The system is an abominable yardstick to measure crew fatigue because it ignores the endless hours spent performing ground duties, such as flight planning, aircraft preflight, troubleshooting, waiting for parts, cargo, fuel, and clearances. On-duty to off-duty times should be used to regulate our exposure to fatigue, not takeoff to landing times. We said so many times, but the response was always "that's above my pay grade" or something similar.

I tell the controller that my test pilot license has expired, that I decline the offer and will return to bed. With an accommodating chuckle, he ignores the remark and asks when I want the crew bus.

I proceed to wake the engineers. Taking a defensive position, Brian peeps with a painful squint into the bright hallway and questions my sanity when I break the news. He then turns and relays the news to Walt. From within the dark comes Walt's incredulous reply.

"You gotta be shittin' me."

Not surprisingly, the two loadmasters, Mike and Jack, are suited up and packed. Their work/rest patterns do not necessarily coincide with ours. They sleep during a cargo flight but have to stay awake if passengers are aboard. Tonight they are rested and ready. They have anticipated the alert by watching the TV monitor in the lobby, which displays the names of aircraft commanders on a first in/first out order. When my name had scrolled near the top they knew the alert would soon come.

As we receive our briefing at the CP, an unsettling message arrives and spreads ripples of concern among the crews. A jet airlifter has crashed on takeoff from a base in Germany, survivors unknown. I immediately grab a phone and ask for a Stateside line to our home base. Wisely, the Mississippi Air Guard has established a standing order for its crews. In case of an airlifter crash anywhere in Desert Shield, we are to report in so that we can be accounted for during the confusing hours immediately following a crash. Knowing also that the news of the crash will soon break in the press, I ask that the families of our crew be told we are safe. The base wants more information, and I tell them what little I know. It was probably a C-5, but some of our people could have been deadheading on it.

We stop by the intelligence shop for an update. The situation in Kuwait is stabilized, but Iraq has mobilized a great deal of firepower. Our buildup is now in high gear but has just started. If they move south now, there is a good possibility that they could overwhelm us. Their late model Soviet- and French-built fighters are easily capable of reaching our flight paths.

The biggest threat may be our own people. We must take care to follow the voluminous procedures issued us in the form of SPINS (special instructions) to avoid becoming the target of friendly fire. We have to make sure that our radios are tuned to the proper frequencies, most of them classified secret, and that our transponder, which identifies us to ground-based radar, is updated hourly with the secret codes. We are keyed for the code words "CLEARED TO KILL" or "WEAPONS FREE" on any of the tactical frequencies we're required to monitor while in the AOR. If we hear those words, we know that hell has erupted. In such case the SPINS detail what we are to do, depending on location, weather, fuel state, and hostile threats. Its authors must have assumed that we would simply take leave of our instincts and our common sense. They have tried to provide guidance for every conceivable contingency.

We leave the CP complex, black bag bulging with flight plans, weather data, and SPINS, and catch the crew bus to the C-5 Galaxy on which we'll deadhead. The C-5 is a monstrous airplane, similar in size to a Boeing 747 but closely resembling a C-141 in basic shape. The plane is so big that it has complete sleeping quarters, galley, and lounge for a relief crew. But as we board, the aircraft commander tersely informs me that the bunks are reserved for his own crew. Sorry, he says, but we will have to sleep in the passenger seats for the seven-hour flight. Someone grumbles as we turn to transfer our gear. "Sure. No problem with us. Keep the bunks, Mike Foxtrot."

As we are stowing our gear, word arrives that the C-5 has a serious problem with its landing gear. While waiting for it to be fixed we accomplish the "mill-around checklist." The procedure calls for several actions that can be accomplished in any order:

1. SLEEP ON AN AIRPLANE BUNK.
Note
You will enjoy it if you like to sweat.

2. EAT YOUR BOX LUNCH.
Caution
Be careful not to eat the box itself, as it all tastes like cardboard.

3. SLEEP ON PARATROOP SEATS (if bunks are taken).
4. READ WALT'S HUNTING MAGAZINES.
5. SLEEP ON THE RAMP (use your helmet bag for a pillow).

WARNING
It'll be cooler, but stay under a wing to avoid being crushed by a cargo loader.

6. REFIGURE YOUR 30/60/90 DAY FLYING TIME CUMULATIVES.
Note
Bones will argue with your results no matter how hard you figure.

7. READ THE COMIC SECTION OF YESTERDAY'S *Stars & Stripes.*
8. EAT THE MYSTERY MEAT SANDWICH FROM ITEM 2.
CAUTION
You swore to leave this alone.

9. PACE TO AND FRO (preferably between the number four engine and the wing tip).
10. ARRANGE FOR A CREW BUS TO PICK UP THE LOADMASTERS (they must go to the chow hall for their third breakfast).

After about an hour we are informed that we have been reassigned to a new mission and a crew bus is being sent out. This news brings on a rash of mixed emotions. We're happy to dispense with the deadhead and the subsequent flight in a jet of doubtful airworthiness; on the other hand we know that this development will add at least two hours to our already lengthy day. We happily bid goodbye to the C-5, return to the CP for a new briefing, and are assigned a mission to Jubail, a Marine Corps helicopter base near the Kuwait border. While the engineers preflight the newly assigned aircraft, we do our flight planning and get the weather forecast.

Walt meets us as we arrive at the jet and escorts us to the tail, where Brian and two young mechanics are looking up at the vertical stabilizer towering four stories above. The jet is hemorrhaging red hydraulic fluid from the tail cone. Brian thinks that a seal in the rudder boost package is afoul. The two mechanics have investigated and tell us that it is simply excessive fluid, not to worry. But Brian and Walt will have no part of it and direct them to dig deeper. The young mechanics call in to their controller with disgusted voices and order additional help. An hour into our next mill-around checklist word arrives that the leak has finally been found, but the ETIC (estimated time in commission) is two hours plus whatever time it takes to locate and get the replacement parts—or "parts plus two."

We're facing a twenty-plus-hour day ahead of us still. We have "burned" five hours already and are still two hours from takeoff at a minimum. I call the CP on the jet's radio and tell the controller to send a bus. We're going back to bed. They comply, as they must when an aircraft commander declares a flight safety crew rest but not before we accomplish a few more mill-around items.

Back at the command post we hear the news of CINCMAC's visit. General H. T. Johnson, commander-in-chief, Military Airlift Command, arrived yesterday and has proceeded to clean out the temple.

He wasn't pleased with how the base was treating us. He found that dozens of rooms had been held in reserve for academy cadets on their summer orientation while aircrews were sleeping in the gym. Heads are rolling left and right. One guy saw him in the class six store where alcoholic beverages were sold. He was enraged, believing that the crews were being scalped, and was walking around, personally marking the prices down. This news makes us feel a little better. Perhaps somebody cares.

Back we go, dragging our bags to the hotel to begin the cycle anew. Our first trip to the Persian Gulf is foiled. A whole day—a day without flight hours—has been trashed. It's the first of many.

Sitting on the balcony alongside a cooler of San Miguel, we watch the Spanish sunup and judge landing patterns. Bones quotes a popular phrase, something to the effect that adversity, indeed, occurs. And Walt invokes the universally understood term in the airmen's world for bad mechanical luck.

"Boys, we're snakebit."

FOUR

DOWNRANGE

Still another day has burned us with more maintenance cancellations, but now we are finally poised to go. However, we've been delayed for over an hour. The flight line was quarantined because of a hot cargo problem of some sort. Bizarre though it sounds, a missile had fallen out of its box. Someone feared it would blow up, so everything had come to a halt while some explosives technicians checked it out. It was one of the momentary episodes of chaos at TJ that interrupted an otherwise steady state of confusion.

We stow our bags and begin the familiar ritual known to all pilots as nest building. First I stow my personal kit—the one with the books and tapes—in the cubbyhole behind and outboard of the seat. I have to stretch for it slightly but can reach it comfortably if I slide the seat aft a little.

Next, I get out the "pubs." From the large storage bags back in the loft, which contain all the information you need to fly almost anywhere on the globe, I fetch all of the charts and booklets needed for the trek.

Then I sort the approach books, which contain the detailed procedures for making approaches to thousands of airports. The procedures are designed so that a safe letdown can be made in bad weather, but we fly them in most places no matter what the weather.

Next I select the "supplements," which are thick booklets containing all the details of individual airfields and facilities; stuff like latitude and longitude, frequencies, runway and taxiway data, load-bearing capacity, notes telling us to do this and not to do that ad nauseam. One of my pet peeves being the sight of a messy cockpit, I take care to arrange the material neatly and in the sequence I'll need it. Bones apparently was a dismal failure in Chart Folding 101. He has a deplorable habit of strewing unfolded charts, booklets, flight plans, and such about the cockpit with reckless abandon. He stacks them on the glare shield and casts them on the center console. He wads them up like great spitballs and crams them down into his map case. Despite my scorn, he shows little improvement.

Once, back at home station, while building my nest, I got annoyed at the way some meathead on the previous crew had stuffed the approach booklets down into the map case. Fishing my hand down into the case in search of a booklet I felt something mushy and moist. I jerked my hand back and saw that it was smeared with stale tobacco juice that had been spit into a paper cup.

That tripped my breakers. I thought of that most wicked and hideous instrument of mass destruction known to mankind, strapped back there to the aft bulkhead—the crash axe—and how I would use it on the vermin who had done this. I had an idea who it was but called the command post and demanded the names of the underbreeds who had last piloted the jet.

I learned that it was the young farmer from New Hebron, the ever-grinning mustachioed Johnboy Turnage, who grew cows, chickens, and young children who tended the chickens, and who had won the highly distinguished Commander's Trophy for being the absolute undisputed Best in his USAF pilot training class. But he also had a conspirator: our unit's resident rotorhead Judd Moss, a convert from the Army, where he had flown helicopters. They were both disgusting chewers and were both qualified in either seat. The task of finding the culprit was complicated, because I knew that each would blame the other for the ignominious deed. And that's precisely what happened when I confronted them with it weeks later. They made a mockery of my attempt to chew their asses out, claiming innocence, pointing accusingly at one another, snickering, cheeks abulge. Since then I never reach into a crammed map case without carefully checking for repugnant booby traps.

The final act in nest building is seat adjustment. I slide mine as far forward as I can, which is unusual for a tall guy, but I like to be close to the panel. Then I adjust the rudder pedals as far out as they'll go. I make the vertical height so that I can just see a small deflector forward of the windscreen. Then I recline the seat back a few degrees and fix the armrests at a slightly sloping angle. In other than this familiar position I feel like a klutz.

The jet is in good shape, and we're ready to try again to launch for the sands. With a few minutes to go before station time, I decide to test Walt's patience.

While he isn't looking I go aft and drain a can of fuel from the single point refueling valve, then walk out and throw the fuel up onto the bottom of the right wing. It splatters, spreads, beads up, and drips onto the concrete, reeking of kerosene. Before it evaporates, it bears a remarkable resemblance to a fuel leak, which is a serious matter on a '141.

I cut the others in on the prank, put on my poker face, and climb to the flight deck, where Walt is reading a copy of *Guns and Ammo*.

"Walt, you'd better go out and check the right wing. It looks bad."

He sees the concern in my face and proceeds out, mumbling something about a snake. Finding the dripping fuel, he looks at me and sighs. He just slowly shakes his head in a disgusted resignation but then realizes that all eyes are on him, not the leak.

Somehow I expected cussing and rage, but I see Walt is not a man of such behavior. I clue him in on the gag, and he just smirks with an "I'll get you back" expression.

The preflight checks done, we sit and wait as the troops board. I look down at the long line of them, shuffling slowly toward the jet from the buses. They're fully decked out in desert camo, complete with the wretched German-style helmets that I just can't get used to; rifles and bayonets, bandoleers of ammo, and other such soldiering truck protrude and dangle from their sacrificial bodies. All of them look exceptionally young—only a couple of years senior to my oldest son. A chilling thought envelops me, thinking that he could be among them.

One is a girl. Incredibly, she is clutching a stuffed animal and laughing with the soldier beside her as if they were at a county fair. I wonder aloud what a battle-hardened enemy would think of this sight and call the crew over to my side window to see the spectacle. These times—I just don't understand them.

Finally we blast out of TJ, loaded with mixed cargo and troops. Our heavy load includes pallets of chain saws and drums of antifreeze. We also have great stores of Gatorade and stacks of food cartons stamped "MRE," a colossal lie: "Meal, Ready to Eat."

We climb out to the east over the serene moonlit mountains and cultivated valleys toward Barcelona and reach our cruising altitude of flight level 330, which is approximately 33,000 feet. Above 18,000 feet over the United States and the high seas, everyone sets their altimeters to 29.92 inches of mercury, which is the internationally accepted standard day pressure at sea level. This "transition level" is much lower in most countries. Above this level, altitudes are called flight levels, because they do not measure exact height above the earth but rather provide a level playing field for all the high-altitude cruisers. It assures me that the Aeroflot flight coming at me up ahead at flight level 350 is actually 2,000 feet above me, and it frees both him and me of the burden of resetting our altimeters to new values as we rapidly pass through areas of changing atmospheric pressures as the low flyers must to maintain accurate terrain clearance.

I start to get a little weary as we cross into French airspace, so I turn the controls over to Bones, disconnect my headset, and lean the seat back. Jeff is asleep in the bunk, so I don't wake him; I just want a short snooze.

A little while later I wake up and find that I'm the subject of a sick joke. I'm smothered in charts. They are piled on me like a stack of newspapers on a homeless bench sleeper. Low altitude charts, high altitude charts, terminal charts, and VFR charts are piled high on me and are spilling over onto the center console and the glare shield. I flail about like a drowning man and emerge from the pile to find Bones, Walt, Brian, and Jeff guffawing like insolent degenerates.

The respite in the seat has left me miserably unrested, so I go back and take the bunk Jeff vacates. I want to be fresh for the first trip into the AOR. Trying to sleep in the '141 is an ordeal, even in the bunk. You have to contend with heat, the deafening noise, and the cozy proximity of high-pressure and high-temperature bleed air ducts. An emergency oxygen bottle and mask are kept next to each bunk in case of rapid decompression. The bottles often leak down pressure, and only the foolish neglect to check pressure gauges before settling in for a nap.

At the altitudes we fly, if we had an explosive decompression, I would probably not get out of the bunk without the bottle, before losing consciousness. The crew would likely be too busy to help, especially with passengers to take care of. Brain damage or worse would result quickly. The outward-opening number two overhead escape hatch, which is located almost over the bunks, has historically been the culprit in most decompression events. That's not a comforting thought as I lie here on my back looking up at it. So I turn over.

Everyone seems to have the same impression of cruise sleep. You lie there trying to log some Zs, listening to the engines and the slipstream, thinking of home, the job you used to have, whatever. Then there's the sickening feeling of someone shaking your boot. Two, maybe three hours have passed. You don't feel like you've slept; you've just been in a cerebral holding pattern. You feel that time has been passed, but you seriously doubt that you're rested.

I grab a bottle of chilled muscadine juice from the cooler and join the crew and a couple of passengers visiting the flight deck. One is the lady soldier sitting in the forward jumpseat wearing a headset, and Bones is busily playing sky cadet, explaining with textbook precision what all those dials are for.

We are over Egypt. The Sahara down below is graveyard dark, lifeless and devoid of lights. But ahead is a weird, puzzling apparition. I have to rub my eyes and strain hard to make it out. Contrasting with the blackness is a long, snakelike fuzzy brightness. At first it seems to be a skyborne phenomenon. But no. It is below where the horizon ought to be. It must be a ground feature.

Maybe Bones has been this way before, I should ask him about it. But he's busy with the passenger. And besides, it wouldn't look good. I'm supposed to be the old head around here. I adjust the red beam from the reading light down so as to study the SPINS but keep glancing ahead at the specter.

The ghostly vision grows brighter and begins to resemble the Milky Way. But it is too low in the sky for that. And I can clearly see the Milky Way higher among the stars.

The glowing snake bends left, then right; narrows slightly, then widens again, and gradually fades out toward the far south. Now individual points of light begin to appear. Soon it becomes obvious that the glowing serpent is actually a long colony of millions of lights. Here and there clusters break out that are brighter and tinted differently. Then it hits me.

I minored in geography and feel pretty stupid for not anticipating this. Of course: it is the fertile, populated Nile River valley. Incredibly, almost all of Egypt's 39 million people live in this long, narrow band of life-giving soil and moisture.

We would fly over the valley numerous times in the year ahead, and in the light of day we could clearly see the green fields and farms contrasting sharply with the yellow featureless desert. It seemed you could stand in a sugarcane field and toss a rock into the desert wastes. I never ceased to marvel over the sight, especially at night when I'm given over to profound ponderings.

The Nile valley is a microcosm. It's a clear and stunning testament to the frailty of all life. Our planet is somewhat like the Nile. We live within such narrow boundaries between life and nothingness. If we stray out into space without protection—like the Bedouin who rides away from the river—we perish. The earth is the perfect distance from the sun; a few miles either way, and we couldn't exist. And the tilt of the global axis, the atmospheric pressure, the chemical makeup— all are precise for us. It would take more faith for me to believe that it was not divinely planned and created thus.

We turn eastward over the river and see a hint of sunrise ahead. Normally this would be a dreaded time. After hours of darkness and the tranquillity imparted by the stratospheric night skies, the sun blasts into the cockpit with a laser brilliance, brutally assaulting weary eyes, coercing them to squint and close; to stay closed until awareness wanes; till neck muscles relax, and the inner ear senses the falling head and rejuvenates the consciousness, snapping the eyes open. Then another dose of solar brilliance immediately begins the cycle anew. It's the scourge of the cargo pilot. S-LOC, I call it: sun-induced loss of consciousness.

But today I welcome the return of the sun because I'm eager to see these mysterious regions from biblical history over which we're going to certain war.

Ahead, beyond a range of serrate mountains, the sun glistens off the waters of the Red Sea. We are flying in the direction that the earth turns, so that the sun appears to rise rapidly. The colors begin to blossom with the sun's return. The turquoise blue of the sea breaks out of the brownish tan deserts, but the mountains west of the sea are a blazing crimson. I don't see a single cloud. Far to the north I can make out the mountains of the Sinai Peninsula, over which we will fly coming back out.

Bones's voice interrupts my musings, demanding a return to the business at hand.

"Red Crown, Red Crown, MAC Alpha 5140, over."

Red Crown is the radio call sign of the U.S.S. *Saratoga,* an aircraft carrier steaming lazily with her task force in what the Navy must regard as more of a bathtub than a sea. We must try to establish contact with her before crossing into Saudi Arabia or risk a visit from her deck of fighters.

"MAC Alpha 5140, Red Crown, go ahead."

"5140 is eastbound squawking 3612."

After a short delay the seaman sitting in front of his console identifies us and clears into the heralded AOR.

"MAC Alpha 5140, you're sweet, sweet. Cleared to cross."

I think that means radar contact/radar identified, but it's only a guess. I was never taught Navyese.

I train my binoculars on objects in the water but cannot pick out the *Saratoga,* only a few southeast-bound cargo ships and some oil platforms. Halfway across we contact Jeddah Control and are given our cleared route across the vast Arabian Peninsula. It is as we expected, thus there is no need to reprogram the waypoints in the navigation computer. We watch George, the autopilot, turn us southeastward as we cross the entry point over the seacoast settlement of Wejh.

The radio is extremely busy with air traffic coming into and out of the AOR. The Saudi controllers have thick accents, but English is the official language of international aviation, and though I become frustrated with them, I sense that they're doing their best to move us through. Bones and I listen closely to each transmission, sometimes glancing at one another with "what'd he say?" expressions on our faces.

It seems asinine, this method of moving millions of dollars of equipment and hundreds of fragile lives around the sky on scratchy, hissing, word-of-mouth instructions. Bones, Jeff, and I banter over the absurdity of it all. Many times we have descended blindly into a valley, with gigantic rocks obscured by clouds all around. As it behooves us, we try to stay generally oriented, but we depend utterly on the radar controllers to keep us clear of both the rocks and the other planes flying as blind as we are.

It occurred to me that the business world would consider such an operation to be a very serious transaction, fraught with financial and personal liability. The controllers bark orders to move a $20 million piece of equipment and dozens of lives blindly and very swiftly through a murky sky filled with mountains and planes. So much is at stake and not least the careers of both those doing the ordering and those taking the orders. The lawyers would have a field day with this if they could somehow exert control over it. Managers, stockholders, and supervisors would insist on carefully constructed and executed contracts.

But what if the corporate world, dealing with millions of dollars and hundreds of lives and careers, conducted business as we do between cockpit and controller? It would be as simple as, say, a phone call from a construction company to the city zoning commission. Something like: "Hello, this is Crashworthy Construction Company, we'd like to throw up a six-deck parking garage at the corner of Sixth Avenue and Eighteenth Street."

"Roger, you're cleared to proceed. Call back when you're done."

But the commission's telephone is on a party line. Other companies are trying to talk to the clerk all at the same time, and the lines are scratchy and hissy. The best the commission can do is record all the conversations, so that if the garage falls in and crushes a couple hundred cars, or if it was built in the wrong place, then blame can be established.

And what if we did business their way? We have the technology to fax documents quickly between ground and air. A computer could supply the basic language and would prompt the pilot and controller for the variables. We would make instant contracts, spelling out the duties and responsibilities of both controller and pilot. Each would sign and fax to the other. There could be no room for—"Micala-ahfiifeunforsero . . . cleeriadBraffofiffate, mintintreetreeseeroreeprt-Midiinah."

I glance at Bones, but he's shaking his head. I look back at Jeff in the jump seat. "Don't ask me," he shrugs, answering the unasked question.

We may be just around the corner from data link air traffic control. No human voices will be heard. Only a message will print out saying: "MAC Alpha 5140, cleared Bravo 58, maintain FL 330, report Medinah."

In this case I think I would welcome such an innovation. But then it'll only be a matter of time before the controller pushes a button and my airplane responds while I sit and watch. Of course I will have emergency override authority, but if I use it, I will have to defend such brazen action in a court of inquiry.

The landscape below keeps me pinned to the window, binoculars at the ready. The geology excites me. We cross great fault block mountain ranges and sail over the sinuous patterns of breached, plunging anticlines and synclines—the long parallel ridges produced by the warping and eroding of layered rocks. Dry though it is, water has played a tremendous role in shaping the Arabian landscape. Countless dry streambeds claw at the uplands, gradually tearing them down into vast alluvial fans. I'm bewildered by the sight of small settlements here and there in the parched valleys. How do the people survive? Bones, who is also schooled in geology, suggests that maybe they have herds that feed on grasses we're too high to see.

Being infidels, we are forbidden to overfly the holy city of Medinah and are routed slightly north. Then we are told to contact Riyadh Control and proceed eastward over Bir-Darb, down Route Blue 58 over the central plateau.

The landscape now is predominately of volcanic origin. Hundreds of black cinder cones dot the yellow desert. Vast fields of hardened, hummocky brown lava testify to a cataclysmic history. I venture a guess that it wasn't too long an interval, geologically, between when the cones last spewed their clouds of molten ejecta and when the first Bedouins herded their animals, as they do still.

Farther, past Riyadh, the mottled lava gives way to immense

swarms of dunes. These are Barchan dunes, which seemingly march—and in a geological sense, do exactly that—across the bleak landscape, their characteristic crescent shapes testifying to the prevailing wind direction.

"There, Bones!" A large circular feature. Three, four, five miles across, maybe. It's hard to tell. It's badly eroded and barely discernible. Possibly it's a huge meteor crater.

The jet ahead of us receives his descent clearance; soon we'll be next. We contact the airlift control element, or ALCE, and pass along our load data and estimated landing time. Jeff gets fresh weather from a met station in Riyadh and gives it to Brian, who falls to the task of calculating landing performance data. Brian then hands the data cards up to us, and I brief the crew on our planned approach to runway 34 right. Afterward I call for the ritual.

"Let us now read from the Book of Lockheed."

Brian knows this is his cue to start the descent checklist, the seventh of twelve such rituals we perform from the time we strap on the jet until we leave it. Bones and I respond dutifully after each challenge.

"ALTIMETERS."

"Set, pilot."

"Set, copilot."

"RADAR."

"On and tuned."

"CREW BRIEFING."

"Completed."

"RADAR ALTIMETER."

"On and set."

"THRUST REVERSER LIMITER."

"Set."

"CONTINUOUS IGNITION."

"On."

"SEAT BELTS AND SHOULDER HARNESSES."

"Adjusted, pilot."

"Adjusted, copilot."

"I'm pleased to announce that the descent checklist is complete."

I buckle my shoulder harness and adjust the seat. You've got to get the seat to the exact vertical position you're used to. Just a notch or two higher or lower and you could grossly misjudge your height above the runway during landing.

The '141 has a long body, one that sits low to the ground. It was designed this way so that cargo and vehicles could be more easily loaded on board. But as a result there is little clearance between tail and ground, which poses a problem when landing. If you continue to apply back pressure in the flare, looking for that smooth "grease job" landing, the underside of the tail cone can easily strike the runway. It's not a life-threatening situation, but smoke, sparks, a costly repair job, and a trip to the kick-butt room are the likely results. Yet we have a choice. We can partially flare the jet, thereby accepting a firm but safe landing, or we can gamble on the "check-and-roll" maneuver.

This thing is not taught in the flight schools but is a recognized acceptable way in both the military and civilian world to land certain long-bodied airplanes. Instead of actually flaring the plane, we "check" the descent with back pressure at about the point where a normal flare would be initiated. Then we release back pressure, reducing the angle of attack. If we judge it right, we'll catch the main trucks on the upswing as the nose rotates down toward the runway and maybe get that delightful grease job. It works best on airplanes in which the center of such rotation is forward of the main gear.

But the trick is to check the descent when the main wheels are about 3 feet above the pavement. That's hard to judge when one's butt is about 30 feet up and angling skyward and descending at 10 feet per second while moving ahead at 200 feet per second. If you check at 5 or 6 feet, you'll pitch down flat on the runway, picking up an excessive descent rate, thereby crunching the main gear and possibly slamming down the nose; check too low and you drive the main gear into the concrete. To hit it right, you have a decision window of about plus or minus a second.

Certain conditions can help or hinder the process. Most of us welcome a mild cross-wind. This allows us to bank into the wind during the check-and-roll maneuver, using opposite rudder to maintain runway alignment. The upwind wheels touch first, followed by the downwind wheels. The result is a cushioning effect and that oh, so wonderful feeling of a great landing. A few pilots will argue that such landings are unsafe because of an involved technicality—something to do with delayed spoiler activation because the aircraft's weight doesn't immediately settle on the touchdown switch. But such folks are not usually gifted enough to execute the check and roll anyway.

A Yankee named Rick Hess came down and joined us from a fighter squadron in upstate New York and proceeded to make consistently perfect landings in the C-141. Had he not been able to find the key to getting along with southerners, we would have run him out of town on a rail. A few others among us, such as Johnboy Turnage, Tom Wallace, and Rob Finch, could hit the landings with embarrassing perfection. Most of us could do it sometimes, and a few could never hit it, but we all somehow managed not to break the jets.

When a fellow pilot makes a bad landing, the code requires that you remain silent if you don't like him, since silence can be the most painful of criticisms. But if you like your flying partner, you might try to ease his chagrin with a remark or two about the various conditions that brought on his misfortune, whether or not they're relevant. Still, it is from the nonpilot crew members—the engineers and loads—that the crude remarks about chiropractors and mangled spinal cords will come. Mercifully, such remarks are normally made on "hot mike," which is a feature of the interphone system that pilots don't normally monitor.

It was on the worst of days—those when the airplane is lightweight and the wind is calm—that I made one of my all-time worst landings. I checked too high and crunched down hard as the wings shed their lift in the rapidly decreasing airspeed. I felt that inevitable red flush and embarrassment as the jet rolled and we reconfigured the flaps for another takeoff. I was exceedingly glad that the "Old Man" wasn't aboard.

Tech Sergeant Hank Woolsey was a flight engineer, and because of his age, which was perceived as advanced, he could and did approach the frontiers of intimidation with his practical jokes on us college boy officer pilots. He kept a "squeaky horn," the kind that made a preposterous rubber duck kind of noise, in his flight kit. The goal of any pilot flying with Hank was to make a landing good enough to keep the cursed squeaky horn silent. And it was quite a challenge, for Hank was an accomplished civilian pilot in his own right. He required near perfection from the more experienced pilots while being a little more tolerant with the younger guys. Still, the horn respected no boundaries of rank, age, status, or talent. All of us—from the lowest second balloon (second lieutenant) to the heavyweights from the Head Shed—were subject to its humiliating teasing.

Relieved though I was that Hank wasn't with us, I still couldn't escape the pitiless horn that day. Just as the flaps started tracking to takeoff position, we heard it coming across the squadron frequency in our headsets, as somewhere the horn was being held next to a microphone.

OWEEHA OWEEHA OWEEHA OWEEHA

I looked over on the parallel taxiway and saw another C-141 taxiing out for takeoff, in the perfect position to observe the immense cloud of blue tire smoke drifting from the site of my bone-jarring landing.

But now the time is over for practicing landings. All continuation training requirements have been suspended. Yet somewhere out here in the tail of the storm I feel that the squeaky horn lurks, waiting for my next cruncher.

Shortly, Riyadh hands us off the Bahrain Center, and the frequency becomes jammed as dozens of aircraft compete for the controller's attention. They have trouble understanding him and ask again and again for clarification. Soon the frequency is a hopeless quagmire, as planes nearing their clearance limits become impatient and call desperately for clearances.

Then, to our surprise and delight a deep, self-confident voice with a Texas drawl interrupts the overloaded Saudis and starts methodically sorting through the communications chaos, like a firm but caring father with his brood.

"OK, EVERYBODY BE QUIET AND LISTEN. Now, who's askin' for lower?"

"MAC Mike 2427, you can expect lower in twenty miles. Break, Texaco 32 go direct Gassim and contact Riyadh 126.0."

"MAC Victor 1834, descend now to two one zero, pilot's discretion to one eight zero. Break, MAC Alpha 4112 fly heading two four zero, intercept Golf fifty-three, expect higher at Bopan."

"Army 26 Romeo Kilo, Roger, cleared tactical, your discretion."

"Now, who else was callin'?"

There it is, straight ahead. At last, the azure blue waters of the Persian Gulf. The yellow-green streaks of shallow reefs contrast vividly with the aquamarine waters. This is far too beautiful and pristine looking to be the most troubled pool of water in the world. It looks so refreshing, so nonthreatening.

Lord, but we're a long way from home.

The Texan hands us over to the Dhahran "Director," whoever that is, who in turn passes us to the airfield control tower. We complete another litany, the approach checklist, and turn on to a twelve-mile final approach, intercepting the electronic beam known as the localizer course, which will guide us to the runway. We don't need it, though; the weather is clear and we can see the vast airfield ahead. We pass over the lavish beach residence of a member of the royal family and perform the before landing checklist.

We slow down and welcome the roar of the landing gear and flaps as they are lowered into the 200-knot slipstream. It signifies that a respite is at hand. Half the long duty period is almost over. A huge seawater desalination plant passes off our right wing as I reduce power and start down the electronic glideslope. We drop low over the bleak sands and cross the runway threshold, stealing a quick glance at the man-made hills just east of the runway.

Here we see the first indication that we have arrived at the much heralded line drawn in the sand. The silhouettes of missile launchers and their attendant acquisition radars are pointed northward. They don't seem so very imposing; the launchers are simply box-shaped, housing the missiles within. But they exude a certain cockiness, an arrogance, like Davy Crockett and his Tennesseans, not really embracing the cause of Texas, just spoiling for a sporting fight. Yeah, that missile battery over there is Davy, leaning across the battlements, sighting down Old Betsy.

But I figure to be back in Tennessee or somewhere like it when Santa Anna charges.

Bones mumbles something about Toto and Kansas as we roll out on the long runway, six and one-half hours after departing Spain. As we turn westward and taxi toward the military side of the field, it becomes immediately obvious that the Saudis have spared no expense on the airport. It has all the modern facilities of any in the Western world, as will almost every place we go in Saudi Arabia in the months ahead. We take care of the post–landing checklist rituals as we taxi past rows of allied fighter planes parked in concrete revetments. Several American-built A-4 fighters bear Kuwait Air Force markings, with "Free Kuwait" painted boldly on their sides.

We are marshaled into a parking space behind another C-141 on a vast ramp teeming with activity. Air Force C-5s, C-141s and C-130s are constantly streaming in and out, often waiting for a parking space to open up. Great jumbo jets bearing the colorful logos of the major airlines look absurdly out of place here, as they disgorge hundreds of troops and thousands of tons of palleted cargo. Trucks, vans, cargo loaders (known to us as K-loaders), tugs, and behemoth fuel trucks bigger than any I've ever seen rush about the ramp, so that we have to be supercautious walking across the tarmac.

We walk toward the great hangar that serves as a staging area for incoming troops and, we would learn, is a favorite backdrop for TV correspondents taping their reports. The noise is incredible, with the scream of idling engines, the throbbing of power carts, the whop-whop of helicopter rotors, and the ground-shaking thunder of afterburners. It seems Dhahran is truly the Da Nang of the Persian Gulf.

As we walk nearer the hangar complex, I can hear, through the din, the intermittent wail of Arabic prayer songs on a distant loudspeaker. The air here seems thick with war.

FIVE

TROUBLED SKIES

ones applies back pressure to the control yoke, and we rise as if perched on the muzzle of a great cannon being elevated for a shot. The 323,000-pound rip-snorting beast begins to run on its main wheels for a distance, allowing enormous cells of high pressure to form under our wings. Then we are flying and none too soon. The end of runway 6 flashes beneath us as I comply with Bones's request to raise the gear. Glancing out to the left, while listening to the familiar groan and plop of the retracting gear, I see that we're still low enough to pick out the white golf balls lying on McGuire Air Force Base's fifteenth green.

We breathe a little easier, now that the mother of all takeoff rolls is behind us, and Bones banks the Starlifter to the east. Torrejon lies eight and one-half hours ahead. As I switch the radio to departure control frequency, I abruptly freeze, motionless, my hand still on the radio knob.

When something goes amiss with your aircraft, you react instantly, if you're well trained. Your eyes go directly to whatever instrumentation can verify the problem. Your hands move immediately to the appropriate switches and levers. Your mind flashes the much rehearsed corrective action. But there is one matter that freezes you like a statue, that reduces you from a refined machine to a simple creature depending utterly—even desperately—on your animal senses. Nothing makes your skin crawl and your brain flicker with foreboding more than the pungent smell of burning electrical insulation.

My eyes shift to one side, then the other while I sniff the air. Yes, there seems to be a very faint odor. But I've been battling nasal congestion for weeks—who am I to judge subtle smells? It's really barely noticeable. I try to ignore it. I'm busy with the radio and the departure procedure. Besides, there are five of us on the flight deck, if the odor is real, surely someone else will notice it.

But who am I trying to convince? It's time to fess up.

"Do you guys smell anything?" I ask.

Like me, they all are waiting for someone else to make the disquieting suggestion.

"Yeah. Just barely. An electrical smell, maybe," Walt replies.

That's not what I was hoping to hear.

Without waiting for guidance from me, Walt sensibly goes down to the cargo bay and into the tunnel underneath the flight deck to examine the tangled jungle of cables and dusty electronic boxes. He reports back that he couldn't smell it down there. That relieves us a bit but heightens our curiosity. We agree that the smell is getting stronger, though it is still elusive.

Trouble usually comes in subtle ways for the flier. It commonly starts out as a sneaky beast. Instead of rearing a big ugly head, it plays peek-a-boo with you. A feeling creeps over you that something is wrong. You rub your eyes, shake the cobwebs out of your head, look around to see if anyone else looks vexed. But trouble is a cunning psychologist. It plays with your mind, tries to convince you that all is rosy, that you're just tired, or that an indicator has gone bad.

And trouble plays havoc with your ego, which is quite hefty, or you wouldn't be here. You feel the need to discuss your suspicions with your crewmates but are afraid of what they might think of you if you're wrong. Then it gradually builds and enlists conspirators such as confusion, fatigue, unfamiliarity, and personality conflicts. External influences such as weather, fuel availability, and conditions on the ground can join in with the swelling, cascading snowball.

I know that every minute we are putting five more miles between us and the safety of the airfield, but the beast is having a field day in my mind. We'd be a laughingstock if we went back and the mechanics found nothing. They will write "cannot duplicate" in the discrepancy forms when their search for a problem from a flight turns up nothing. I hate that. It suggests that I'm a jittery flier or that perhaps I'm someone who just wants to cause trouble for mechanics.

And then there's the fear of that old specter, fatigue. You know it'll catch up with you in the long hours ahead and you don't want to do anything to hasten it or intensify it. If we go back, they may throw us onto another mission, lengthening our crew duty day another three or four hours. But worse yet, they may dump us back into crew rest, which is something we dreaded at McGuire. Such are the mind games that insipid trouble plays on a flier, urging him to hold his inertia, to stick with the course.

But I know the crew is troubled, especially the conservative Brian back on the engineer's panel.

"Let's go back," I finally say to Bones.

As New York Center clears us to turn 180 degrees for a direct course back to McGuire, the loadmaster, Mike Hall, announces that he has found the source. Many loadmasters stand back and watch when something like this happens or until an obvious calamity breaks out but not Mike. Maybe his survival instinct is driving him, but whatever, I'm delighted by his initiative. I turn and look, seeing him on hands and knees, sniffing, like a dog, at a circuit breaker panel just behind my seat. Then I notice the blue haze forming just above the deck, and I issue the order that I should have made minutes earlier.

"Crew, get your oxygen masks on. Check regulators 100 percent."

The mask, with its attendant smoke goggles, hoses, and cables has an acute way of boosting your awareness when you wear it. It grabs your lapels and slaps your face—pours a bucket of cold water on your thick, lethargic noggin. It gives you a vigorous shoulder shaking and makes you realize that your margin for error has narrowed and a high level of performance is now in demand. The hissing of your breathing and your muffled voice in the mask ram reality home and rivet your attention to the task at hand.

Now we are desperately busy. Bones transfers control of the jet to me and begins to copy new weather, while Brian calculates landing performance data and Walt continues to investigate the smoke. We barely have time to run the approach checklist. The weather has dete-

© Walter Sitauvik

riorated since we took off, so rather than the quick visual approach
that we hoped for, we have to set up for a lengthy ILS (instrument
landing system) approach.

We follow the radar vectors from McGuire Approach Control and
intercept the glide slope beam. As we lower the flaps and gear, the
smoke thickens. The runway is wet and we're extremely heavy. It
would be nice to get rid of some of this fuel, but there is no time. Even
if there were, it would be questionable whether we should open the
dump valves with a fire somewhere aboard. Brian says that we should
be able to get stopped, but there won't be much room for error.

The tower reports stiff crosswinds. This we definitely don't need,
because the crosswind requires extra speed that will gobble up precious runway. We break out of the clouds at about 400 feet into a heavy
rain, and I begin to fight the gusting winds. I push the throttles up,
then bring them back again and again to control the sink rates and
airspeed transients. The yoke moves fore and aft, left and right under
my hand in a struggle to maintain attitude. Bones switches on the

rain removal system, and the tremendous howling of the pressurized air blowing across the windscreen claws at my concentration, but it clears the rain away.

With a clear view I can see that we are approaching in a big crab because of the crosswind. Our nose is pointed well to the left of the runway, though we are tracking the center line. We cannot land like this. Seconds before touchdown, I push the right rudder to the floor and roll the yoke hard left. The left wing goes down, and the nose swings to the right—too much. Now we are angled a bit to the right of the runway centerline. I release a little right rudder pressure and apply a slight back pressure to the yoke. The landing is smooth, not because of my skill, but because of the extra airspeed we've had to carry.

Immediately I throw all four engines into maximum reverse thrust. The reversers are clamshell like doors that close behind the engine's exhaust pipe and direct the jet blast at a forward angle much as a spacecraft slows by firing a rocket in its direction of travel. But then the snowball gets bigger.

Bones notices the amber warning light and yells that the number four reverser has malfunctioned. This forces me to discontinue reversing on the number one engine, to avoid running off the left side of the runway because of asymmetric reverse thrust. Now the smoke is the least of our troubles. We have a heavy bird, a wet runway, excessive speed, and half our reverse thrust.

I begin to apply hard brake pressure at about 110 knots indicated airspeed, far above the maximum 60 knots for brake application. I hope the antiskid brake system will hold up. I remember how it failed me in a similar situation a couple of years ago, but we were lucky then. If the tires blow I might not be able to control it. I pull the inboard throttles back so hard I feel like they're about to bend. Predictably, we hear the popping explosions as the compressors begin to stall, and the engines spit enormous fireballs ahead of the plane. As the runway end approaches, we begin to slow enough to turn off safely, but the snowball hasn't stopped rolling yet.

Knowing that the brakes will be white hot and in danger of catching fire or even exploding, I stop as soon as we are clear of the runway and call for a quick evacuation. We shut down, jump out, and are passed by firemen as we trot away from the jet through a cold rain. We inhale deep lungs full of freshness and dampness; it never felt better. We laugh and slap one another's backs there in the rain, like sailors delivered through a gale. We've ridden the snowball. We've "cheated death once again," Mike chants.

The mechanics quickly find the charred wire bundle in the AHRS circuitry. There will be no more flying for us today. The flight surgeon has grounded us temporarily because of the smoke. And before the brakes have cooled, it seems, the rumors have started about us. One crew we meet at the motel has heard that we were recalled and grounded because we were drunk. Another brings us false news that we are to be decorated. Later we learn that we have been killed.

The doc releases us a couple of days later, and they throw us into the fray again. We had a minimum crew rest at Zaragoza and are now headed back downrange.

"MAC Bravo 5518, you are cleared direct Barcelona, Upper Golf 33. Maintain Flight Level 330."

We've reached our cruising altitude, and the Spanish controller has cleared us to proceed along route UG23 to the eastern boundary of his airspace. I look at the computer-generated flight plan for a review of our route clearance, which reads: ZZA UG25 QUV UG23 ALG UB35 CRO UA1 METRU W727 DBA B12 KATAB UA451 LXR W726 WEJ B58 KIA. It looks fairly simple. Barcelona is tuned into both our navigation radios, and we are flying directly to it. Beyond that, with the concurrence of the respective countries, we will continue along UG23 through France and Italy, switching over to Upper Amber 1 (UA1) at Crotone, which is on the toe of Italy's boot. I'm not sure why we sometimes substitute colors for standard aviation phonetics (like "amber" for "alpha") when referring to these international routes, but I do it because I hear other pilots doing it. I suppose it's a way to be a little rebellious in our rigidly structured world without causing too much consternation.

After Italy, the controller's accents begin to get thick and confusing as we cut southeast through Greek airspace. At point Metru, UA1 changes designation to Whiskey 727 and funnels us into El Daba, Egypt. Then we pick up Bravo 12 to Katab and Amber 451 to Luxor, followed by Whiskey 726 across the Red Sea to Wejh and Bravo 58 to Riyadh, which is our destination. Some of the points identified in our route clearance are just points in the sky—"fixes"—that are unrelated to anything on the ground. The giveaway is the five-letter length. Other points, which are identified by three letters, represent actual navigation stations on the ground and are usually named after the closest towns.

The navigation en route chart is complicated to the point of intimidation. A sheet of Mozart's music would make more sense to me if I didn't have so much experience at reading these things. The charts are cluttered beyond reason. Lines run asunder in every direction, like a pattern of fallen fiddlesticks, each marked with its identifier, course, distance between stations, changeover points, and compulsory and noncompulsory reporting points. Data boxes, latitude/longitude coordinates, flight information region boundaries, prohibited areas, and restricted areas are splattered everywhere. Ominous threats lie within mysterious shaded areas, such as:

WARNING
UNLISTED RADIO EMISSIONS FROM THIS AREA MAY
CONSTITUTE A NAVIGATION HAZARD OR RESULT IN
BORDER OVERFLIGHT UNLESS UNUSUAL PRECAU-
TION IS EXERCISED.

And worse:

WARNING
AIRCRAFT INFRINGING UPON
NON-FREE FLYING TERRITORY
MAY BE FIRED UPON WITHOUT
WARNING.

Islands and coastlines are indicated only by subtly shaded lines that are impossible to see in dim light, but they are not considered important. This is a chart of airspace, not ground features. I get rankled when Bones and his generation of young fliers refer to them as "maps." Rand McNally makes maps; mariners and aviators navigate by charts. Don't they teach these things in flight school anymore?

The five-hour-and-twenty-nine-minute flight will take us across 2,952 miles through six countries. We will burn 10,154 gallons of fuel. We will change course sixteen times, navigation frequencies fourteen times, and communication frequencies thirty-one times.

We have no passengers because we are carrying "hazardous cargo." The jet is loaded with pallets stacked with guided missiles. We can't see them; they're enclosed in metal cases stenciled with the usual strings of numbers and codes of the logistical language. But the word "Patriot" is embedded here and there in the printed gibberish.

Those were Patriot batteries we saw at Dhahran a few days ago. These are bound for Riyadh, the Saudi capitol. They really are serious about an Iraqi air attack. From the sleep-inducing training sessions I'm occasionally required to sit through, I have a vague idea of what a Patriot is. It's a radar-guided surface-to-air missile designed to ruin the day of an attacking pilot out to do an honest day's work. But I can't imagine that Iraqi aircraft will be a real threat. Their air force is the YMCA flag league; ours is the NFL. I decide that the missiles are being sent over as a contingency, probably just to soothe some nerves.

Back behind the stacks of Patriots are a few cases of another kind of missile, a smaller one called the "Stinger." This is a "shoulder launched" missile that can be carried by one person. He aims it, bazookalike, at a low-flying aircraft and lets it home in on the aircraft's engine heat "signature." It only has a small warhead about the size of a hand grenade, but it's enough to bring down most helicopters and some fighters. Stingers proved deadly in the hands of Afghan tribesmen against highly sophisticated Soviet aircraft. It shouldn't take a rocket scientist to figure out what we and our cargo would be worth to a terrorist group.

We often haul hot cargo, which can be anything from acids to nuclear weapons. And lately we've been hauling a lot of it. In peacetime, thorough precautions are taken. A whole chapter in our "you'd better do it this way or else" manual is devoted to them. Volumes are written about precautions for the load planners to follow. Great effort must be made by the crew to see that there is proper documentation, and the destination must be informed of the dangerous stuff. It must be annotated in the flight plan, relayed by long-range radio en route, and relayed again, in detail, just prior to landing. We are required to park in special remote spots to load and unload. At one Stateside base we must taxi over a mile through some scenic, forested countryside, as if on a Sunday drive, to reach the hot cargo ramp.

I remember my first hot cargo flight. I was a new C-130 aircraft commander hauling 10,000 rounds of 30-millimeter antitank ammunition to Canada for a joint exercise. We waited with engines running in the remote parking spot at the Canadian base and soon spotted a truck approaching from the front with a gigantic trailer in tow. The trailer, we deduced, was an external power unit—a big generator, bigger than those we were accustomed to—that could be hooked up to the aircraft to provide power when the engines were shut down.

A strange thing happened as it approached. I wanted to shake my head vigorously, to draw nearer to the windscreen as if to get a better view. I looked over at Larry Beall. The stoical "Beally," as we called him, would light a cigarette and watch a thermonuclear attack as if it were a mediocre fireworks display; it took much to impress him. Now he was staring ahead with a speechless, steadily broadening grin.

The trailer, seemingly in slow motion, detached itself, swerved gently to its right, and passed the truck, as if being driven by an impatient ghost who summarily intended to ram us. The truck stopped as the driver watched helplessly, wanting to steer clear of what was about to transpire. The kamikaze power cart, with its ghost pilot Murphy, gathered speed and bore down on us with our cargo of pyrotechnics.

Our four big propellers, each with four blades that resembled huge paddles, were spinning furiously, as turboprops like to do even at idle. Anything running into the props would tear them asunder, scattering debris at bullet speeds. Our load of sleeping 30 millimeters would not take kindly to such intrusion. With about a hundred feet to go, the errant trailer slowed, veered to the left, across our nose, and toppled into a ditch. Ole Murph shook his fist in frustration at us.

Since the start of Desert Shield, the book on hot cargo had all but been thrown overboard. In the Middle East, a "bad moon was risin'," as the old song goes. I sure felt it. And the ammo had to get there fast. No longer were we parked in remote areas or bothered with busywork. The powers that be had decided, in the interest of expediency, to keep the flow moving as fast as possible and hoped that ole Murphy would lie low.

For the most part he did, or so some would believe. But the truth is that we—those of us who flew and supported the air logistical tail— were simply better than they thought we were. The Pentagon planners had crossed their fingers and sat nervously in their chairs, hoping that the giant scheme would unfold with some measure of success and a minimal loss of life and property. But their apprehension was entirely unwarranted. The first team was on the field. And we were coming through like the champs we were since the day the red flag went up.

We've exchanged our hot cargo for cold cargo. We're westbound across the pond, headed back to the States. The stars are out by the blue zillions tonight, but no one is noticing. Our thoughts are dwelling on the objects in the rear.

There are four stainless steel boxes in our cavernous cargo bay. We're carrying HRs—the Air Force's warm and sensitive code for dead bodies: human remains. The war hasn't even started yet, and already we're bringing home gelatinous masses that used to be human beings.

The loadmasters are in the bunks; there's no reason for anyone to be back there. We have no other cargo or passengers. But nature calls, so I unstrap and, leaving the jet in Bones's charge, climb down the flight deck ladder. Turning toward the lavatory, I stop to view the scene.

The cargo bay lights have been turned off to preserve the bulbs, except for a few near the front. The din of the engines assaults the aural nerves. Brian wastes no effort trying to regulate the temperature back here, from his engineering station up front. It is cold enough to make your breath fog.

A third of the way back, the four boxes are chained to a steel pallet that is, in turn, secured to the cargo floor mooring locks. There are no flags draped over them, but there is a computer printout attached with each occupant's name plus an accounting control number of some sort.

There is a very hot rumor circulating—intensely talked about everywhere we go. The government has ordered 10,000 of these cold, loathsome containers. In a few weeks I may be looking at a plane packed full of them, a vision that chills me more than the cold air could.

The two boxes on the left contain the remains of two fighter pilots.

They were killed on a training flight somewhere in Saudi Arabia. Their F-15 apparently just flew into the ground while they were maneuvering at low altitude.

I speculate that the desert did it. Deserts are real killers to low fliers. Taking quick glances at the ground, one who is not familiar with the desert environment can mistake brush and small scrub trees for the large trees he was accustomed to. Instead of being 50 feet above a 100-foot tree, he may be 5 feet above a 10-foot tree. That doesn't leave a lot of room for error. Yes, of course they had a radar altimeter, but in the heat of the fight or the excitement of the chase or whatever—well, it just takes a second's worth of diverted attention. Yeah, I think the desert is to blame for this.

Arabian deserts are all the more dangerous. I heard that the Saudis have to import sand for concrete; theirs is too fine grained. I believe it, because their sand is airborne about as much time as it's not. The ultrafine particles lift into the sky, borne by winds racing unchecked across the landscape, the grains becoming finer with altitude. The result is an absence of horizon. There's only a pale blue zenith that gradually changes to a pale yellow earth below. Your judgment has to be flawless when flying low and fast through such a surreal world.

Judgment is just one event in the flier's survival sequence. Eye must first see the situation or the threat. The image is flashed to the brain. The brain sorts out the image and makes a decision based on sensory data stored in its memory cells. The decision takes the form of an electrical signal sent through the nerves to the muscles, which in turn grip and apply pressure to the stick, the rudder, the throttles. These linkages move wires, cables, and hydraulic actuators that activate flight control surfaces and fuel control valves. The flight control surfaces flex, resulting in aerodynamic pressures that exert force on the aircraft to change its flight path. The point at which flesh meets metal in the sequence is not important. The only relevant factor is the final result—the flight path. The flier and the craft are merged. They're one. And they live or die as one.

The F-15 is moving at 600 miles per hour, maybe faster, 50 feet above an alien, indistinct world. Was it a millisecond's inattention? A heartbeat of a hesitation? I don't know. They just flew into the ground.

I wonder if there is anything more in those boxes than a few

©Walter Sotamund '94

A-7D Corsair

charred fragments of bone, boot leather, and helmet. I pose the question to Bones. But he just shrugs, and I regret asking, feeling that I've violated some unspoken sacred code.

I almost flew into the ground once. I was young and quite stupid at times and wanted to impress my boss. I was tapped to fly as number four in a flight of four A-7s. The flight would be part of an experiment. An especially modified C-130 transport would launch an unmanned radio-controlled drogue that would fly across the gunnery range, spewing out chaff in a long corridor. Chaff is like thousands of tiny slivers of aluminum foil that hang for long periods in the sky, like clouds. It is invisible to the distant eye, but radar can see it within certain frequency parameters. Our mission was to delineate the chaff corridor on our radar scopes and fly so as to remain within it. The idea was that enemy air defense radar would not be able to isolate us within the cloud until we dove out of it onto the target, thus reducing our vulnerability to radar-guided antiaircraft weapons. We were trying to learn from the hard knocks of Viet Nam.

My role wasn't important, even though I would be the only plane actually to attack the target. Delineating the chaff cloud was the main objective. We just didn't know if our A-7 radars could do it. Colonel Mike Nelson, my squadron commander, was in the lead Corsair, and the wing deputy commander for operations, a very powerful man, was flying as number two. My squadron mate Duane, the number three man, would accelerate out ahead of the formation and fly across the range, visually checking for souvenir collectors and illegal aliens who often crossed the ranges, coming up from Mexico.

Other experiments had also been inaugurated in this post–Viet Nam era of adjustment. On a few occasions we had practiced the "pop-up" deliveries that are now standard practice. It was a thrilling maneuver in which you flew very low to avoid hostile radar, relying on your inertial navigation system and chart-reading skills until you were close to the target. Then, with an abrupt pull-up, followed by a daring roll to the inverted position, you acquired the target visually while upside down or nearly so. Swiftly rolling wings level, in a thunderous dive, you released the bombs and rolled hard back to the deck to escape. No other fighter tactic made a pilot's aggressive juices pump with such intensity. The thrill was proportional to the danger, but the risk could be minimized by thoroughly planning and thinking through the attack beforehand. Such was my near fatal downfall.

As Duane called the range clear, I impulsively decided to make a pop-up attack instead of the usual high dive. The bosses were looking; I could easily impress them. The target was an old Korean war vintage F-84 jet parked on a runway in a desert valley. I broke away, dove for a low line of hills south of the target, and leveled off as close to the ground as I dared. The dry washes and scrub brush of the desert floor flashed underneath the nose in a blur. Cliffs of yellow sandstone scurried past the wings.

The underpowered A-7 is no speed demon compared with other fighters, but flying at 500 knots down in the "weeds" shocked my adrenalin glands. My arteries pumped like the jet's hydraulic systems. Something akin to an electrified blaze of light flowed through me, buzzing and bubbling like the immense, pressurized stream of fuel to the insatiable engine. I was intensely alive.

But as I smoked up the valley, I began to realize that I hadn't thought this out enough. Where was the target? The inertial measurement system, or IMS, indicated that it was straight ahead, but the black box could be a mile or more in error and routinely was. Could it be slightly left or right? And how far? Where should I start the pop-up? It depended on the type of ordnance and delivery. The details were fuzzy. I didn't want to foul this up and get lost with the brass looking on. I should have stuck to the plan.

A slave to my ego, I was committed. When the IMS distance clicked down to about two miles, which was much too late, I pulled the A-7 hard up, watched the altimeter needle race with a blur past 4,000 feet, then rolled inverted and pulled the nose down. I couldn't believe it. There in the windscreen, beyond the dancing green symbols in the head-up display, was the inverted image of the F-84. I immediately flexed the stick and slapped the earth back underneath. Within a few wild heartbeats the metallic blur evolved into an onrushing, expanding frame of wings and tail, complete with faded numbers and rows of rivets. I was viewing the final second of my earthly existence through a powerful, zooming telephoto lens. "Target fixation" would be the conclusion typed on the investigating committee's report. And as usual, they would be wrong. This was more like target stupidity.

I don't know if it was through instinctive habit or an inflated ego, but even as I began a desperate attempt to emerge alive, I pressed the strike. Holding down the bomb release button, I jerked the stick back into my gut, grunting under the tremendous "G" pressure pressing me down into the seat. The G-suit swelled furiously around my thighs and belly, staving off the blackout. It was so intense that my vision narrowed as though looking through a hideous tunnel. My heart pounded, and I felt flush with fear, stupidity, and embarrassment.

In a few seconds, with the nose pointed safely up, I managed a glance over my shoulder and saw where the twenty-five-pound practice bomb had impacted. The white smoke was flowing in a wicked curl up into the wake turbulence created by my near collision with the parked F-84. If the bomb had been a standard 500-pound Mark 82, I would have been blown out of the sky by its fragmentation pattern. It was a perfect hit—a "shack." But the boss, fiddling with his radar high above, noticed neither the direct hit nor the near crash.

When we stepped into the crew van back at the base, Colonel Nelson asked how the attack went, and I croaked a response. But Duane just looked at me, expressionless, then slowly shook his head. He'd seen it. He knew he was looking at a sweating, quivering, imbecilic tester of fate's ragged boundaries. I remember that brush with fate as clearly as if it were yesterday. Somehow I escaped the desert's snare. But those guys back there didn't.

We bore on through the North Atlantic night, pondering the cargo, unsuccessfully trying to restrain our imaginations from their twisted propensity to probe the contents of the boxes. But the dead fighter pilots aren't really what bothers me. I know they probably have weeping, heart-shattered relatives waiting—teary-eyed children maybe. They died in the cockpit; their deaths are sufferable. And of the third box I know nothing other than that it is someone from the armed forces in Europe, a traffic victim perhaps. It's the fourth box that really haunts me. It is short and small—as if it contains the body of a child.

They gave me a new crew and a new mission after a couple of days at home, and now we're headed west again after another mission downrange. The weather across the Northern Hemisphere is becoming wintery now. That's good news if you're flying eastbound with the winter jet stream and bad if you're going west against it. And it's just plain bad-all-around news if you're planning on landing anywhere in Europe or the U.S. eastern seaboard.

I'm relaxing in the seat, listening to my tape player. We've discovered that the little micro speakers will fit neatly under our military headsets, and if we turn the aircraft radio volume up a little higher than the music, we can still hear any radio traffic that might be intended for us. Of course we wouldn't do this during a critical phase of flight such as takeoff or landing, but still, it has become a tremendous source of relaxation during the long cruises. Some headquarters desk jockey has discovered that the crews were listening to music with their cassette players while flying, and he issued an order to cease and desist. The bureaucrats are trying to get into our cockpits with their paltry regulations and fly for us. We know which rules are prudent for safety and which we can snub. Some were made to be broken, and this is one. We blow it off.

Greg Carpenter, my new copilot, is known to us as the Baby Pilot. BP is such a young-looking lad that we constantly jerk his chain about his boyish appearance. He often finds pacifiers attached to his helmet bag or a bottle in his flight lunch, but he always reacts with a gigantic grin and joins the laughter. He is as unpretentious and unassuming as a person could be. You'd have to be a colossal jerk to get the Baby Pilot sore at you.

BP hears a familiar voice working Cairo Control and alerts me. I take off the speakers and listen closely to the transmissions. It's Tommy Sledge. Elated, I transmit on Cairo's frequency and ask him to come up on Channel 10.

"Tango Sierra, if that's you, come up and talk to me on Button 10."

We're not supposed to use Channel 10 for personal conversation, only for official stuff like weather checks or communication relays and such. Countless factions of unfriendlies all along the Mediterranean and down into the AOR could monitor the frequency, and doubtless they do. But Sledge is my buddy, and I want to palaver. One thing we will do, however, is avoid using real names, knowing that they would probably be recorded somewhere in a dark, smelly room by a guy with a cigarette, a stubbled growth of whiskers, and an AK-47.

Tommy recognizes my voice. "Is that you Tidy Boy?" This is a crude reference, practiced by Sledge and certain other of my associates, to "Tide," as in Crimson Tide.

"Yeah. Hey, Hammer, did you hear about the Ole Miss graduate who married the Greek gal?"

Across a couple hundred miles of airspace he suffers me to continue.

"Well, they wanted to give their son a name which reflected each of their respective cultures, so they called him Zorba the ——."

"MAC Bravo 2557, contact Jeddah on 133.9." It's Cairo, interrupting the punchline on the VHF radio. I repeat it after Sledge responds to Cairo's instructions.

But he knows the joke, and I know that I have gotten out of my league. Sledge is not one to be challenged to a collegiate joke slugfest. He fires a stinging retaliation against my alma mater, as the bewildered man with the cigarette shakes his head and records the strange American secret codes.

We dwell for a while on Sledge's favorite topic, Southeastern Conference football, and then catch up on bits of news around the squadron. Unlike the active squadrons, where friendships are kindled and quickly left dangling as people come and go, a Reserve or Guard squadron is a family. Many of us have known one another for years. News about where our comrades are and how they are faring is important, and we seek it at every encounter.

"Have you seen hide or hair of George lately?"

"No, but I saw Blair Jernigan yesterday. He claims a Fondren sighting last week at Rhein Mein."

I miss George, I want to see him, to sip his Kahlua coffee with him, to talk of the late great oil business.

Then comes unhappy news. "Did you hear that Steve Watkins got released?"

A vision of Steve's grinning face flashes in me. I will not see him again.

"No. Why? His kids?"

"Yeah."

To be released from service after the president had called us into active duty was a very difficult transaction. It could only be done for reasons of health or extreme family problems, and the decision was made at a lofty level in the command chain. And once released, there was no returning. Steve was gone. I grieve for his loss, but I understand. It has been about seven years since that tragic night when the weight of the universe slammed down on Steve's shoulders.

He had been with us for a couple of years, had separated from the active service as a B-52 pilot, and had settled down in his hometown of Crystal Springs. There he became active in the family furniture business and indulged weekly in the gratifying pleasure of flying the C-130s of the Magnolia Militia. He was a quiet fellow in those days, very soft-spoken, with an ever-smiling, cherubic face. But even after the inevitable "new guy" period—usually a year—passed, Steve still acted a bit like an unsettled stranger. We didn't know much about him. We would ask him about the furniture business. He would reply that it was good, but with a subtle measure of discontent in his face. Beyond that I never intruded.

Steve was out flying when it happened. It was a three-ship, formation airdrop mission at night. The supervisor of flying had received the call and transmitted a radio message directing Steve's plane to land. There had been a natural gas explosion in the furniture store. Steve's wife, mother, and sister had been killed in the blast, which leveled the building. Steve was led away from the operations room in a daze, oblivious, his life changed forever.

The town of Crystal Springs was shattered, and the Guard unit was beset with sorrow for the man we knew so little of. For weeks we kept track of Steve through Stan Papizan, another of our pilots who lived in Crystal Springs. Our questions peppered Stan whenever he appeared. And always: "He's coming along well. He has a strong faith in God which is pulling him through." And I kept wondering what I would say to Steve when at last he came back to continue his flying, supposing he did come back. Would I try too crudely to express sympathy, which might prompt an emotional response? I couldn't just pretend nothing happened. I've always been inept in such matters, and I didn't relish the thought of seeing him again.

I don't remember when I saw him after that; the memory is fuzzy. But I know that our paths rarely crossed for several months until one day when Steve seemed to have been reborn. He was indeed a new Steve. He was sporting a new look. He had tanned a lot, changed his hairstyle, and lost weight. He grinned, laughed, talked, and participated aggressively in the flying and training activities of the unit. He told me that he had decided to put the loss behind him as well as he could and get on with his life. And the new Steve was an extrovert, a favorite personality of our squadron, and a highly respected flier. He led the charge in the difficult conversion from C-130s to C-141s, becoming among the first C-141 aircraft commanders in our unit and the first to become air refueling qualified.

Then word came that he had remarried. His new wife was the TV correspondent who had done a special report on his tragic loss and his subsequent recovery. It was a Christian program that documented Steve's faith as his sustaining factor. He spoke often of her and how his children had taken so well to their new mother.

And as he grew in favor with his comrades, Steve continued to flourish. He landed a trophy job with Delta Airlines, flying 727s out of New Orleans. Steve's life had changed so markedly that it was a marvel both to him and to those of us who knew him. It was pure pleasure and an inspiration just to be around him.

But now, Sledge had brought word that he was gone, that he had been released. It was a time when many were looking for an excuse to get released, but we knew Steve was not among that crowd. If anyone wanted to do his share in this giant operation, it was Steve Watkins. He would not have asked for discharge unless a higher priority called.

It was the children. Airline flying they could accept, but the daily portrayal of war and foreboding on the television had cast them into a grim fear of being orphaned.

Yeah, I knew Steve wanted to fly with us, to see this thing through, to make a long career of the Guard, to remain in the Guard family. But his love for his kids was greater. With regrets, he opted out. And we lost a brother.

Visions of Steve's sobbing children still linger in my mind as we land at McGuire AFB, New Jersey. But they are abruptly displaced by more stunning news. Shocked, I hang up the phone at the command post window and turn to break the news to the crew. Their gleeful postflight banter stops as soon as they read the seriousness in my face and voice as I talk with our home base command post.

The wife of one of our flight engineers has committed suicide. No details were passed to me. I didn't know her personally, but I had known the flight engineer many years. He is not on my crew, but I had flown with him often in more placid times. The ride to the billeting office is a somber one; all thoughts are turned homeward.

I've given very little thought until now about how this whole situation is affecting my Ellie. She's running the household, the budget, the kids. That's all nothing new to her, but this not knowing when I'm coming back—the unknowns of the war that lies ahead and my role in it—has got to be taking its toll.

When she married me, she married flying. And she knew it. Over all our years together I don't remember a single complaint, though complaints have often been warranted. She never begrudged a penny of the tons of money I've thrown into airplanes, sometimes money that we needed elsewhere. That simple faith—that trust of hers—keeps me coming back; it anchors me. But she deserves better.

One of eleven children, she came from a family of hardworking Kansas Mennonite farmers, all devout, dedicated conscientious objectors. Yet she married a fighter pilot. The family never expressed ill feelings toward me about my job, but some things we just didn't discuss.

After we had married and moved away, I stopped in one weekend on a cross-country proficiency flight. My father-in-law, Harold Esau, and two brothers-in-law came out to the base to pick me up. Yes, the brothers said that they wanted to see the jet, but Harold strolled out to the flight line reluctantly, motivated only by his insatiable curiosity about all things mechanical. While the brothers asked a few questions and marveled at the big camouflage-painted fighter, Harold walked around it slowly, saying not a word, with hands clasped behind his back: a clear body signal of a holding back, a symbolic keeping of his distance. I tensed when he stepped in front of the gun. I'll never forget his expression of sorrow as he paused and stared down the sinister rifled barrel of the 20-millimeter rotary cannon.

Ellie wasn't a natural flier, but she misled me on our second date. I dumped her into the back seat of an Aeronica Champ out at Woodring Airport and put her through a few wingovers and whifferdills. "Oh, that was fun," she lied charmingly as we taxied the Champ back in. In the years ahead, flying would be not much more than a quick way from A to B for her, and she would never feel comfortable with it. But most important, she accepted it as my way of life. I could ask nothing more of her.

Surprisingly, she began taking lessons a few years ago. Her excuse was that she wanted to know how to land our plane if I slumped over incapacitated, though I believe she really needed to prove to herself that she could meet the challenge. For one of the biggest events of her life, her first solo, I wasn't there. I was thousands of miles away, flying C-130s around South America, and so I didn't experience it with her.

She soloed only three times. On the third flight the canopy popped open with a loud bang just as she became airborne. Thinking it was an explosion, she declared an emergency with the control tower and landed the Grumman amid a host of speeding, wailing, red-flashing fire trucks. She was terribly embarrassed by the episode despite my reassurance that she had done exactly as she should have done. Instead of panicking, she remembered the prime directive: fly the plane, then work the problem. But that was the end. She never again had the desire to fly alone. I didn't press her. If she accepted my love for flying, then I needed to accept her indifference to it.

I've always tried to be reasonable and discreet about the time spent at the airport. The Grumman always needs to be tinkered with or washed. A short flight is always in order to keep the seals and gaskets lubricated. And it's imperative that I put in occasional hangar talk with the airport crowd. It keeps me in touch with my roots. But one Saturday afternoon, as I was planning to slip away to the airport, Ellie asked a simple question. I was struck by it.

"Are you going to the flying field?" she asked.

It wasn't a pointed or suggestive question; there was no resentment over my proposed pilgrimage to the field. It was a simple request for information. The follow-up was a request that I bring home some milk.

I stopped and pondered the wondrous sound of it. She didn't say airport, nor airfield, nor aerodrome—*flying field,* she said. They were such beautiful words; words that sent my heart soaring; words that told me she understood; she cared; she knew. I loved her tremendously for it.

She never took well to the military lifestyle. The job and the planes were bearable but that abominable officers' wives club, the OWC, was beyond the call of spousal duty. She wanted to be herself. She had little interest in being on the cutting edge of fashion and social life. Keeping the club fashionably decorated and furnished and scheduling highbrow social functions were of no concern to her. And she cared not in the least that fighter pilots had the impudence to wear their flight suits in the dining room and get rowdy in the casual bar on Friday nights. The OWC Gestapo, as the pilots called them, was out to banish such low-bred acts of peasant behavior, and participation in its activities was expected of her. The OWC pecking order was a disgusting reflection of the husbands' chain of command. Ellie didn't fit in. And like her family, she was a pacifist at heart.

Because of her Mennonite family's solid antiwar convictions, I was a little concerned about her reaction to the Persian Gulf situation. A few months after it all started I was home for a few days, burnt out. I had reached the magic 330 hours in ninety days and had been sent home to recoup. While I was there, we watched the antiwar protests and demonstrations on TV. Then we saw a kid burning the American flag somewhere in California. She became enraged at the sight. I had never seen her so mad over a news event. How could anyone do such a thing, she demanded, while brave men and women risked their lives for that flag? I loved her more, as she voiced her anger and rage, than I had ever before. She truly was the air under my wings.

A close friend was once discussing the marriage institution with me over lunch. He had divorced and remarried. When I told him how committed I was to Ellie, he cautioned me never to say never. "Read my lips," I told him.

"Never."

SIX

ZARAGOZA

My watch says it's 0115, but it's set on "Z," or Zulu time, which is military slang for Greenwich mean time. The longitudes of the world march across our lives so relentlessly that Z time has become our sole reference to the passage of the hours, the days. I think you add two to Z, to get local time at Zaragoza, so it must be about 3:15 A.M. here. Or do you subtract two hours? But then, is Spain still on daylight saving time or not? My body stays so soaked with weariness that even simple determinations are error fraught.

Typically, I crash for three or four hours after coming in from the West but then wake up and languish in the dreaded half-sleep, half-wake fog for another two hours before surrendering. Thinking I'll take a walk, I stir, looking around for my sweats, and discover that Curt is awake as well. At his suggestion we check out the gym keys from the security police and come over here to kill some time.

Curt is in the weight room, working out. There's a set of exercise machines in there, the kind with the chains and stacked bars, but the gym staff has seen fit to lock away the inserts. Why in creation anyone would want to steal the little steel rods that you stick into the stacks to select your weights is beyond my comprehension. Curt is furious about it and is taking out his frustration with the free weights.

I'm dribbling a basketball and listening to the bounces echo off the walls of the empty, half-darkened gym. I think it's the loneliest sound life serves up: no exuberant shouts, no buzzers or crowd swells, no squeaking tennis shoes, not a murmur or a whisper, just that solitary bounce and its echo. Yet there's something about the sound that sustains and consoles. Even so, it's the sound of solitude: a slow dribble, a pause, a twang off the hoop, more dribble. Maybe it will be the final sounds the world eventually breathes—we'll go out with a bounce, not a bang.

Of all the fine traveling companions I've had the honor to fly with, Curt Kennedy is one of the most delightful. He flies for USAir as a DC-9 captain. He's stocky, a good runner, and a lover of sports. The loquacious Curt is an Ole Miss–educated lawyer who loves people, conversation, and humor, yet is wonderfully unpretentious. He is a philanthropist of southern-style friendliness, establishing goodwill and warm feelings with everyone he meets but not without a skillful touch of diplomacy with the higher-ups. A couple of weeks ago down at Torrejon his mitigation skills met a big challenge.

A stranger boarded their crew bus at the billeting office as they finished their bag drag and sat down for the trip in to the command post. Oddly, he was in civilian attire, and Curt appropriately decided to inquire. The man could have been a spy or a terrorist or maybe a plant to test the crew's vigilance. Curt's approach as he extended his hand was characteristic: "Hello, sir, I'm Curt Kennedy. Who are you?"

The man shook Curt's hand. "Glad to meet you Curt. I'm H. T. Johnson."

Curt pondered the name, didn't recognize it, and pressed further but still with a mild manner, as if he were catching up with a distant but interesting relative. "Well, pleased to meet you too, sir, but what, ah, what are you doing here?"

"You mean you've never heard of me?" he replied.

"Well, no. I don't believe I have."

"I'm CINCMAC, your boss."

Curt vaguely remembered that CINCMAC was the acronym for commander-in-chief, Military Airlift Command. From this man it was only about three more levels up to the president. The general probably didn't expect every one to recognize his face, but certainly his people should know his name. CINCMAC was visibly agitated. "Oh, yes." Curt responded enthusiastically, extending his hand again. "Well, we certainly are glad to have you here, sir. Will you be going with us downrange?"

He wasn't.

Curt then began to pump the general with questions ranging from the nature of his visit to the health of his wife and children, allowing him little time to respond. Soon the rest of the crew followed Curt's lead and joined in, and a friendly banter developed as the general's irritation melted. It was a smooth recovery.

Curt was like that. He could talk up a storm, never allowing your attention to drift or your participation to wane. Yeah, I flew my most enjoyable missions with Curt.

He loved to tell the story of his encounter with the southern humorist Jerry Clower. Again, it was a characteristic Curt Kennedy reaction. Approaching his gate in the terminal, Curt noticed a crowd gathered around a talking, gesturing figure. Moving in closer, he recognized the "Mouth of the South" carrying on in his flamboyant manner with everyday people just as if he were onstage. Curt's story was entirely believable, because I had once seen Clower joking in a doctor's office. Listening in, he heard the subject of Jerry's clowning. It was the old rivalry between Mississippi State, Jerry's alma mater, and Ole Miss. Jerry was telling the crowd of travelers that it would come to fisticuffs if he ever had to sit next to an Ole Miss graduate.

Curt asked the ticket agent for the seat beside Jerry, and the stage was set. Jerry had settled in as Curt had stowed his bag in the overhead bin, then he took a stand in the aisle and raised his fists.

"OK, put 'em up, Jerry."

Jerry didn't fight. In fact, he probably found a kindred soul.

Curt and I tire quickly and leave the gym for the murky dampness of the Spanish night. We walk back, listening as a departing C-141 shatters the silence. The plan was the same. We would try again to bank some sleep before we became legal for alert. We were coming to loathe Zaragoza. It was a beautiful place when the weather was good, but lately it had remained gloomy. And the base was small. We felt confined, even during our short stays. Zaragoza became the epitome of fatigue. It was never a haven, never a restful respite, only a place in which to recover to some mediocre level of revitalization.

We grew tired of the fare in the chow hall and began to eat in the NCO open mess (the officer's club had closed its kitchen). The evening before we had had a curious encounter there over which Curt continued to muse.

We had ordered the special: ribeye steaks, always a bit stringy and overdone, but the unique appeal of a multicourse meal, savory or not, was that it killed time. And the club was a relatively pleasant place to sit and stretch out a meal while the minutes clicked down to alert time.

When the waiter appeared, we thought we had been cast in a Pink Panther movie. He could easily have doubled for Peter Sellers. The thin black mustache, the Mediterranean accent, the large rolling eyes, the white cloth folded over the forearm, pencil and order pad in hand: it was all suggestive of a movie set. And when he spoke we had to suppress a snicker.

"Ant how vould you like youh stake done, sirh?"

"Medium, please."

A short pause followed each question as a distinct mark was made on his pad.

"Bekt potato or frensh fries?"

"Baked, please."

"Souah cleam or buttah?"

"Sour cream, please."

He regarded us with astonishment, as if only a second before he had informed us two simpletons of the sour cream's unavailability.

"Ve haf no souah cleam!"

Curt's eyes and mine met. By golly, this *was* a Peter Sellers movie.

"Then butter will be fine."

Fifteen minutes later, french fries arrived. Curt politely sent them back.

Then the baked potato arrived—with a great scoop of sour cream atop.

"How's Heidi and the kids?" I asked. Curt had just returned from a couple of days at home. He perked.

"She's fine. But she broke down the other day."

"How so?"

"Well, she expected me to be home longer, I guess. When they called I was in the shower. She lied to them, told them I was gone, didn't know when I was coming back. When I got out of the shower she was hysterical. Said that she had lied, that we would both be going to prison, but that it wasn't fair for them to call so soon. I called them back and smoothed things over."

I had never met Heidi, but hearing this I liked her.

I don't know exactly what it is about Ole Miss graduates that sets them a bit apart. Not above, just beside. Certainly there's an air of Faulkner about Curt, his anecdotal eloquence, I guess. But I've known others as well who seem a bit novel. I think maybe it's their short tolerance for one another. They're civil, to be sure, but there's a hint of rivalry among them. Still, one needs only to attend an Ole Miss Homecoming up at Oxford—as I have—to witness their camaraderie. Yet I've seen them exhibit a bit of shifty-eyedness toward one another. I attribute it to their propensity to be jealous achievers. It was here on the Zaragoza flight line a couple of months back that I watched two of Faulkner's boys do battle.

Curt was deadheading with us from Jackson to Zaragoza. He was assigned at the time not to my crew but rather to the pool of pilots stationed there temporarily. Each time we transited Zaragoza, or the other staging bases, we were assigned a pool pilot to augment us for the long round trip downrange and back. Being assigned a tour as a pool pilot was a dubious honor that I had been grateful to avoid. Some liked it because it was a way to build flying time more quickly and to enjoy the luxury of a single room at the staging base. But the pool pilot was a maverick. Each mission, he was assigned a different crew, whose members most likely were total strangers to him. Each time he flew, he would have to prove himself worthy and reliable and to yield his own well-being, reluctantly, to an unfamiliar aircraft commander. He or she was required to be a *first pilot*, at a minimum, a rating that allowed him or her to fly either right or left seat, unlike a *copilot*, who could fly only in the right seat. However, many pool pilots were either aircraft commander rated or even instructors. It was a lonely job; the pool pilot had no sense of belonging. We further degraded his status by referring to him as a "rent-a-pilot." Curt's tour would be about two weeks.

Though he was not obligated to do so, he relieved Bones and me at the controls during the long journey. Along with us was newsman Bert Case and a cameraman from WLBT in Jackson. Bert had somehow wangled a trip downrange at a time when only select media people from the national wire services and networks were being allowed in. It was a media coup of sorts—a crew from a local affiliate going to the war zone. But then, Bert had a knack for bringing such things off. It would be big news, a documentary of an airlift mission to the Gulf.

Curt and Bert hit it off well during the journey, both being natural jabberers, and before long discovered some sort of common ancestry between them. By the time we touched down at Zaragoza, Curt had concocted a scheme to get himself to the top of the pool pilot list so that he could accompany us downrange. I doubted he would be able to pull it off, but with Bert's help he persuaded the crew stage manager to put him at the top of the list, and into crew rest we went.

But the next morning as we flight planned for the sandbox turn-around mission, another pool pilot showed up. He was at the top of the list before our arrival and had been alerted for our mission by mistake. I guess Curt's plan fell through the cracks when the shift changed at the stage manager's desk. In walked Ole Miss graduate Charlie Decker. As the two met, opposing fingers were pointed, and the two men simultaneously asked, "What the hell are you doing here?" It was more a demand for an explanation than a question.

Both wanted badly to fly the mission with their hometown comrades, but the stage manager stood adamant in his resolve to allow only one to go. I could hear an ongoing furor in the next room even as Bert interviewed Bones and me on camera about the mission. Finally, we held a conference with the stage manager, who favored Charlie for the trip. With courtroom finesse, Curt convinced him that his kinsmanship with the newsman was a newsworthy event back home and would make for good publicity, but Charlie argued that he alone was the rightful pool pilot. Finally, the manager threw his arms up in disgust, wishing to be done with us, and dispatched both Charlie and Curt to crew the mission. But that was not to be the end of it.

Out on the flightline as Bones and I threw switches and punched buttons, I looked down at the tarmac and saw them there. I couldn't hear what they were saying, but lips were moving furiously, simultaneously. Fierce gestures and threatening body language portended a new civil war in the making. I sent the loadmasters down to stand off and be ready to move in if a struggle erupted. I didn't know what the argument was about, thinking that all problems had been settled to everyone's satisfaction. Then I concluded that each had perceived that the other had offended his honor, and that honor would be restored to the winner of this war of words. Soon the pointed fingers began to peck minute punches into one another's chest, and the loads moved in closer. Then the two seemed to realize our concern and stopped, peered up at me, smiled accommodatingly, and shook hands. Civil war had been averted. Face and honor were preserved. Faulkner chuckled and winked.

We laugh again at the encounter with Charlie as we turn in for what we hope will be a good couple of hours of oblivion before alert time. But it seems that only a few minutes have passed when the buzzer on the wall brutally throws me into convulsive movements. Rising, I hear Curt sigh and see him roll his pillow overhead as the Spanish-accented voice addresses me through the speaker.

"Major Cockrell, call the command post, please."

Down in the lobby on the hot line, I take the mission. We are to take a C-141 inbound from the States—due in one hour—and proceed to Abu Dhabi. Our pool pilot will be Captain Lemanski, who is in room 130. I note that he is only a few doors away from my room, which is 238. I don't know this Lemanski (he is evidently from another unit), but I am to alert him along with the rest of my crew. The crew bus will arrive in half an hour.

I return to the room and relay the information to the stirring Curt. He agrees to alert the rest of the crew while I find Lemanski. I get into my flight suit and proceed to his room. He doesn't answer the knock. Again I rap furiously on the door, but there is no response. I'm perturbed over this. The pool pilots know the rules. Like us they're supposed to remain in their rooms during their "legal" period (usually a twelve-hour window), or else notify the command post if they venture away from the telephones. I knock again and test the door. It's not locked. I peek inside. A young man is lying unconscious on the bed. The air reeks of alcohol. A whiskey bottle lies on its side on the bedstand. Clothes and flight gear are strewn about the room. I touch the foot and shake it.

"Lemanski. Lemanski, wake up. This is an alert, man." He moves not a whisker. I shake him again violently, yet still he doesn't move. My God, I think. He's dead! I look around for signs of drugs that he may have taken with the liquor, but there are none. Then Curt appears in the open doorway.

"Curt, I think he's dead."

Curt comes over and shakes him vigorously, spoiling my search for a pulse. Then the man resurrects. Eyes slowly open and stare at me through a stupid glaze.

"He's drunk as a skunk!" declares Curt, informing me of the obvious. We shake him some more and raise him to an upright position.

"Lemanski, don't you understand, we've been alerted. The crew bus will be here in a few minutes. You gotta get going, man!" This was a serious breach of the Uniform Code of Military Justice—somewhat like being drunk on guard duty. I know we are all under tremendous stress, and some handle it better than others. I don't want him to be caught, but he is too far gone.

Curt continues his prodding. "Come on, Lemanski, GET UP! GET UP!"

I interject, rebuking him. "Lemanski, I can't handle this. You're not fit to fly with us. I'm gonna call the command post and tell them you're sick. Understand?"

"Leave him alone, Curt," I admonish as we leave the room. "He's too far gone."

But then we look back, and there he stands in the door, looking like death warmed over. His lips quiver and try to formulate a word. Curt goes to his side. "What is it, man? Come on, spit it out. What is it with you? Don't you know what you're doing?"

The words come slowly, painfully from a dry, writhing tongue: "Wh-who . . . are y-you?"

"For God's sake, man, I'm your aircraft commander. You've been assigned to my crew."

A hand goes up to an obviously pain-laden head. "A-aircr . . . com . . . wh-what kind of air . . . craft?"

Curt and I eye one another. Something is very wrong here. "Why, C-141, of course. You're a pool pilot, right?"

"P-p-p-pool pilot?" He gropes for words. I look up at the number on the door. It's 230. Lemanski is in 130, on the floor below. I look back into the room. The crumpled flight suit bears a Strategic Air Command patch but has no rank on the shoulders. The man is a tanker crewman, a boomer. And he's recovering.

Painful babble begins to issue from fluttering lips as the glazed eyes search for telltale signs of a bad dream. Listening intently, as if trying to garner secrets from a dying prospector, we're able to glean a few clipped words from the gibberish. "I . . . I . . . I . . . what you're talkin' ab . . . twenty hour . . . missi . . . refuel . . . fight . . . I didn't even t-touch . . . gr . . . man, for eighteen—hey man, who . . . who are you? What you want fr' me?"

I think quickly.

Still using the name of the man down below, I proffer a hurried explanation. "Lemanski, there's been a great mistake. The MAC command post gave me the wrong room number. I'll have their asses for this, don't worry, buddy. Get on back in there and get some sleep. I'll straighten this mess out right now." We usher him back to the bunk.

We find the real Lemanski, who somehow learned of the alert, already moving bags down in the lobby, and join in the bag drag out to curbside, where the bus is waiting. On a shuttle back into the lobby, we see that the boomer has come down to see us off. He stands there like the creature from the black lagoon but still looks confused. I don't know if he intends to attack or what. I grab a couple of bags and call out to him. "Lemanski, get on back to bed, son. We'll check on you later."

"What?" the real Lemanski shouts from the doorway.

"Huh? Never mind, I'll explain later. Let's get out of here."

SEVEN

PAIN OF A DIFFERENT DEATH

*When a pilot dies in the harness, his death
seems something that inheres in the craft
[flying] itself, and in the beginning the
pain it brings is perhaps less than the pain
sprung of a different death.*
Antoine de Saint-Exupéry,
Wind, Sand, and Stars

Our Starlifter is cruising back uprange, straight into the setting sun, away from the gathering storm of war. Ahead is the Red Sea with the jagged, ocher Egyptian mountains beyond. Cockpit instrument lights are being turned on. Sunglasses are being stowed. We're prepping the jet for dark flight.

Unencumbered by haze and pollutants, the sun departs with a great brilliance at this altitude. But the panoramic splay of crimson and orange lasts much longer tonight because we're chasing the sun. We will of course lose the race; the earth turns twice as fast as our speed, but the lingering spectacle inspires a kind of silent reverence through the cockpit. Only the rush of the slipstream and the occasional crackle of modulated radio voices intrude on our sunset ponderings.

"MAC Victor 6522, Red Crown, you're radar contact, cleared area transition."

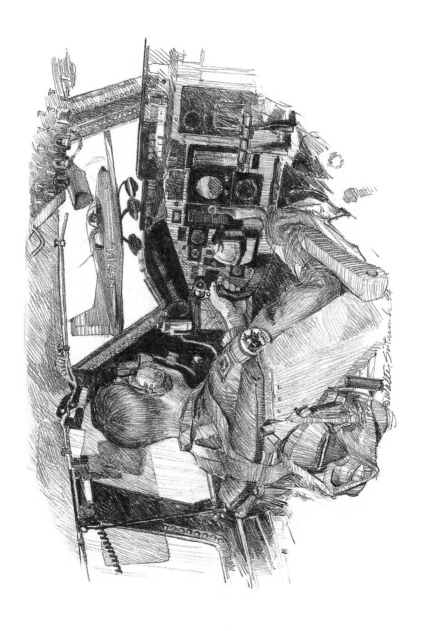

"6522, roger," I reply, staring at the sunset, with visions of Dave's little plane silhouetted against it. It seemed we were always flying late in the evening, the closing of the day forcing us back to the world.

And I remember how we, the group of us, sat there on that old concrete fence rail until the sun went down, watching the Cessnas take off and land. Watching with envy. Trading dreams. Breaking out of the egg of adolescence, feeling a calling swell within us. Certain that it would be fulfilled but electrified with impatience, we sensed our day was coming.

We were about evenly endowed then with the traits of future professional fliers. And if God had combined the three of us into one pilot, Gene Key would have been the brain and I the hands. But the heart—that would have been Dave DeRamus.

The three of us were cut from the same mold: products of financially comfortable working-class families, the oldest sons, townies who lived at home while attending college, the seeds of flight planted in us by fathers who themselves were occasional fliers. But Dave was different in a delightful, inspirational way.

He was the extrovert, the talker, the dreamer, the romanticizer. And he grew to love flying with every fiber of his being. While Gene quietly, confidently calculated his course in life, and I ambled toward my goal, depending on luck and divine help, Dave swaggered ahead with bold declarations and unabashed single-mindedness, leaving in his wake a reputation of cockiness.

Dave had a stocky athletic build. He had a passion for football and water skiing and pursued them with intensity and determination, as he did everything. Yet his eyes were soft and far-focused, as if he were discontented and a bit melancholy. His slight smile was always there except when he was directing scorn at his two favorite targets: government bureaucracy and rotten flying weather. He had a tremendous sense of humor and loved to laugh but was also moody. In those early years Dave was a model young Christian who was active in church. He often delivered the invocation at our Air Force ROTC social functions. But change came. An elective course in religious studies, he claimed, had opened his mind. He questioned some of the teachings of his faith and left the church after someone told his mother that Dave was going to Hell for doubting.

His intellectual departure from traditional belief troubled Gene and me, who stayed the course, but we all remained steadfast friends, bonded by our passion for flight.

And finally our day came, but the Air Force sent us to different bases for flight school and later gave us sharply different flying assignments. Gene became an instructor, I went to tactical fighters, and Dave was assigned to the secretive world of electronic warfare. Soon Gene and I had taken wives, while Dave chose a single life. But we stayed in touch and visited when we could.

On one such visit Dave and I met in Spokane, Washington. I recall so clearly what he said that crystal clear afternoon, there in the beautiful, forested mountain countryside north of Spokane. I had a weekend off from the rigors of Survival School at Fairchild AFB, and he had driven over from Malmstrom AFB at Great Falls, Montana, to see me. Neither of us yet had an airplane of our own. We noticed a lone biplane performing aerobatics over a large deserted meadow. Dave and I stopped and watched as the red wings rolled, looped, and spun, the little engine reverberating in the silence of the valley. The pilot obviously intended his private air show for the eyes of God only, but we watched, beholden. And as the plane finally faded away he remarked that he expected his life would end some day in the cockpit of an airplane. I berated him for being a fatalist. Now I wish he had been right.

I got a letter from him while I was stationed in Thailand. He had bought an airplane, a used Grumman Yankee. He wrote of the plane's sporty handling characteristics and fighterlike appearance. I decided that if he could afford one on first lieutenant's pay, then so could I. And so I too bought a plane as soon as I returned Stateside, an old Cessna 140. But when I visited with Dave and flew the wonderful little low-wing two-seater that embodied the sheer joy and exaltation of flight, I knew I had to have a Yankee as well. I sold the '140.

We flew together military style whenever we met, wing to wing with only a few feet of separation, waltzing in cumulus-studded skies, pursuing one another in mock air battles. Afterward we would sip Mountain Dew, which was his drink of preference, and rap at length about the stuff of flying. As always, I listened mostly and watched the flash in his eyes as he talked about aspect ratios, power loadings, and corner velocities. He would sketch out dreams of elaborate modifications to his Yankee and talk of plans for air journeys to fascinating places. And he talked of new friends he had made. Friends, he said, who were open-minded and unpretentious, who shared his spirited views and philosophies.

Dave was clearly jealous of me when I landed a fighter assignment out of pilot training. He was a good flier, but there were no fighter slots available for his class, so he settled for flying EB-57s. The old 1950s vintage twin jet bomber had been converted so that it could carry electronic equipment to test the defensive capabilities of the more modern interceptors of the North American Air Defense Command. Dave's ho-hum job, as he described it, was to fly around and be blown out of the northern skies by imaginary missiles. And I knew, as I learned and practiced fighter tactics in the southwestern deserts, that he felt destiny had forsaken him. But Dave had a plan to find his way into a fighter cockpit and eventually to his ultimate dream: test pilot school.

We took chances in those days that we would never take now. We flew cross-country one summer in formation from Montana to Alabama. Low clouds stranded us in Springfield, Missouri, and we became impatient. Neither of our planes were equipped for safe instrument flying. While waiting we began to compare the planes and discovered that, together, we had the basic tools to make an instrument flight. He had a good attitude indicator; mine was mushy. I had a transponder; he didn't. We both had VOR receivers. We could back each other up! We didn't have the capability to make a precision instrument approach but reasoned that it didn't matter because the weather was reported to be improving along our intended route. We would make our two planes one. We would pierce the gray clouds glued to one another's wings. We had both done it in Air Force jets. Why not now? We decided to file an instrument flight plan and launch in formation.

The guy at the flight service station counter looked over our flight plan and pointed to an obvious error. We had written in two different aircraft numbers in the box reserved for such identification. Dave advised him to read on, and he would see why. We had written in the remarks section "Flight of two AA-1's." The technician was incredulous. He, like most general aviation people, thought of formation flying as two or more planes separated by a couple of city blocks of airspace at a minimum.

"No, no. You can't do that," he responded.

We assured him we could.

"How you gonna see each other?" he demanded.

We explained how we proposed to do it and assured him that we regularly did it in the military.

He finally accepted that we were serious but, doubting that our plan was legal, he phoned the Kansas City Air Route Traffic Control Center and informed them of the suicidal request he had received. He came back to the counter and removed his glasses.

"The center says the military does it all the time but they had never seen civilians do it. They said they don't know of any rules against it. So I guess I can't stop you if this is what you want to do."

A few minutes later we were taxiing out together under a 300-foot cloud ceiling, and Dave took our clearance from the tower.

"Grumman 5713 Lima Flight is cleared to Greenwood, Mississippi, as filed, maintain five thousand, squawk 0133."

The tower controller seemed to understand that we were a flight of two, but after giving us takeoff clearance, he was aghast when we taxied onto the runway together.

"One three Lima, are you taking off in formation?" he queried.

"Yeah, that's how we filed" was Dave's response.

He told us to stand by. Obviously, more phone calls were being made as legalities were being checked and our sanity was being questioned, but a minute later he came back up.

"OK, one three Lima flight, you're cleared for takeoff. Maintain runway heading. Good luck."

We launched into the murk with me on the wing. I could easily see his dark blue plane in the clouds, and I stayed glued to his wing for almost an hour until we broke into the clear. But still there was a solid undercast beneath us. A little while later we flew over a hole that looked to be a few acres in size, through which we could see the green Mississippi woodlands below. Out ahead of us there was little sign that the undercast was breaking up as we neared our refueling stop at Greenwood, so we canceled instrument flight rules with the center.

We were then on our own, but visual flight rules required that we remain clear of all clouds. Dave was cautious. He radioed me that the hole looked so small that he didn't know how we were going to descend through it and maintain cloud clearance. I knew he was assuming that we would use a normal shallow descent profile that would put us back into the cloud deck before we descended through the hole, but that's not what I intended. I was a fighter pilot; I knew how to get through the hole.

I told him to follow me and broke away from his wing. I rolled the Yankee nearly inverted, closed the throttle, pulled the nose down and dove through the hole as if in a dive-bomb attack. He followed. Luckily no one was cruising along under the cloud deck near the hole. But I didn't think anything of it. Such maneuvers were normal for me but not for him. When we landed he was ecstatic about it, and he laughed about it often as time went by.

A few days later we were out skirmishing over Lake Tuscaloosa. The two Yankees rolled and dove, unnoticed, I'm sure, among the scattered cumulus high above the bass boats and skiers. It really wasn't much of a match. I was pulling a high side "yo-yo" maneuver to gain a tracking solution on him when he decided to reverse his direction of turn. It was a reckless move. I unloaded the G-pressure on my Yankee and reversed my turn in unison with him, rolling out with a perfect lead on his plane. I smiled and pressed the mike button, uttering the three words that told Dave he was beaten.

"GUNS, GUNS, GUNS."

Dave knew far more than I about aerodynamics, flight theory, and such—he had an aerospace engineering degree—but he simply had no experience in air combat science. He rolled out of his breaking turn, and after a minute of silent straight flight, he keyed his radio.

"How'd you do that?"

Later, over Mountain Dew, I explained it, as he nodded in pensive analysis.

A couple of years later, Dave had succeeded in finding his coveted fighter job: an F-106. The '106, or "six pack," was said to be the Cadillac of the fighters, definitely the prettiest fighter plane ever made, and unlike the ponderous brown and green tactical fighter that I flew, it was designed to defend the homeland against bomber attack.

Later in its years, during dissimilar air combat training, the Six proved to be very adept at preying on other fighters, as well. This was Dave's big break, and he proceeded to make up for lost time. We compared notes often. His mission and mine were acutely different. Dave was a liberal political thinker. The politics and tactics of the recently ended Viet Nam war was always a hot subject with us, and such discussions led him to remark that he could never drop bombs on folks, innocent or not. But he loved to vow, with a squinty-eyed grin—as if it would be great fun—that if a Soviet bomber ever threatened his mother or anyone else's, he wouldn't hesitate to "hose the sons-a-bitches down."

Once again, we were home on leave when I called him one morning and explained that I was flying my brother to Jasper and would return to attack the VOR at eleven o'clock. The VOR was an unmanned navigation station with a distinctive antenna that resembled a great inverted ice cream cone. It was a challenge to air combat, of course. No more needed to be said. But he allowed as how he planned to go water skiing and had no time for such games. I knew it was a smoke screen.

At about 10:45 A.M. as I approached Lake Tuscaloosa I tuned my radio to the control tower frequency and, sure enough, heard Grumman 5713L receive takeoff clearance. The cork had been sucked under, as I suspected. My juices started to flow. I retuned my radio to 122.75, the civil air-to-air common frequency, and dropped down low. I maneuvered to approach the station from the east. He wouldn't expect that, since the route down from Jasper was from the north. I began weaving left and right, with each turn "checking six": looking behind for signs of Dave's blue Yankee. He was not to be seen; the plan was working.

With the target almost in sight, it seemed I had a clear shot. Then with about a mile left and a good head of speed, I popped up to a thousand feet and began a left roll to bring my nose to bear on the station. As I rolled out in a shallow dive, my headphones erupted with his triumphant shouts.

"GUNS, GUNS, GUNS, YOU TURKEY!"

It was I who had taken the bait. Expecting him, and still I had been ambushed. It was indeed a turkey shoot. I needed to get back into this fight quickly, needed to salvage some dignity. I ignored his guns call and pulled up, broke hard and checked six. There was Dave about a thousand feet back, his nose pulling a deadly lead on me. I had fallen for the oldest trick in the proverbial book, allowing him to attack from out of the sun. I was aghast at my stupidity. But I pressed the fight, turning, breaking, rolling, yo-yoing to gain an inside advantage, all to no avail. He wouldn't be shaken loose. Then I began to realize that the playing field was more than even. Dave now thoroughly understood fighter tactics and spiced his performance with application of a superior understanding of his Yankee's aerodynamic characteristics. Countering my every maneuver, he zoomed higher, dove faster, and turned tighter than I could. I simply couldn't match him.

Cleanly whipped, I finally declared Mountain Dew time, and we recovered in a formation overhead pattern, to the delight of the weekend airport bums. We taxied the two petite Grummans onto the ramp and shut down, and Dave waited gleefully while I jumped out of the cockpit and vaulted over the leading edge of the wing, as Grumman pilots are disposed to do. Dave leaned against his Yankee with a smirky grin looking like the cartoon coyote gorged on roadrunner. We exchanged a few irrelevant clipped sentences, each waiting for the other to make the first comment about the fight. But then he unlatched his cowling and showed me the new 150 horsepower engine that had replaced the stock 108 horsepower, which is of course what I had. He was charitable enough to attribute his performance to the extra power, but I knew that I would never be equal to his skills, engines aside.

The years went by, and we all left the active duty Air Force. Gene eventually landed his dream job with Delta Airlines, and Dave became an instant Boeing 737 captain with an upstart no-frills airline called People Express (PEX). He joined a Guard unit but served only a couple of years.

Although he was flying his beloved F-106, Dave was unhappy in the New Jersey Air Guard. I never knew exactly why. He complained of the same things that he did on active duty ("too much paperwork, too much bullshit"), which puzzled me. I was in a Guard unit also and was very happy with it. I knew it was radically different from the active Air Force. He just didn't fit the military mold, I figured. But Dave had always been profoundly different, a self-proclaimed marcher to a different drummer.

Finally one day he up and quit the Guard. His story was classically DeRamus. He had flown his Yankee into Atlantic City Airport and called the Guard Base, asking them to come over from their side of the field and pick him up, as they usually did. But he waited for an hour, and becoming impatient, he impulsively decided to walk over to the personnel office, which was nearby, and file separation papers. He then crawled back into the Yankee and left the military forever.

He made the papers and TV when he flew PEX's inaugural flight into Birmingham. It was a godsend for him. He could then live in Birmingham and commute to his base in Newark, and the publicity seemed to him a warm invitation to come home to the South and settle. And despite his despondency about his new employer, Continental Airlines, which acquired PEX, he seemed to be happier than he ever had been. But something was happening to him.

I called him and learned that he had just gotten over a bout with pneumonia and was on extended sick leave from the airline. But he assured me that he was doing well and in fact welcomed the respite as a chance to begin writing a book. The book would be about flying, of course, a techno-thriller about a Russian bomber pilot. It was something he had been inspired to do after he had met Victor Belenko, the heralded Soviet pilot who had defected in a MiG-25 several years earlier.

I didn't think too much of the news of his illness but was a bit curious. He was not a sickly sort of person. But as the months went by, Dave didn't go back to work. He reassured me. "I'm doing well financially. I've saved quite a bit of money and my Loss of License Insurance is paying off. I'm in no hurry to go back to that rat race. The doc wants me to just take it easy for a while." Something was terribly wrong.

Then there was another stay in the hospital with a collapsed lung. I decided to go see him after he got out. But on my way up to Birmingham I stopped in Tuscaloosa and invited a friend to go along for the flight. I would introduce him to Dave, and the three of us would have lunch. When I saw Dave I regretted bringing the friend. He had lost weight. Curiously, his hair appeared to have grown out. I could see through his facade that he was ill. And with the stranger present he would be reluctant to talk candidly about his condition.

Yet there in that last visit with him, he remained the cocky overflowing DeRamus that he had always been: still poking fun at the military establishment; still talking of vast dreams; still adamant that he, Gene, and I would somehow come up with $100,000 each and buy Glassair IIIs to make a formation aerobatic air show team. I wanted to believe it. It would have been the ultimate of dreams come true.

He began to grow tomatoes, which was totally out of character for him, but it was a newfound joy, he proclaimed. And the writing continued feverishly. But even as his mother moved in to care for him, he sank lower, and finally, with another collapsed lung and spinal meningitis he entered the intensive care unit, never to leave. Eventually, the beeps and squiggly lines on the oscilloscopes went steady and the sun finally went down on Dave's dreams.

In the end it wasn't a mid-air collision, an enemy missile, a failed engine, or a test flight gone bad that got him, as he had prophesied. It was AIDS. I knew it had to be. Gene and I compared notes. We had had the same suppositions all along. I wondered if he might have told me that last time we were together—the day we met for lunch—had the stranger not been there.

His manuscript, "Red Star Express," was good. I could clearly see him in his characters. But it fell victim to the collapse of communism and went unpublished. He would have been a fine author.

But my most vivid memory of Dave was the way he was always asking those tough questions about life—the ones that most people stuff into the closets of their souls, not willing to confront. He had a quest for the Truth, with a capital T, as he expressed it. Yet he knew the Truth.

I slip the microspeakers of my Walkman under my headset and listen to some Moody Blues. Dave loved to listen to their distinct harmonics and exuberant lyrics while he flew his Yankee.

"MAC Victor 6522, Jeddah, contact Cairo now, on frequency 134.6."

Their music seemed intended for fliers.

I know he's out there somewhere—somewhere in the sunset.

"MAC Victor 6522, Jeddah Control, I say again, I say again, call Cairo on 134.6, do you read? Over!"

I really miss him.

EIGHT

THE PROBABLE CAUSE

I'm plowing through the tail of the Storm, seated across the cockpit from the only black man I've ever come to know well. He's talking of his upbringing in the poverty-infested Delta. It's not a delta in the geologic sense but is actually a large triangular-shaped region characterized by the low, flat, fertile floodplains of the lower Mississippi River. Hope is a sparse commodity for a black kid growing up in the Delta. Where once picking cotton was the only viable way of life, now aspirations are focused on the catfish processing plants, where the wages are often bad. But at least it's out of the sun, and it's steady work, as long as the city dwellers in Jackson, Memphis, and New Orleans don't lose their taste for the ugly, bewhiskered, pond-raised but damned succulent little devils.

Brady Tonth set his sights higher than the fish factories. He was descended from a tarnished history of bondage and hate-mongering that most prudent Mississippians find at least disconcerting, if not repulsive. But fueled by a great resolve to succeed, Brady emerged from the poverty trap, earned an education, the silver wings of an Air Force pilot, and later the four stripes of an airline captain. The six-figure salary was a nice fringe benefit.

Those first months were terribly apprehensive and uncertain. He was the Mississippi Air Guard's first black pilot. He met with no rudeness or overt expressions of prejudice, but the attitudes were there; he could feel them. He occasionally overheard racial jokes and detected subtle condescension. Still, he avoided confrontation and instead revealed his exuberant personality. Yet he didn't know for sure whether he was making any progress bucking the headwind of prejudice, especially among certain of the enlisted contingent who often flirted with the boundaries of insubordination in their relationship with him. But one night at the all-ranks club he found out.

The entire squadron was at the Gulfport Training Center for our drill weekend. A lavish boiled shrimp feed had just concluded, and many of the crewdogs migrated into the club and began to mingle with the local crowd. The big room was crowded and loud with country music. Although he was one of the few men of color there, he was enjoying himself immensely—so much so that he invited a local white girl to dance while her male escorts were away. I had remained on the patio with the more sedate of my squadron-mates, but I heard the skirmish when it began.

The two men, both burly and intimidating, had returned and had found the girl on the dance floor with the festive Brady. The spectacle must have affronted whatever puny values they harbored, for they wasted no time in clearing the dance floor, then commenced to teach Brady a lesson or two. Brady thought that maybe he had overstepped and now was about to pay dearly. But no sooner had the brutes seized him than Robert Evans and Mad Dog Mashaw, our two scrappiest loadmasters, dove into the fray, followed quickly by a host of crewdogs, driving the thugs away. Then Brady knew that he was indeed among friends. They might be yet a little crude and a bit insensitive, but he belonged. It meant much to him.

Still, he never forgot those of his brothers and sisters who remained trapped in despair. He tells me how they need to know that they can break out, as he did, that all they need is encouragement and a good role model. He tells me about his efforts to instill hope in the forlorn faces of the black youth around Vicksburg. He talks to them on the street corners and addresses them in schools and churches. He has a splendid gift of gab; he smoothly engages total strangers in conversation as if he'd known them all his life. He tickles me the way he talks of serious subjects of the heart and head and then, deciding the conversation has become too weighty, without pause switches to unmitigated bullshit.

We have had many such freewheeling discussions—from brain to bull—in the cockpit during the long cruises and in the quarters and eateries of a half-dozen air bases. I had tried to explain the paradoxical pride I felt for my southern heritage. I told him about my great-grandfather, who had had little or no formal education but had nevertheless expressed himself well with the pen and had written of the pride for the "cause" for which he had fought the Yankees. Yet he was only a dirt farmer—didn't own anyone. There must have been more to the Cause than I can account for.

I wanted Brady to understand what I couldn't comprehend myself, how I could identify so closely with such a long lost thing. The harder I reasoned, the more disdainful the Cause became, yet the more I realized that I belong to it. It must be that the Cause with which I identify bears little resemblance to that which motivated so many in 1861. Or maybe, even in those troubled times, the Cause had many and varied meanings.

I don't know, maybe the Cause is simply that which drives me to express my threatened individuality, to preserve and protect my freedom, to persevere in the face of overwhelming odds, like that inspirational feeling a Southerner has when he or she is the underdog. Maybe we just like being underdogs. When I see that impassioned flag with its crossed bars and blue stars, I don't see hatred and bigotry, though I see them in the faces of the wretched people who use the flag to justify them. Rather, I see courage and honor. I see it the way my great-granddaddy saw it.

Brady accepted and tried to understand my feelings. But he explained, with deep sincerity and logic with which I had to agree, the feelings of his culture. We didn't agree on everything, but we were able to talk about such things without confrontation, with open minds—a characteristic, I believe of maturity, the Christian values to which we both subscribed, and of true friendship.

Brady has a way of characterizing bigotry with humor. He related a story from his days in UPT. Nearing graduation he was scheduled for the big event, the T-38 solo out and back. He had about thirty hours' solo time the day his instructor released him to fly the "White Rocket" alone to Craig Air Force Base in Selma, Alabama.

Brady was a bit unnerved about flying to Selma. The city had been in the national spotlight because of great racial turmoil and violence. The very word "Selma" had come to symbolize hatred and struggle.

But Brady had no time for that. His paramount priority, like that of all UPT students, was to get through the program and graduate. The challenge was tremendous; the washout rate was high. But he was relieved that his itinerary was to refuel expeditiously and return to Columbus. The flight was uneventful. Brady had hit his checkpoints and set the '38 down on one of Craig's long runways. He taxied to the transient parking ramp and shut down the engines. Then, looking down, he saw that the service personnel were civilians, not the Air Force airmen he expected. No doubt they were citizens of Selma. And they were white. As he unhooked his oxygen mask and raised his sun visor, the men stopped and looked up at him incredulously, mouths agape. Brady knew what they were thinking. "That niggah done stole that T-38!" he guffawed.

I told Brady about the first black pilot I had ever met. I too was a student in UPT learning to fly T-37. Although our instructors, clad in their helmets, masks, visors, and hoses, often appeared to us as beasts, they were very much human. In fact most of them were only a year or two older than I. Many of them were "first assignment" instructors, meaning they had never flown anything but trainers. Because of a good UPT performance—but one maybe not quite good enough to get a fighter job—they had been retained to teach their newly acquired jet flying skills.

For the most part I didn't care for these guys because I sensed that they were frustrated with their jobs. They really wanted to get out and "fly the line" like a real pilot. Their attitude often resulted in a strained relationship with their students. UPT was challenging enough without your having to put up with a guy who was trying to prove that you can't walk and chew gum simultaneously, let alone fly a jet. Such was my attitude when Captain Brown came.

A slight hush fell across the training room when he walked in. He was a tall, broad-shouldered man with a bushy hairstyle that must have pushed the haircut regulations to the most liberal of interpretations. His eyes were the color of coal tar, and he carried his big frame as if he were on the backside of some great achievement. He smiled diplomatically but yet at the same time looked slightly annoyed; he was here among us, casting an imposing presence, but was subconsciously elsewhere. And he was intensely black.

This was a time of widespread racial turmoil and upheaval. Black people in any prominent position in society were exceptional, and black pilots were almost unheard of. The potential for confrontation was clear. Captain Brown was obviously the new instructor we'd been told to expect. The changing of instructors was a common practice, and we never knew when we would be assigned another one without explanation. I just hoped I would not be the person to find out what this bold new pioneer of his race wanted to prove. I wasn't prejudiced. Naa, not me. I had always regarded black folks as my Dad had taught me: they were human beings and deserved respect. But there lingered a reservation back in the dry bays of my mind that maybe black people were better adapted to things other than flying.

My pulse began to race with anxiety. I was from Alabama, for cryin' out loud. My governor, George Wallace, was running for president on a states' rights platform, which everyone knew was a smoke screen for segregation. In those days if you mentioned Alabama, people thought of a smoldering children's Sunday school room and bloodstains on the Edmund Pettus Bridge in Selma. Both were the work of a few pitiful zealots, but the images were devastating. And here I was caught in between. Maybe I could lie to him about where I was from, but I could never cover my accent.

Presently Captain Brown and the flight commander emerged from an adjoining office into the big room. The flight commander pointed at me, and Captain Brown came to my table.

Why me, Lord?

He extended his hand, smiled warmly, then sat down and with a calm, completely reassuring voice began to melt my silly concerns away. I saw immediately that this man was a far cry from those first-assignment instructors. He was a seasoned combat veteran fighter pilot of a hundred missions over North Viet Nam. He had flown Phantoms, had seen friends perish in fiery crashes, and had watched some men parachute into the hands of a tortuous and vengeful enemy. His countenance was that of a man who had glimpsed Hell and knew now what was important in life and what wasn't. Yes, I could sense it. Here was a man who stood far above petty prejudice and vindictiveness.

He captured my respect at once. He began to cultivate a pilot-to-pilot relationship with me, not the instructor-to-dumbshit type that prevailed at the other tables. He stressed that I was going to be the beneficiary of his greater knowledge and experience. It was as simple as that. I had logged about fifty hours in the Tweet, including a few solo flights, but that first flight with Captain Brown was to be my first lesson in aerobatics. Normally the lesson would make students apprehensive, as aerobatic training was a totally new experience. But as we took our chutes and helmets, and walked out to the jet, I marveled over how relaxed and unpressured I felt.

He didn't say much while I started the little jet up and flew it toward our assigned airspace over the town of Pond Creek. Then, with his coaching, we put the Tweet through thrilling sequences of loops, rolls, immelmanns, split S's, cloverleafs, and my favorite cuban eights, high over the plains of northwest Oklahoma. The freshly harvested wheat fields, neatly dissected by straight roads and fence lines, rolled lazily across the top of our canopy, rushed straight at our nose, and fell away as quickly behind our tail. Cumulus-studded blue sky and yellow field spiraled and oscillated in a swirling kaleidoscope of color, as we rolled and looped like a blissful young dolphin in a boundless ocean. We were pilgrims, fresh out of bondage, turned loose in a promised land, where the uncompromising gods of airspeed, altitude, and power jealously demanded our devotion. Yet sin we did, forsaking the margins of our concentration to self-indulgence and, awash in a resplendent freedom, drank of the joy and laughed wildly within our souls.

Years later I would stand in some of those same fields down below, beside my future father-in-law, and watch those same Tweety jets waltz high overhead, revealed only by an occasional reflection of sun on canopy, their engines barely heard above the prairie winds. And I would remember Captain Brown's calm, patient, and clear-headed instructions as he chatted into the mask microphone as if he were teaching me to oil paint.

"OK, a little more back pressure. Thaaat's it. Now lay your head back against the headrest and look as far back as you can. Just wait. Here comes the horizon now. Pick out a section line and pull straight down through it. Can you believe they pay us to do this? Incredible. It ought to be the other way around. Now, when your nose passes through that green-roofed farmhouse, the one there beside the pond, unload and roll out. Great. Now, hold your dive angle. Watch your airspeed. Start the pull again at 250 knots. Thaaat's it."

I glanced at Captain Brown a time or two, during his demonstrations, as if I could somehow see his face through all the trappings. The cockpit shadows retreated across his helmet as the jet rolled sunward, and all I could see was the reflection of myself in his visor. My image looked exactly like his. I knew that he was smiling, that he loved what we were doing. Yes, this man was different. Whatever he had, I wanted it.

That night in my room, as I watched the grim TV reports of racial strife and struggle, I reflected on the events of the day. We had both reluctantly returned to earth and to the realities of Newtonian physics. But while I was infused with new confidence and fresh inspiration, I realized that Captain Brown had indeed returned to bondage. And his shackles were far worse than mere chains. He was bound by attitudes of hatred, prejudice, and closed-mindedness. Then I knew why Captain Brown so passionately sought the freedom of flight. The jet doesn't care about the race of the man who merges with it to become one creature. The wind, the sun, the billowing clouds, and the vast blue skyscapes are color-blind guardians—they cast away the shackles of all who fly into their courts with heavy hearts, seeking sweet release.

I knew then that, although I had the fuel and spark built in me, Captain Brown engaged my starter and brought up the rpms. And I owed him for much more than just the gift of self-confidence. I was forever indebted to him for opening my eyes as well. I doubt he ever knew it, but he had unlocked some shackles of mine. From that point onward I constantly searched my thoughts and attitudes for telltale signs of subtle prejudice and prejudgment. And in doing so, I discovered the joy of relating to others as God intended. We are all his children. We are all siblings. Together we seek, and together we are given. Or forgiven.

A few weeks later I was assigned another instructor and Captain Brown was gone as quickly as he had come. But the fire in me continued.

NINE

BERNOULLI BAPTISM

T his is a rare treat. The need for men and equipment to support the Alabama Air Guard's deployment of their Phantoms to the Persian Gulf has brought me home. But it's only a quick stop.

The marshaler stands in front of us and holds one of his orange paddles down while waving the other fore and aft over his head. He is commanding me to turn the Starlifter very tightly to bring our nose around to the west. Off to the left I notice several small planes tied down in a grassy area and take special care not to use too much power in the turn. Our jet blast could easily send them rolling like aluminum tumbleweeds.

I complete the turn very slowly, a bit too slowly for the marshaler. He now vigorously waves the paddles overhead, motioning me to taxi farther forward. I gently nudge the throttles about a knob width forward and hear the four big Pratt & Whitney turbofan engines dutifully spool up in a muffled whine. It's uncanny how you can tell from just listening that there's more than one engine back there. They seem to harmonize, as if in song. One of the little pleasures in flying this great creature is taxiing her. I marvel in the awesome feeling of more raw power literally at my fingertips than most people could ever imagine.

The marshaler stands his ground as our radome nose approaches to within a few feet of him. Then he crosses his paddles, indicating that he is finally satisfied with our position and we are to stop. Looking down on him through the windscreen, I'm reminded of that little cartoon mouse, the one who presents the finger of contempt in a final act of defiance as a fierce eagle is about to consume him. I set the parking brake and flip the four ridiculously small switches on the overhead panel that choke the big engines into silence.

The crew entrance door is opened down below, and the shrill of the engines as they spool down mixes with the metallic clinks of seat belts and shoulder harnesses being unfastened. I take the flight-planning kit and descend first the flight deck ladder, then the crew door ladder to the tarmac, and stretch in Birmingham's cool breeze. The diesel throb of an external power cart bursts into life, as a number of people swarm about the jet, preparing to service it. The loadmasters are already busy far to tailward, where I hear the high-pitched scream of the hydraulic pumps waver slightly as they labor to power open the enormous clamshell cargo doors. The copilot remains on the flight deck, programming the navigation computer for the transoceanic journey ahead, while I start for the operations building.

The small planes in the grass naturally catch my eye as I pass. Suddenly I stop, transfixed, mouth agape, eyes bulging with wonder, like a man spotting a long-lost, almost forgotten lover. Sitting there in the grass is a Cessna 150 bearing the seal of the Alabama Wing, Civil Air Patrol, and the number N7195F. I'm stunned motionless. I want to grab someone and point to it, to proclaim loudly that that's the plane I first soloed. But no one's nearby.

How many years has it been? Twenty? Twenty-five? I was a junior in high school when I first flew alone. No, not at all alone. I was with 95 Foxtrot. She belonged to a flight school down in Tuscaloosa then. And she's still alive. And here. Talk about a chance meeting. Unbelievable. I haven't thought of her in years.

I walk over and gently touch her, like a boy cautiously but delightedly caressing his new dog. Her skin is rough and weathered. She needs a paint job; the interior is well worn. She has doubtless given birth to hundreds, maybe thousands, of fliers since I was with her last.

That summer day of my youth, with four hours and fifteen minutes of flying time in my log book, 95 Fox and I flew together, just us. And on that day I glimpsed God's chart table and saw the course of my life plotted on it.

Cessna 150

Some people dazzle the air show crowds; others make megabucks hauling hundreds of trusting souls; a few have the red stars of MiG kills painted below their canopy rails. But it makes no difference who they are or how glorious the job. They owe it all to a clattering crate of a puddle jumper sometime in their past. Somewhere there was a start. Something, someone—a friend or relative, a book or a model—planted the seed. A flight instructor cultivated it. But an airplane provided the baptism, in a river of sky.

The first brick in the formation of any great flying career was laid by beings such as Aeronica Champs, Cessna 150s, or Piper Cherokees. But all too often, amid the excitement and challenge of the big iron, the roots are forgotten. "Slow and simple" is eclipsed by the excitement of an F-15 or a Boeing 757.

How often have I heard them? The disdainful comments. The condescending questions from the "it's not worth it" crowd:

"Why do you do that? Don't you know that little plane can ruin your career? What if you screw up and bust a Federal Air Regulation? Why, the FAA would pull your license in a second."

Then there's the "tired of it all" bunch:

"Are you kidding me? When I get out of this cockpit I don't even want to see another airplane, big or little, until I have to come back here."

Finally, from the most nauseating group, the space cadets:

"If I can't yank, bank, and roll, fly fast and feel the awesome power of that afterburner, man, I'd rather not fly at all."

Then so be it.

But there's a propeller over there in the grass for me.

I bought my first plane, a thirty-year-old 1947 Cessna 140 for $2,900, while assigned to a fighter squadron flying state-of-the-art A-7D Corsair II jet fighters. The '140 flew at 100 mph up to a maximum altitude of 6,000 or 7,000 feet. The A-7 flew 600 mph up to 40,000 feet. The '140 was not stressed for aerobatics; it couldn't do much of anything exciting except land in remote places. The tough, combat-engineered Corsair could loop, roll, drop bombs, fire missiles, shoot cannon, and withstand up to seven Gs. Most people wouldn't consider the two as the same species of creatures, nor would they think it justifiable even to compare them.

Some of my buddies in the squadron couldn't understand the attraction. Why would I waste the time and money? A few of them did get interested when they realized that the little craft could expediently get them down to Rocky Point, Mexico, for a fishing trip. But I was unenthusiastic about lending it to them for that purpose. To be fair, some of them thought the plane was a novel idea, but no one ever asked to go flying in it. And when I offered, there was always grass to be mowed or a tennis date to be kept.

Yet heroes and comrades we were, ready to sacrifice it all tomorrow. We were the passionate envy of almost every eye that looked up at our neat four-ship formations thundering across Tucson. Here I was, a member of that elite club with the right stuff and the right hardware, living amid the exclusive, closed society of fighter pilot brethren. And yet my best friend was a civilian with a simple private pilot's license. But friendship is something that ought to transcend boundaries of status and ego.

He certainly had a name any fighter pilot would envy: Vroom. Dave Vroom. He was employed as a mining engineer but had an aeronautical engineering degree. He had first soloed at an early age, but less than perfect eyesight had blown his opportunity to fly the fast jets that he had admired while growing up around Tucson.

Coming to know Dave, I began to realize that the yearning for flight, the passion for it, the joy it brings, is not limited to professional flying or to the fast, powerful machines. More often than not the true fulfillment of the wing is found on the grass strips and the dirt runways where birdsongs echo through aged hangars and fabric wings tug gently at carefully tied ropes.

Yet I met him not on an airfield but in the small church Ellie and I attended. As I came to know him, I could tell Big Dave admired me because, I suppose, I was what he had dreamed of becoming. And I was always amazed at his genius with things of a mechanical nature. There seemed to be nothing he didn't know about engines, metallurgy, and fabrication. He was highly skilled at both grease monkey mechanics and drafting table designing.

Unlike the top guns in the squadron, Dave was delighted to take a spin in the Cessna 140, and he immediately caught the fever. He had been flying for years, but not until then did he become consumed with the idea of having his own flying machine. A couple of weeks later he called and asked me to fly over to the small strip on his side of town. We landed, shut down, and looked around for him. Suddenly a Cessna 120, an aircraft almost exactly like mine, emerged from behind a hangar with Big Dave's grinning face behind the controls, his petite wife in the right seat. She saw us and shrugged her shoulders in a resigned smile. Their savings for his planned consulting business had taken a hit. At that moment I knew I had cultivated a true friend, had found a brother. What the top guns couldn't understand about me Big Dave did.

We made the most of the freedom our little taildraggers offered. We explored the desert Southwest, chasing coyotes and landing on dirt roads or sometimes just open areas. We flew about without knowledge of a destination. In what we began to refer to as "treks," we pointed the noses of our tiny Cessnas in whatever direction moved us and flew until we crossed something interesting or until night encroached. We camped in the desert and on riverbanks, caught fish for supper, slept under our wings—Dave beneath the wing of his plane, me under mine, as if they were sacred spouses to whom we had pledged fidelity. We experienced what flying used to be, what it was meant to be. Through the marvel of those simple wings and that wide open country, we were delivered to the frontier of unbridled freedom.

But Dave got us into trouble once, and our salvation came from an unexpected source. He was leading while I flew tightly on his wing. We crossed a plateau and dropped down, following the contour of the land until we crossed over Lake Meade. It happened too quickly.

Suddenly I noticed a marina below us. The bobbing masts of a nest of sailboats shot beneath our wheels, not dangerously close, but far closer than the rules allow. I cautioned Big Dave on the radio, but he happily continued out over the water and I stuck to his wing, hoping that the boat people were airplane fans also. I was certain that the numbers on the sides of our planes were readable at this altitude. We pressed on across the lake to the dirt strip on the east side that we had spotted earlier in the day, which would be our campsite for the night.

Two weeks later the dreaded call came. It was an FAA investigator in Las Vegas. Was N3117N my plane? Was I flying it that day?

"Yessir."

"Were you aware of the boats and marina?"

Silence.

"Yessir." Mistake, I thought. Shouldn't have admitted that.

"Have you ever heard of FAR Part 91 concerning minimum altitudes?"

I swallowed hard.

"Yessir."

"Do you have an explanation?"

"Well . . ."

"Is there an airport there? Maybe you were in the process of taking off or landing?"

Silence.

"Yes. Yes, there was an airport and . . . and we were on final approach for it."

"Hm, hold on a minute."

I heard the sound of a chart being unfolded. I was sweating bullets, 20 mike mikes.

"OK, I think I see it here. Is it Cottonwood Landing?"

"Yes, yessir, that's it, all right."

"That's quite a final approach you had there—five or six miles!"

"Yessir, ha ha."

I cleared my throat.

"OK, well, I'm satisfied. I think I can close this one out."

Dave got the same call.

Whoever that FAA guy was, he was one of us: a brother. We owed him one, Big Dave and I did. And we raised our mugs to him and planned the next trek.

It was twenty years after I first soloed 95 Foxtrot that I experienced the greatest satisfaction of flight. It was not the result of fast, powerful maneuvering, or flying to exotic new lands, or exploring as the spirit led. It came when I passed the gift along to someone else.

A flier who builds a trophy aviation career but never passes on the light is losing out. True, not everyone is cut out to instruct, and some who do it shouldn't. Moreover, as a vocation, it's a slow way to starve. But I decided to do it as a sideline. I wanted to feel what it was like to teach someone to fly, not just to check him out in a new military plane or merely to administer proficiency training, like the instructors in our Guard unit. To start from scratch with a student—that's what I had wanted for years. When I did so, I discovered a whole new way of relating to another human being and the revelation of seeing that person discover a new life and a new world. And I found the culmination of that experience when I passed the torch to a longtime, trusted friend.

"OK, Schneeflock. How does a wing lift your butt off the ground?"

"The Bernoulli Principle. When the velocity of a fluid increases, its static pressure decreases and, since air is a fluid, the resultant low-pressure area over the top of the wing sucks the wing up to fill the void. The fuselage is attached to the wing, and my ass is attached to the fuselage, therefore I fly. Now, if you're finally satisfied with my aerodynamic wisdom, can we go work on prowess?"

It was near dusk and a high overcast was developing. The winds had begun to die down. The conditions were right, but was the Schnee ready? The first few landings that day had been inconsistent; a pretty good one, then a not-so-hot one, and so on. But my coaching hadn't been needed, and that was the important thing. A couple of lessons earlier he had progressed to being able to land without my physical assistance on the controls, but I needed to wean him of verbal dependency.

"All right, I'm not gonna look this time. I mean it. I'm covering my eyes! You're on your own, buddy. We live or die together—I'm depending on YOU this time!"

BLAM! Bounce. Bounce.

I looked up and removed my hands from my eyes. I pinched myself, then him. I grabbed his arm and shouted in mock jubilation.

"We're alive. WE'RE ALIVE, Schnee! Thank God!"

He glanced at me scornfully. But the tactic succeeded; it diffused some anxiety. He proceeded to make two additional independent landings. They were not pretty, but they were safe.

Again we turned onto final approach, and I decided that if this one was safe, I would release him. I would have done so yesterday but he didn't have the consistency. I haven't mentioned the S-word to him. He knows we're in the zone for it, but flight students don't like to think about that until the time comes. And it always comes before they think they're ready.

We ambled down final approach in the tiny Cessna 152 and made another bouncy but acceptable touchdown. As we rolled he moved the wing flap lever to the UP position and started to push in the throttle for another takeoff, but I put my hand over the throttle and closed it. The little engine idled back down and he shot a puzzled glance at me. I told him to turn off at the midfield intersection. I could sense his relaxation. He felt the ride was over. He could get back down to the office and wrap up a few loose ends before calling it a day. But as we cleared the runway I applied the brakes, stopped the Cessna and unlatched the door handle.

Before soloing a student the instructor always has the lingering feeling that maybe his student is not ready. Maybe I'm being premature about this. The man's life is in my judgmental hands. Perhaps another few landings or even an additional flight lesson would relieve some of the subtle doubts. I knew this feeling was natural because I had soloed other students before, but Bob was an old friend, almost family. It was a little different this time. I know this feeling is normal, but I had to take care that he saw nothing but absolute confidence in my face.

As I opened the door, I had to raise my voice to overcome the engine and prop wash.

"Taxi slow. Give me a chance to get up to the tower. I'll wa—"

"WHERE'RE YOU GOIN'?" he interrupted, shouting, demanding.

"Make two touch-'n-go's and a full stop. If you have a question I'll be in the control tower."

Before leaving I cautioned him that the Cessna would perform differently without my additional weight. The comment caused his expression to change from astonished disbelief to one of deep soul-searching. He looked at me but his eyes were focused about a thousand yards beyond me. I slapped him on the shoulder and slammed the door. The Schnee was alone with the Cessna. His birth was at hand.

I guess my reaction when I first soloed was about the same as anyone's: a fast pulse; a giddy feeling; wanting to laugh, hold my breath, and grit my teeth all at once until it was done. That magnificent feeling of achievement—it's something that never left me because I always reached still higher: the instrument rating, the commercial license, the multiengine, the airline transport certificate, flight engineer, flight instructor, aircraft commander, bigger and faster airplane checkouts. There was always a challenge, always a test. And after each, there was that same feeling, although some tests were not without adversity.

I sat on the bench outside the flight school and watched as he taxied the puddle jumper in and shut it down. I knew better than to go out and help him tie it down. I let him savor the few minutes alone with the plane. He finished and walked toward me, glancing back at it. He was wearing that characteristic grin of his—the one that suggests he knows something about you that you don't know he knows. But that time there was a gleam in his eye that exceeded the one from his best oil discovery.

He stopped and just gazed at me for a moment. Bob and I went back a long way. We had been classmates together at the Capstone. Sometimes words were not necessary between us. From that day onward he called me "Dad," and those who overheard him thought it a private joke of some sort, since he's a couple years my senior. Schnee paid them no mind. They would never understand.

TEN

MAIDEN FLIGHT

We are several weeks into the Desert Shield operation now, and some measure of routine has settled in. For example, we can expect to be deployed for two to three weeks, with several days' recuperation at home afterward. And we can anticipate about three trips downrange from the European staging bases before rotating back Stateside. On the other hand, one thing has become less certain: our company in the cockpit. My original crew has been broken up and scattered asunder. Each new cruise, now, presents new faces, some of them people with whom I've flown in earlier times. But loadmaster Mike Hall will fly on and off with me until the end.

Mike is an exuberant, energetic young man with an overflowing personality. Sometimes he verges on cocky and brash, and occasionally he causes ill feeling among his peers as a result, but he is a great traveling companion. Life is never dull around Mike. And like most enlisted people in our unit, he has a casual relationship with the officers, which is unofficially acceptable in the Guard. But Mike is disciplined enough to respond well to good leadership.

Our officers regularly roomed and socialized with enlisted men. All were on a first name—even a nickname—basis. Such an admission would send an active career officer reeling in horror, but that kind of relationship worked for us. Together with our active duty counterparts, we were chalking up an unprecedented track record of safety and reliability. Our success was proof enough. Still, every fresh face in the cockpit presented a new twist to life. And sometimes a new challenge.

More black airmen, including several pilots, had followed Brady's trail. They established a record of reliability, competency, and leadership. But even more profound personnel changes were taking place, changes that required severe adaptations. Some of the entries in my logbook are marked with a star to indicate that something unusual or worth remembering happened. A double star entry had initiated an abrupt change in my attitude the year before.

It was an eastbound Atlantic oceanic crossing. The autopilot was doing an admirable job, allowing us to relax and settle in for the high seas cruise segment. I was studying a navigation chart when I heard it. The half whisper, half cry of the flight engineer's astonished voice electrified the interphone.

"Dear . . . GOD!"

I looked up from the chart and over at Milo, not sure who had uttered the sobering remark. He was peeling away his Ray Bans and peering behind him, disbelief written across his face. I careened about, as well, and looked back. Four sets of eyes were agog, fixed upon the object in the middle of the flight deck floor.

A crumpled flight suit was lying there, the olive green Nomex material piled on itself; patches and zippers showing here and there. Then all our heads lifted up to the top bunk on the aft bulkhead, whence the zoom bag had been tossed. The drawn blackout curtains were bulging and pulsating with movement from within, as if a solitary struggle were in progress.

Then our eyebrows arched higher as a brassiere was flung from beneath the curtains and fell onto the flight suit. We stared incredulously at the growing heap and flinched again as more female undergarments plopped onto the pile. Various imprecations and utterings of disbelief issued from our lips into the plane's interphone system. The loadmasters inevitably arrived to check out the strange exclamations from the flight deck. For the next hour we wondered and laughed, speculated and bet, eyes periodically cutting back toward the bunk. Would she ask for the garments to be handed back up when the nap was over? Would we comply? A loadmaster paced the flight deck, threatening to fling the curtains back and teach this teaser a lesson.

But we forbade him; much was at stake here. We didn't know this person very well. And we were puzzled and confused by this striking sign of change in our preserved world of engines, wings, and throttles.

Bob Moore smiled and slowly shook his head. Once a farmer, he had grown milo, among other crops; I had coined his nickname. His face and thinning hair were as red as his Mississippi Delta dirt. His warm smile was genuine and contagious. He didn't talk much, and his humor was subtle. I liked him because he and I were so much alike and because he reminded me greatly of my brother, Steve. Over the years, while we flew together in the Guard, Milo was a banker and, early on, a lending officer to farmers, while I was a geologist with an oil company. Later, discontented with the corporate world, he turned to farming, much as I turned to consulting. Then both his business and mine had crumbled. Together we felt the pain and frustration as our once-needed, noble, and respected professions were trampled underfoot by political ineptitude, wild swings in markets, and the ruthless struggles of power and greed. Together, Milo and I blew off the old persuasions and threw caution to the wind; what did we have to lose? In abrupt, upheaving, heart-ripping midlife changeovers, we became airline pilots. Milo went to the silver birds, I to the Friendly Skies. But brothers we remained.

Finally the curtains began to ruffle. Fingers appeared, then the sleepy, green-eyed she-pilot, hair bedraggled, appeared, smiled, and extended an arm outward, asking for the garments.

But no, no, no was, of course, the answer. We cut eyes toward one another and chuckled; the time was at hand to turn the gag back upon her. We were so clever. "No, ma'm, you'll have to come down for them yourself." Snicker, guffaw.

She pleaded with us, and still we refused. Then she questioned our decency and sense of humor, all the while clutching the curtain around her neck. She was exasperated; her gag had gone afoul.

As I was beginning to feel that it had gone far enough, she began a desperate act. She detached the blackout curtain from its hooks and wrapped it about her. She then carefully lowered herself to the flight deck and ambled to the pile of clothes with only her bare arms, feet, and ankles showing from the makeshift smock. I thought I noticed a whimper and a tear. I felt bad. Then, as she stooped to pick up the clothes, the curtain parted.

"LOOK AT THIS!!" the engineer sitting near her yelled. He reached inside the wrapping toward her leg and grabbed something. We all strained from our seats looking with curious and bulging eyes. He had grabbed a handful of olive green nomex material. SHE WAS WEARING A FLIGHT SUIT! The sleeves were cleverly rolled above her elbows, the legs in a similar fashion above her knees so that she looked naked beneath the curtain. The other clothes had been stashed in the upper bunk to set up the prank. She flung off the curtain and collapsed into the lower bunk, laughing uncontrollably.

We were no more than fish hanging on her stringer—she, the happy and skillful angler. But now at least we knew something of this newcomer. She had ably staked out her territory among us, and for that we respected her.

Such was my introduction to Ginny Thomas, the first female military pilot I'd ever known. She was from Alabama, and as the only two Bama graduates in a sea of Mississippians, we established a rapport pretty quickly. But still, I wasn't sure about her. This was too new. She came from the active Air Force, a tanker pilot. She had a good reputation, having been decorated for saving a Navy fighter plane running low on fuel. But like the rest of us, she wasn't the career type and had turned to the best of both worlds: flying Uncle Sam's jets in the militia.

And a bold move it was. The Mississippi Air Guard was a decades-old male bastion; a fortress of walls lined with haughty men—me among them—closely cradling our guns of pride and watching with curiosity and skepticism as this maidenly newcomer rode in, bringing with her a profound change. But we quickly saw that she was not the type who wanted to prove something. Oh yes, this we expected; this we wanted. We were scrapping for a fight. Sacred boundaries had been spit across. We knew it was a hopeless battle, but we reveled in being the underdogs. We wanted to point and shake our arrogant heads, to jump on her case, to extol our superiority and magnify her weaknesses. And we did it sometimes with a cruel resolve. We strangely forgot about all the hard landings we had made when we saw her prang it. When she strayed above the glide slope, we sneered the sneer of self-deceived perfectionists. She went through hell and never tried to fight back, never dared us to knock the feminist chip off her shoulders, because there was no such chip. She just wanted to be one of us, to be accepted even as we ourselves wanted to be accepted by the group. We allowed this during the off-duty times, the layovers, the long drill weekends. But in the cockpit, for a longer time than should have been, we regarded her as something of an intruder and, subconsciously perhaps, a threat.

I shed my zoom bag and crashed into the small German bed, utterly exhausted from the night crossing. I was well aware that I would sleep like a piece of granite porphyry for six hours only to stay awake all night until the 0600 takeoff. Then, before the mission would even have begun, the freshness would be depleted, and I'd be wasted again. Yes, on other occasions I had agonizingly forced myself to stay awake another six or eight hours, so that I could get a normal amount of sleep just prior to alert time. It's no good for me. I would just wrap up in the soft German comforter and cast off from reality. I'd drift away into blessed slumber and let sleep run its course. But there was a persistent rapping at the door.

I staggered over and swung the door open. Miss Ginny stood there, wearing her touring clothes and a cheerful grin. She had sunglasses at the ready and camera shoulder-slung. She started to talk, but I preempted.

"No, no. Go away." I started to close the door, but she threw her weight into it and resisted, pleading with me to forsake the gloomy room and accompany her into the German countryside. I replied that the very idea was insane, as I managed to force the door closed. Finally I pushed it to the latch and turned back for the bunk, but the rapping and pleading continued. Then they stopped but resumed on another door across the hallway. I snickered, knowing that Milo was then being accosted. I heard his door open as she implored him to come out.

A few minutes passed, and I was roused again by the relentless rapping, and again I ambled to the door, resolved to put an end to it. But there, behind her, emerging from his room was the defeated Milo, donning his jacket and Raybans.

"Come on out of there!" he shouted. "If I've got to do this, you're coming too."

I conceded and made ready, while she found a more willing companion in Jerrell, a loadmaster, who had slept during the crossing. The four of us hopped a train bound for Heidelberg. We followed and watched in ignorance as she conversed in fluent German with the local citizens. She had done her share of the flying last night, yet she snapped pictures, talked incessantly, and ran up castle stairways with the energy of a child. But there among the mountains and castles, we forgot for a while about the fatigue, and we became a little less concerned about the new face standing next to us on the fortress walls.

The last we heard, Ginny had been assigned to George Fondren's crew, along with our second female pilot, Mary. That would be an interesting combination. One of our guys says he'd like to be a little gremlin hiding behind a switch in that cockpit, listening to the master bullshitter and the quick-witted she-pilots. But I suspect George is more subdued these days. The times are indeed a'changing—and George and I are having a hard time keeping up.

ELEVEN

MY KIND OF FLIERS

W e wait in front of the billeting office at "0-dark thirty" for the crew bus that will take us to our 162-ton chariot. A chilled wind is blowing, and low ragged clouds are racing overhead. I never thought Spain could have such lousy winter weather. We shiver with the dampness and anticipate the fatigue of the twenty-hour mission ahead.

The dreaded sound of the crew bus diesel engine grows, and headlights appear in the mist. Another cursed bag drag is at hand. We drain our styrofoam coffee cups and with burnt-out moans begin to pick up the B-4 bags, the duffel bags, the chemical warfare bags, the pubs kits, the mission kit, and the coolers. As the bus parks, we see that it contains an inbound crew. The lights inside come on, and simultaneous shouts arise from within the bus and from among us.

"It's one of our crews!"

These were always welcome words, and when we heard them, our spirits bolted upright. With renewed energy we greeted our old comrades from the Deep South. We slapped backs, shook hands, and horseplayed like shut-in brothers.

"How long ya'll been out?"

"Left the house yesterday. How 'bout ya'll?"

"Sixteen days and goin' back downrange today."

"Shee-it."

I look around for the pilots and spot the aircraft commander. It's Pink Floyd! The all-American kid next door; the red-haired and temperamental yet abundantly friendly Pink. Beneath his youthful face he hides a great self-confidence and a bit of an ego, which is expected and acceptable. I followed his fast progress from the day he showed up as a raw second lieutenant. He progressed quickly to a captain, then aircraft commander, and soon became an instructor.

Shortly after joining us, he found a real job and became an insurance adjuster. He made pretty good money and proclaimed it a great job. But it was easy to read the discontent in his unassuming face. The truth was that he was hungry to fly professionally, and just prior to the callup he had landed a lucrative job flying for Federal Express.

Seeing Pink I always remember the Greenwood air show, where we were both once big stars. It was one of those rare occasions when we could show off a little and have some fun. He was a new jet jock with an ardor for center stage, but the spotlight focused more sharply on him than he anticipated. It was the result of a simple slip-up; he wasn't even responsible for it—if he is to be believed—but in the Mississippi Air Guard the teasers will hose you down when you blunder. I would have my turn at the hose.

I had just transitioned from C-130s to C-141s and had checked out as an aircraft commander, which is the equivalent of captain in the airline world. Pink was fresh out of pilot training and more recently the C-141 copilot school at Altus Air Force Base.

One Sunday afternoon I reported for a proficiency training mission that was scheduled to go out to Oklahoma and back. Pink was already at the base and had vigorously completed the flight planning and paperwork. With thinly veiled excitement he informed me that an air show was under way in Greenwood, his hometown. He knew the air show coordinator and had arranged for us to make a brief appearance, before we winged it for Oklahoma. Pink had okayed it with the supervisor of flying. Everything was arranged. We would appear at precisely 1:30 P.M.

It sounded fun to me, so I briefed the crew on what we would do at the show. We would approach from the south, make a low slow pass overhead with the gear and flaps down, generating a lot of crowd-pleasing noise and smoke. Then we would "clean up" the jet, retracting the flaps and gear, and return to the airport from the north at high speed. We would pull the nose up from a low approach and roll the

Chief Master Sergeant Charlie Watson

beast toward the crowd so that they could see the top profile. After this "pass-in-review" maneuver, we would climb out at maximum power, bathing the airport in thunder. Chief Master Sergeant Charlie Watson and his student engineer scrutinized the plan with concern, but I assured them that we could do it safely if we all stayed alert and did not exceed certain parameters. Pink was beside himself with excitement.

At 1:25 we contacted the show coordinator and were informed that an aerobatic act was ending and we were cleared to come in. Peering out of his window like Kilroy as we passed, Pink was stunned at the size of the crowd and the variety of show planes parked on the field. This was truly a big event for his hometown. The pass-in-review maneuver went as planned and as we climbed out toward Oklahoma, satisfied that the crowd had been amply impressed, the happy Pink remarked that he would get a copy of the videotape of the show.

Curiously, weeks went by, but my promised copy of the tape was never produced. I kept reminding Pink, but he conveniently kept forgetting. Finally, after incessant cajoling, he gave me the copy.

It was beautiful beyond expectation. The deep southern drawl of the narrator, Jim Burris, could clearly be heard, his booming voice echoing and reverberating across the airport on the public address system. As we approached on the high-speed pass, the experienced Jim anticipated the maneuver and warned the crowd.

"This is your camera pass, folks. Have your cameras ready."

As the image of our Starlifter passed in a graceful, turning arch and started its climb-out, applause could be heard, and Jim's voice boomed again in tribute to the town's native son.

"Beautiful! Beautiful pass. There he goes folks, Greenwood's very own Lieutenant David Floyd, the *aircraft commander*. Don't you know his daddy's proud!"

Dave would return and do the show again in a couple of years, this time as the aircraft commander indeed, and again he would do the town proud.

I have never let him forget that. But maybe I won't press it this morning. He looks burnt out. I can see it in his eyes. In a little while Dave and his crew will be in the bunks we so reluctantly left, and we'll be in the seats they gladly vacated.

C-141B Starlifter

Another trip downrange faces us like a relentless taskmaster. We will throw our backs again into the harnesses, but our pyramid seems to have no taper. We've built it higher than any other, but still there is no end in sight.

After a long hiatus, we find ourselves coming back through TJ again. With Zaragoza to pull away some of the traffic, TJ has settled down a bit. The Wild West atmosphere is long gone. Our pistols are now checked with the security police armory before we leave the flight line. Thankfully, we're down to only two to a room.

The base services officer has finally recognized that some crewdogs, like jet engines, must spool down. She has ordered the erection of a beer tent on the lawn in front of the billeting office. The activity under it has waned with the cooling of the weather, but the "inbounds" still congregate under it before turning in. Last night there was some sort of a fracas out there. A lieutenant is walking around this morning with a great shiner under his eye, delivered, reportedly, by a sergeant from our unit.

Weather forecasts and flight plans in hand, we leave the operations room and start for the bus, but ahead is a face that rejuvenates me. I was hoping I would cross paths with him, and now there he is, looking like he's back in Jackson, weathering out another dull drill weekend. He leans against the wall in the hallway of the command post facility, hands buried in the pockets of his flight jacket, gazing passively but not unkindly at the antlike activity around him. He nods at familiar faces and waits, like a neglected but patient puppy, for a passerby to linger for a bit of flying talk.

The epitome of a dashing aviator he's not. He wears his hair and his mustache a bit too long for Uncle Sam's austere taste. He always seems to have a five o'clock shadow. And it seems to me that he wears a flight suit a couple sizes too large. His appearance is deceiving to those who think great pilots ought to look like square-jawed, steely-eyed Steve Canyons. He cares not and in fact enjoys the illusion. He doesn't talk a lot and isn't inclined to discuss abstract or philosophical things. Born in an aviation family, endowed with an innate talent for flying, and possessed of a passion for the wing, Tom Wallace is my kind of flier. He's the quiet, confident type who knows he's good but doesn't try to convince the world of it.

I watched him once while the squadron was going through its annual small-arms refresher training. While half the group was popping away with the pistols, the rest of us lounged lazily a distance away. Tom had fetched a chair from inside the shooting range shack and was leaning back in it, arms folded, legs crossed, eyes gazing out to nowhere in particular. His pose looked like that in old photographs I've seen of Civil War soldiers. A small pocket of chat about taxes, politics, and other such paltry topics was in progress near him, the voices rising and falling to stay afloat over the din of the volleys. Quite suddenly, someone started talking about a new airline engine modification. Tom's ears perked. His head swiveled toward the crowd. He uncrossed his legs and listened to another sentence, then sprang from his chair and joined happily in the discourse on fuel flow efficiency and power-to-weight ratios.

And his skill matched his knowledge. He had once been dispatched to fly to the large regional air show in Birmingham, his mission being to place the jet on public display. Arriving at the show site, he put the big Starlifter through such a graceful suite of maneuvers that the air show officials marveled and awarded him the esteemed arrival show trophy. Incredibly, he had outshone some of the world's newest and most sophisticated fighter planes.

To Tom the brotherhood of fliers is not all-inclusive. He cares little for those who settle for mediocrity or less than absolute dedication to the profession. He's especially disdainful of those who use wings purely for monetary or political gain. Those people are like putrid smoke in the pilot lounge, driving him out into the purity of the flight line.

I tell the crew to hold the bus while I greet Tom. He is inbound and I'm outbound. There's not much time, but we catch up with one another as best we can, and he is eager to tell me about the mission to Riyadh he flew a few days back. It seems that Tom's devotion to the brotherhood was severely tested on that trip. He faced what might have been a dilemma for some of us but not so for Tom. Fellow pilots were in trouble. He knew what to do.

The airlift control element (ALCE) staff were people under tremendous daily pressure. The flow of the huge jets was unceasing. The ALCE controllers had to see that the jets were parked, unloaded, serviced, fixed if they were broken, and turned back uprange as soon as possible. They worked twelve-hour shifts, around the clock. They were blamed by their superiors when things didn't flow well and were subjected to the grumbling of aircrews when servicing went afoul. Few people envisioned an airlift operation of this magnitude. There was not enough forethought, knowledge, or hardware to handle this smoothly. Mindsets were not prepared for it. The controllers had to innovate and experiment. When they guessed wrong or miscalculated, they caught flack. Nerves were strained to the limit, and as the months went by, the fatigue, the endlessness of the operation, and broken promises of relief brought on despair. Of all the people in the Persian Gulf operation, none were driven so severely and continuously as those who anchored the receiving end of history's greatest air logistical tail.

And there was no outlet for their tensions and frustrations. There was no officer's club or NCO club at which to unwind. There was nothing to do or see around town. Indeed, much of the time people were restricted to the installation. It was a lousy existence, especially for fliers, which is what they were. The ALCE jobs required pilots, loadmasters, and engineers—people who wanted desperately to be doing what we were doing.

The commander of the Riyadh ALCE had found two of his pilots drunk, or at least he suspected that they had been drinking. Alcohol is illegal in the Kingdom of Saudi Arabia, and our military leaders had declared that U.S. forces would honor the host country's laws. Officially, booze was taboo. Many commanders looked the other way, but some took the policy seriously.

It wasn't clear where the guys had procured the booze. They certainly couldn't buy it in Saudi Arabia or on the military base. But occasionally aircrews coming down from Europe would carelessly put a six-pack of beer or a bottle of some sort of firewater into the aircraft's cooler. I know this happened again and again with my crews, and I had to severely discipline them for being so negligent. I considered it my duty to inform the ALCE discreetly when I found alcoholic contraband on my aircraft so that it could be properly confiscated. And I always marveled at how such disclosures seemed to result in quick fuel service. Still, it was possibly from such stocks that the two pilots had chosen to release their tensions.

Tom knew nothing of the circumstances. Maybe the men had been drunk on duty, or maybe they had been caught having a casual one in their tent. But it was clear that they were being made an example of. Upon his arrival, a colonel had presented Tom with two ampoules of blood and ordered him to take them back to Germany for analysis of alcohol content. The colonel had made arrangements for a medic to meet the aircraft. Tom signed for the samples and assured the colonel that he would deliver them expediently.

The unloading and fueling completed, Tom and his crew started up and departed for the long trip back uprange to Germany. After climb-out he asked if anyone on the crew had any experience in the care and handling of biological specimens, but no one had had any such instruction in the course of their training. Tom reasoned that since humans are warm-blooded creatures, then blood samples must naturally be kept warm—who could argue with such a deduction? So he placed the tubes on his glare shield, where the intense high-altitude sun could keep the blood fresh. But soon night fell across the skyscape and Tom began to worry that the blood would become chilled. He then ordered that the oven in the plane's galley be warmed up to about 300 degrees and placed the tubes therein for the duration of the long trip.

The medic waited as the plane blocked in at the German base, and Tom presented him with the two ampoules full of a baked brown crusty crud. He shrugged at the puzzled medic's proclamation that the samples were useless. He had done his best. And of course he had. He had, in fact, succeeded. The careers of two brothers had been saved. It was no big deal to Tom, just a simple act of loyalty.

TWELVE

HERCULEAN DREAMS

We are waiting for takeoff clearance at an airfield in the tiny United Arab Emirates. We have delivered several tons of fresh vegetables, air conditioners, aircraft parts, and mail to the C-130 unit based here. This place is a long way from Kuwait, but I guess the fighters, with their much shorter endurance, get priority on the closer bases. The C-130s here are flying a few intratheater airlift hauls and some training flights. But mostly they wait. I'm exceedingly glad that my stay in this place has only been two hours. Yet I'm envious of these guys in a way that only those who have flown the '130 can know.

I've grown to love this old jet I'm strapped to. I didn't at first. It was the biggest thing I had ever flown, and its vastness intimidated me. But with airplanes, familiarity breeds affection, not contempt. And as a seasoned colonel once counseled me, "Son, whatever airplane you're flying is a good airplane." Translated, I believe that means "Do not covet another pilot's plane, but delight in what you have been given." Makes sense.

But as I watch the flight of three C-130s glide overhead and pitch out, fighterlike, I remember what it was like. And I'm not alone in such musings. All of us who flew it—pilots, flight engineers, loadmasters, all—remember the happy times we had in the Herc.

It seemed big then. Certainly anyone standing near it wouldn't regard it as small. But the most striking feature of the '130 is its props. Each of the four turboprop engines spins a propeller with four broad

C-130 Hercules

paddles. The ponderous props are governed to spin at the same rpm, regardless of whether flying or just sitting on the ground. Only the pitch—the "bite" of air taken by the blades—changes. This results in the curious propensity of the '130 to be noisier just sitting on the ground at idle power than when flying. You can hear the distinctive drone of a '130 across a great distance, and sweet music it is. But when the noise ceases, the pilots have either shut down or advanced the power to takeoff.

It's the props that make the C-130 so much fun to fly. I considered just taxiing the beast pure pleasure. The big props were my happy servants, ready to respond to the most whimsical twitch of my fingers on the throttles. I found myself often pushing up the power very slightly while taxiing just to hear the props sing their accordionlike whine as they changed pitch. And then I'd pull them back into reverse and listen to them abandon their whine and enter into a great blowing belch.

And in the air the Herc was a fine handling machine, much more sensitive than the '141. It was good for formation flying because of the instantaneous thrust when power was applied (as opposed to a turbojet engine, which requires "spool-up" time). Often this instantaneous power feature was the savior of the third aircraft in a CDS drop.

It was arguably our most hazardous maneuver. The CDS, or container delivery system, was a low-altitude drop (about 500 feet) in which pallets loaded with large metal containers slid out the rear of the plane, their huge parachutes opening just prior to impact. We relied on gravity to pull the CDS from the cargo floor, and in order to achieve this, we had to slow the aircraft down to a critical speed with little or no flaps, so that our angle of attack caused a high deck angle. It's very unsettling, doing that at such a low altitude, and the planes in the rear of the formation had the problem of fighting the prop wash and wake turbulence of the planes ahead. Numbers two and three "stacked high" in hopes of flying over the turbulent air, but still it happened.

You're out there in the dark just a few wingspans above the cottonwoods, with your right hand full of throttles, your left with seventy-five tons of bucking airplane, eyes darting from altimeter to airspeed indicator, from compass to fuel flow indicators, then quickly refocusing on the ludicrously dim formation lights of the guy ahead. Thoughts that should have been left on the ground play around the periphery of your mental focus. You try to forget about the account that you lost today and the boss's foreboding over the business downturn. But the distracting thoughts continue to probe for a crack, an inroad through which to gain access to the critical core of your concentration. And then, as the navigator calls "one minute warning," it happens.

You feel it before you see it. The airspeed decay causes a loss of lift, a sinking feeling. One of the invisible but devilish curls of wake turbulence seizes your wing tip and rolls you violently. Your mind clears; you're in the survival mode now. You counteract with opposite aileron, but now, because of loss of lift, you've sunk down into the teeth of the raging vortexes, forcing you to fight to keep the Herc upright. Instinctively you ram the throttles forward and feel the four big Allison turbines thrust you into blessed acceleration. And as you battle to maintain altitude and formation spacing, you try to follow the navigator's meticulous heading instructions. He's down on the deck beside your seat, kneeling on all fours, his head pressed against the lower quarter window, watching for his computed release point. Every few seconds he keys his boom mic and directs a heading change. "Four degrees right, steady, two right, two left." It's almost preposterous, fighting the invisible tornadoes while trying to turn only two degrees. You do the best you can.

The one minute seems like an hour, but finally comes the nav's command. "GREEN LIGHT!" The copilot switches on the green light in the cargo compartment, and the loadmaster jerks the lanyard, which releases the heavy load. You hear an awful roar, like something is ripping the aircraft apart. As the load separates, the '130 lurches forward, rejuvenated, rid of its burden, and pitches abruptly as the center of gravity suddenly shifts about fifty feet.

Then you push the throttles to max power for the escape maneuver. While you close the distance to rejoin the formation, you listen intently for the drop report.

"Twenty at nine, three," comes the transmission from the DZ officer, who is also a C-130 pilot from your unit.

Your load has impacted twenty yards left of the bull's-eye. Not bad, but the navigator will blame you for the error. He takes responsibility for the six o'clock to twelve o'clock errors, because those are timing problems, but the three to nine errors are heading problems and thus yours, assuming he has given you the correct heading commands (which of course he always assumes).

Despite the hazards, we all delighted over the formation airdrop missions. Those evenings were sportive occasions. Three complete crews, totaling fifteen or twenty crewdogs, assembled for premission festivities, which usually included palavering over fast foods picked up on the way over from work. Then the briefing was delivered by the aircraft commander of the lead plane in the formation. Some stayed after the mission for beer or went over to Harvey's, the crewdog hangout. We enjoyed one another's company. The times were good. But one such night still stands out clearly. It was a night when complacency gave way—as is its tendency—to terror.

A line of thunderstorms was slowly crossing the Mississippi River to our west, but according to the forecast, we would have clear but hazy weather for the low-level route and the drop. The night was very dark with no moon, and haze blotted out most stars, yet the air was smooth. Our call sign was Ruler 12, number two, in a three-ship formation, sitting at the standard 2,000 feet in trail behind the leader. Ruler 13 was another 2,000 feet behind us. This was a visual formation, but we were using our station keeping equipment (SKE) as a backup, to monitor the position of the other planes in the formation. The SKE information was displayed on the radar scope, but our scope was inoperative that night. It was not a problem, though, since the scopes in the other planes worked, and we did not anticipate weather penetration. Visual contact was all we needed. All was well until shortly after we dropped down to our standard 1,000-foot altitude for night operations.

The warning was ever so subtle. I momentarily lost sight of Lead's lights as some soupy cloud flashed by us. But such conditions weren't unusual this time of year. It must have been some patchy fog. There were no thunderstorms forecast for this area until much later in the night, "Right, Jeff?" I sought reassurance from my copilot.

"Right."

We knew that the leader had a good radar and hoped he would not lead us into something nasty. I relaxed as the fog disappeared and the security of Ruler 11's formation lights reappeared. But then Hell paid us a visit.

Lead's lights disappeared again. Something grabbed us. The huge claws of some giant demon into whose stormy lair we had blundered gripped us and began to shake us savagely. The Herc lurched, jolted, and slammed, as if the weather demons were using us in some sinister demolition game.

"CLIMB! CLIMB!" yelled Russ Gatlin, my navigator. As he spoke I was thrusting the throttles forward and rotating, knowing that I had to get away from the ground immediately. But the Herc was bucking so hard that I couldn't read the gauges. The pitot-static instruments were fluctuating wildly, what I could see of them. I fought off a twinge of panic, trying to modulate the back pressure to get a climb going but not too much, lest I overrotate and let the airspeed decay.

As I fought the storm, I tried to remember the procedures for inadvertent weather penetration. Since I was number two, and slightly on the right side, the procedure called for me to turn right forty-five degrees, hold that course for one minute, and then resume the base heading. Three would do the opposite. This would give the formation—now dangerously blind—a much safer spacing. But that procedure obviously wasn't going to work here in the throws of a struggle for survival where we couldn't even hold a steady heading.

About that time I heard the leader's frantic radio call. "Everybody turn south, NOW!"

South was the direction from which we came, thus the direction of good weather, but there was a big problem with Lead's order: it did not separate us. All of us turning south at once would be like a platoon of soldiers executing a right face. They all turn yet remain in the same proximity to one another. But I knew that Lead was fighting his own battle for control and had no time to devote to separation.

The plane was climbing, but I did not want to make the turn Lead had ordered, at least not abruptly. Under the rolling, tossing conditions I felt that too much bank would induce control problems. I tried to hold about a ten-degree right bank and hoped the awful bucking would slack as we climbed. It worsened. Then the horrifying thought struck me that Lead was turning into us.

Knowing better, I glanced up. Taking my eyes off the instruments was an invitation to vertigo—a state of confusion and disorientation—but it was an instinctive move. I was expecting to see lights emerge from the murk. For a few horrid seconds the storm was the lesser threat. They would be into us in a heartbeat: life ending and eternity beginning in a savage collision; a ripping and tearing of metal; his props devouring us; our wing tip piercing him; tons of fuel detonating; an enormous furnace of twisted metal plunging out of the maelstrom.

And as I glanced back again at the pitch black gloom, the sky flashed with a nuclear brilliance and the plane shuddered in a deafening blast. The ride became even more violent as the flashes and booms continued to thrash us. At one point the generators faltered under the electrical onslaught, and the cockpit went dark. But the blackout was only momentary. Yet I knew that if we lost power for any longer than a few seconds under these conditions, we would become hopelessly disoriented. We would roll over and enter a high-speed dive and probably pull the wings off in a desperate attempt to recover. Aviation history was replete with such accidents.

We were too busy to realize how tense our body muscles were, how clenched our teeth were, and how gripped we were with fear until it was over. And over it was, as quickly as it had begun. The gloom departed and the glorious lights of rural Mississippi lay before us. The air smoothed, and we became aware again of the hum of our props. Then the shock set in when we saw Lead sitting out there a couple thousand feet below us—on our right side.

We learned later that Ruler 13 had watched the whole escapade on his SKE as he executed his escape turn. He saw the lead plane's symbol on the scope merge with ours. Only the altitude had separated us. And we never managed to find out why Lead's navigator didn't see the thunderstorm on his scope. The next morning I sat at my drafting table pouring over geologic maps, but my mind was still back in the cockpit, fighting the storm. It could have been bad—really bad. But one thing was certain, I thought as I correlated electronic well logs, and it made me smile: I wouldn't trade places with anyone.

The squadron was a fairly kindred group—not as fraternal as a fighter squadron but close. Still, we were split into two factions: the afternoon fliers and the night fliers. The afternoon guys were those who had jobs with flexible hours or maybe no job at all. That mission launched at 3:00 P.M. and landed at 5:00. About that time the night guys, those who more closely fit the "weekend warrior" stereotype, began to arrive. Their mission launched about seven. The two groups became two different societies, sometimes seeing each other only on drill weekends, rarely flying together. And a measure of rivalry developed. The night fliers thought the day fliers were pretentious, overrated bums. The perception stemmed from the propensity of the day fliers to participate more than was required. Because they weren't shackled by restrictive jobs, they could fly any time the Guard wanted, and as a result they were the most experienced of the two factions. And the day fliers shunned night flying, doing only the minimum required, claiming that it was exceedingly stupid. I was among the nighthawks until the oil business went bust.

Although our unit had established a solid reputation for reliability and safety, there was one major blemish on our record. A deplorable scandal struck us in 1984. We never fully recovered. It all started innocently enough. Three crews were gathered for a three-ship nighttime drop mission to Bull Run Drop Zone. The briefing was completed, and all were milling around, waiting for the engineers to complete their preflights.

Lieutenant Colonel Jake Bland had stopped by the convenience store off base and bought a box of fried chicken and Tater Tots. He intended to eat them as time allowed, but unwisely set the box in the open and left the scene.

Jake was nearing retirement, but his enthusiasm for minute detail and absolute compliance with the "regs" had never waned. He was a "full-timer," an employee of the Air Guard ("technician" was the accepted term). And he was also chief of "stan/eval": the man in charge of a group of pilots, flight engineers, navigators, and loadmasters who administered periodic flight checks and written tests to the rank and file. Jake was a workaholic, full of energy and initiative, but was highstrung, and when he focused on a task, it was hazardous to distract him. His fastidiousness made him a target of the practical jokers—of which we had many—and although he did have a sense of humor, it was a little shallow. Nevertheless, those who took the time to know him discovered a gentle, caring man who was a model of integrity, hard work, and dedication. There was always something that Jake needed to do. Rarely did we see him relax, even for a meal.

When he finished his duties and opened the box, he gazed down at the spoils. His blood heated and eyes bulged as he surveyed the stripped bones lying among the debris of a plundered biscuit. And the Tater Tots: gone.

His sense of decency told him that someone else had also picked up a chicken dinner and had substituted their finished box for a quick laugh. He would be calm. He would play along until his box was returned. He had heard people speak of a thing called patience. He knew he must have some, somewhere. He would call upon it. They would have their silly laugh, then he could have his meal and get on with the mission.

Fully five seconds passed when the patience gave out. The explosion was volcanic; the rage spewed like scalding lava over all within his range. Not knowing who did it—that was the worst for him. Most of them slunk away and drifted toward the planes, a few of the braver ones remaining behind to question him as breaks in his wrath allowed.

As the drop mission launched and progressed, stinging accusations were fired across the squadron frequency. Of the two other aircraft in the formation beside his own, ten people had access to the radios. Jake could not know who was taunting him. He tried to maintain his composure, to be calm and professional, but the teasers were relentless. Jake's radio tortured him as they made their way across the dark Mississippi landscape.

"Cluck, cluck!"

"Cluck, cluck."

"Cluck, cluck, cluck."

"Paawk."

As the weeks went by, the caper mushroomed into a monumental travesty. Jake didn't deserve it. Certainly no one blamed him for being so sore about it, but it followed him like a skulking shadow, and whenever he entered a room fingers abruptly pointed at suspected culprits, and accusations zipped like bullets. The great chicken raid became the ultimate topic to which all conversations evolved. And even as the weeks turned to months, our drill weekends were center stage for the spirited debates, which Jake astutely avoided. "Who done it?" was the question on everyone's lips. A few tried to own up to it, but these we dismissed as depraved souls who were simply starving for attention. None who confessed would have had the guts to pull the deed off. As time went by, two prime suspects emerged from the investigations, and finally, several years after the unhappy event—even after Jake's retirement—a trial was held.

A visiting general was asked to serve as the judge. The defendant, Harold (Hac) Cross, our squadron commander, was represented by one Tom Clayton, who could talk loud and persuasively but whose tongue often became disengaged from his brain and ran afoul of authority. The prosecutor was Bill ("Chalky") Lutz, a smooth, articulate lawyer in civilian life, and the star witness was John Tarr, himself a major suspect. Then the trial began, officially taped by the base audiovisual department. We jeered and shouted as the grim facts unfolded and the judge rapped for order.

The first evidence was introduced and our flight surgeon, Doc Krueger, testified with a shocking graphic description, that they were indeed the bleached bones of a chicken. More testimony followed. But despite Clayton's pitiful attempts to implicate Tarr, the evidence mounted against the defendant. Tarr's observation that Hac had been seen that evening with grease on his fingers was corroborated. A witness for the defendant reported seeing a Tater Tot fall from Tarr's helmet bag yet produced no hard evidence. Witness after witness was questioned, and when the proceedings were finished, Cross was convicted. His sentence: the tab for the post-trial kegs and a career of shame. It was entirely too lenient.

Yet many still had lingering doubts and watched Tarr carefully until the day he retired, his preference for the domesticated yardbird not going unnoticed. Hac showed no remorse and—as was his way—skillfully convinced many that he had gotten a bad rap. And the victim? He ignored his subpoena and chose not to attend the trial.

But even that was not to be the end of it. Until a couple of years ago—before so many faces changed—you could ignite an instant heated debate in any group by dropping a whispered suggestion as you passed, much as Tevye did about the sour horse deal in *Fiddler on the Roof.* Just pass by a friendly conversation already in progress and interject "Tarr did it." The response would be instantaneous.

"It was Hac!"

"Hell no, it was Tarr."

"You dunce, you weren't even there that night."

"What do you know? You weren't even in the unit then!"

"You're both wrong. It was Jimmy Taylor."

"Taylor? Aw, get outta here!"

And so it went until long after you had left.

Thank God, there was one group among us that seemed to provide some measure of maturity and stability. For the most part, its members stayed to themselves and smiled with amusement at the antics, only rarely becoming actively involved. Yet they were not aloof, just apart. They were our navigators. Sadly, we lost them with the C-130s. On the C-141 they've been replaced by machines. But they were special people—highly skilled officers who knew a great deal not only about navigation but about air operations in general. The nav was often the aircraft commander's chief counsel, from whom he could garner a unique and fresh perspective. At times the copilot's opinion could be tainted with ego, inexperience, or even patronage. But the nav was more likely to be honest and unbiased, to offer counterpoint, to play the devil's advocate, to tell the AC what he didn't necessarily want to hear. And for that reason alone, the navigators were priceless.

Without a doubt the most unusual nav we had was Venn Fortinberry. Tall and dark-complexioned, with a weathered outdoorsman appearance, he looked like a young Gary Cooper. He held the rank of major and was a country gentleman farmer who showed up to navigate C-130s across continents and oceans, said as little as possible, and then withdrew into the Walthall County woods. Yet a maverick he was not. The taciturn Venn must have considered his role in life to be the impeccable performance of his job and to speak only when he had something relevant and obligatory to say. Thus when he did speak, heads swiveled receptively in his direction. It was his way to bait us with a pause while he spat tobacco before getting to the meat of his brief messages.

I once concocted a brilliant but risky scheme to expose Venn's emotions to the world, hoping that the disclosure would not be ugly.

When one pulls a practical joke on such a man as Venn, one must be prepared for the possibility that one will have to choose between administering an ass-whipping and receiving one. And I suspected that Venn was an able administrator. But I planned to be drunk with laughter at the conclusion of the affair and thus utterly defenseless. In this way I had avoided reprisal in past such antics. I hoped Venn would exhibit similar restraint. Nonetheless I proceeded.

The scene of the deed was Howard Air Force Base in the Panama Canal Zone. Volant Oak, as it was called, was one of the Air Force's best-kept secrets. It was an ongoing operation in which the militia were the star players. Air Guard and Reserve C-130s were dispatched in flights of four with eight crews and a complement of mechanics to the tropical base for service with the Southern Command. The two-week rotational tour of duty featured several airdrop training missions, with an occasional supply run down to South America to service the embassies. In between the flights the crews enjoyed numerous rounds of golf and tennis interspersed with lavish cookouts, marathon poker games, and occasional forays up the Canal in pursuit of the big tasty peacock bass. It was a veritable paradise for sun worshipers, slumber seekers, tapestry shoppers, joggers, bingeful imbibers, and especially those who simply needed a respite from the rat race of their usual jobs. Howard was a world removed: an exotic, esoteric place of escape and release, masquerading as a site of duty and toil. It was, as we proclaimed, a thankless job, but someone had to do it. And it was there at the officer's quarters high on a bejungled hillside that we discovered them.

Out of the rain forest they came; first a bold vanguard, then the others. We watched with fascination as they slowly moved closer to our building, foraging in the grasses as they came. They were the most ridiculous-looking creatures I had ever seen, a hodgepodge of unrelated species thrown together as an afterthought from leftover parts in God's bench stock. The body was that of a monkey, with long, strong hind haunches that raised the rump and tilted the nose to the ground. The head was doglike, with a slender snout, featuring the ludicrous ears of a bear. The long tail, striped like a raccoon's, stuck straight up and swayed like a whip antenna on a sheriff's cruiser. One or two among us had heard of these strange creatures, but the closest name we could tag them with was kootymongas. I researched it later and learned that their proper name was coatimundis. But despite this revelation, our crude characterization stuck, and enticed by our alms of crackers and breads, the fanciful kootys became regular but wary visitors.

Venn's particular fascination with the kootys prompted me to roguery. He leaned on the railing outside his second floor room for hours each day chewing his tobacco, spit cup in hand, watching the kootys below as they became ever bolder in their approaches. I tested my plan by coaxing the beasts with cookies thrown down in a trail, and it worked splendidly. I found that I could lead them almost anywhere. But would they continue to nibble at the cookie trail up a flight of concrete stairs? The answer had to wait until Venn next flew at a time when I was off.

When that condition was met, I seized the opportunity. Venn was due back at about 1600, and I started half an hour earlier. I succeeded in wheedling a half dozen or so kootys, mostly young ones, up the stairs and down the walkway toward my room, sowing the cookie crumbs all along. When I paused to open the door, three of them spooked and plunged head first over the side, crashing to the ground, but nonetheworse for the fall, they all scampered away. However, a large adult and two pups followed me into the room. Snickering like a deviant schoolboy, I led the three cookie monsters through the connecting kitchen from my room into Venn's and shut the door, feeling as if I had left a box of hand grenades on a hot stove.

Venn didn't show at 1600. I waited. After a while I began to worry that the cooped-up kootys would destroy the room, and I became tempted to abandon the scheme. But then he came.

Fearing that my uncontrollable giggling would alert him I staked out down on the lawn and watched as he climbed the stairs. By the time he was inserting his room key I had followed him up and was peering from around a corner. I sprinted down to his window as he entered the dark room and shut the door behind him.

The encounter began with a sharp imprecation followed by a sound like a rocking chair coming down on a cat's tail. Then the grenades went off. The struggle instantly escalated into an awful pandemonium of thumps, crashes, tears, screams, and grunts. Listening to the clamor of falling furniture and stampeding feet, I leaned close to the window and saw the curtains suddenly jerk, then plunge to the floor bearing a terrified kooty. Soon the door blew inward as if the room had been sucked of its air and two screeching streaks of fur propelled past me at the speed of heat and catapulted over the ledge.

I lowered myself to the deck on weakened knees holding my ribs in the delightful pain of reckless laughter, as the haggard Venn, ignoring me, emerged and leaned against his rail. A wretched thing I was, lying there beside him helplessly guffawing, but I caught a breath and paused long enough to comment on what cuddly creatures they were. But then the third kooty came bounding from the room and blew out past Venn's boots into the airspace over the lawn like a torpedo shot from the deck of a destroyer, and again I was beset with hysteria.

Still gazing toward the jungle, Venn extracted his tobacco can and loaded an enormous chew but said not a word to me until after I had assessed the battle damage to his room. "You know," he spat, then continued in a low-toned, contemplative voice, as if the foregoing had never occurred, as if he were merely picking up where yesterday's musings were left off, "I'd like to turn some of them rascals loose down in Walthall County."

Soon afterward the jets came. The navs left us. Panama and the kootymongas became memories. The day fliers remained distinct from the night fliers, but many faces changed. We flew the jets either around the flagpole or around the world, it seemed, seldom in between and never again to Bull Run Drop Zone. It was deactivated.

We grieved for the loss of the Hercules. But the old colonel was right. The airplane we're in is indeed a good airplane. I'm just glad to be here.

And of the chicken heist? I know who did it. But name, rank, and service number are all you'll get out of me.

THIRTEEN

EYE OF THE STORM

scud: NATO designator for the Soviet SS-1, short
range mobile launched surface to surface ballistic missile.—Department of Defense

scud: (skud), v.i. [scudded, scudding], 1. to run or
move swiftly. 2. to be driven or run before the
wind.—*Webster's Dictionary*

My roomie, Mike Hall, and I are awakened by running
and shouting in the hallway. It's 0200 local time on
January 16, a day since President Bush's January 15
deadline had passed. We fling open the door and learn
from a passerby that the mother of all battles is at last under way. Mike
rushes to turn on the TV, but all we see is a test signal. It must be on the
radio. Mike then dives for the clock radio, but after fiddling frantically with it, he declares it's "tango uniform." We finally find a good
radio in the laundry room and requisition it back to our hole. We
quickly learn that massive allied air strikes are in progress in Kuwait
and Iraq. Even after all the months of preparation, the reality is hard
to grasp. This is no skirmish, no antiterrorist operation, and not a
guerrilla action. It is a massive, full-blown conventional war, complete with killing fields. Later the TV comes to life, and we watch with
the world as the Persian Gulf furiously explodes. The whole thing is
incredible. Even after the months of flying the desert missions, I have
trouble believing it is happening.

While devouring the news reports, Mike and I speculate as to what the immediate future holds for us. We recall our squadron commander, Lieutenant Colonel Dwight Sisk, briefing us about this mission prior to departure. Though hostile action was imminent, Dwight told us he had been assured that MAC would not risk its "strategic airlift assets" (big jets) during the early, uncertain days of the war. And again, when we arrived here at Ramstein Air Base, Germany, the stage manager had echoed the concern. "Relax," we were told. "Until some of the smoke settles, you'll probably get a breather, at the most, maybe a run back to the States." We wonder how such a massive deployed force could go even a few days without strategic airlift support. We've been in uniform too long to swallow everything they feed us, but we accept onlooker status for the next few days.

We finally get to sleep in the late morning, but at about 1500 we are alerted by the command post for what we assume will be an Atlantic crossing. We should know better. In spite of what we have been told to expect, the destination is Dhahran. We are, of course, very familiar with the place. We've been there many times. But in light of the developments of the previous hours, the orders are ominous.

While Mike and the two engineers, Larry Bleakney and Dave Cameron, preflight the Starlizzard, Rob Cox, the other pilot, and I, meet our rent-a-pilot and proceed to the CP for our intel briefing.

Intel updates us on the status of hostilities and issues our SPINS. The briefing, usually a ho-hum affair, has our attention thoroughly captured this time. We are about to plunge into what we think is just the edge of the maelstrom known now as Desert Storm, but I know that in modern warfare, the edges are ill defined. I must admit I'm excited about this, but I have a gut feeling that the whole thing is pregnant with disaster. I figure that if I'm to be a casualty of this mess, it will likely be a result of our own inattentiveness or of friendly fire, either of which is just as terminal as an Iraqi bullet.

The three of us report to the jet at 1700 and find the rest of the crew wrapping up their preflight duties. The soldiers have gone to the chow hall and left a guard at the jet to watch over their weapons. Dave warns us that the guard is particularly jumpy and has been pacing nervously and mumbling to himself. We don't know if he is worried about the war or the flight, but he has a loaded M-16 and bears watching.

At 1800 hours German local, with twenty-five "grunts," 35,000 pounds of cargo, and 158,000 pounds of fuel aboard, we taxi onto the runway in an extremely heavy condition known as EWP gross weight. EWP means "emergency war planning." Not just any war, mind you, but *emergency* war. What more grave and desperate endeavor can the human race be involved in than emergency war? Because EWP is such a risky operation, from the standpoint of structural stress and reduced performance, I always fancied that if we ever used it, the world would most surely be at the brink of nuclear war. But I was wrong. It wasn't much of a war, but it was all we had. And it had obviously been determined that, to that end, we and our C-141s were expendable.

This EWP thing is serious business. The wings have to lift ten tons more than what they are normally designed to do. Metal is a funny thing. Unlike wood, which forgets about stress, metal remembers, and the damage is cumulative. Add the effect of the cracks that already exist in the spars and the potential for a catastrophic failure begins to loom as a greater possibility. It may not happen today, but next week or next year disaster could result from stresses accumulated today, especially if the airplane is henceforth subjected to marginal conditions such as turbulence. And the stress of EWP operations doesn't apply only to the wings.

For an EWP takeoff, we have to use maximum takeoff-rated thrust, or TRT. This is our maximum safe power. If we pushed the throttles as far as they will go, the engines may rip themselves apart under the tremendous internal heat and pressures. But even at TRT the engine turbine blades, under the increased heat and centrifugal force, actually become stretched and cracked. The blades can sling off the compressor and turbine wheels, causing massive engine disintegration. We know that every TRT takeoff reduces engine life and increases the possibly of a catastrophic engine failure, so whenever possible we take off with reduced thrust. But today we wouldn't get airborne by the French border with reduced thrust.

And there's more still to think about with an EWP takeoff. You're so heavy, it takes the square root of forever to get enough speed to fly. Runway length becomes critical, and the crew's margin for error narrows if something goes wrong. This will be a dreaded "split marker" takeoff. Larry and Dave both calculate the takeoff performance criteria with their Hewlett Packard calculators, comparing results. Rob and I do the same with the computer terminal on our center console, known as the Fuel Savings and Advisory System, or FSAS. Rob sets his airspeed indicator marker at 122 knots. This will be our "go" speed. If a problem develops before we reach this speed, we should be able to stop the jet before we run out of runway *if* our calculations are correct and *if* we do everything exactly right. Should a problem occur after 122 knots, we are committed to continue the takeoff. But we cannot lift from the runway until the speed scrolls down to the second marker, which I have set at 140 knots. This will be the "rotate" speed. The calculations indicate that we will reach this speed just prior to the end of Ramstein's frighteningly short runway.

We poll the crew to ensure that all are ready, and point our nose westward down the runway, which lies in a misty valley between parallel rows of hills. This is a place of death, where three Italian Air Force pilots and many spectators died last year in a tragic air show accident. More recently, some of our own died at the end of this runway. We hold the brakes and advance the throttles to TRT. Five sets of vigilant eyes carefully scan the white tapes on the vertical display engine instruments as the jet trembles and strains at the brakes. We check the exhaust pressure ratios, N_1 and N_2 rpms, the enormous fuel flow readings, and the exhaust gas temperatures; all are as they should be. We're conscious of the extraordinarily loud twang of the engines, noticeably higher at TRT than at normal takeoff thrust. They seem to be appealing to us to get on with it—to get this done and over with before it's too late. We swallow hard and release the brakes.

The 343,000-pound beast begins to shed its static inertia and ever so slowly picks up forward momentum. The heavy weight causes every crack and bump in the runway to be amplified by the nose gear strut. As we wait for the lethargic airspeed indicator to awaken, the distance-remaining markers begin to pass by:

7,000.

The bumps increase in frequency and intensity as we gather precious speed. We're driving the engines like wicked taskmasters, pushing them to their pain threshold. They scream in protest.

6,000.

Noticeably faster now, the airspeed indicator is showing signs of life.

5,000.

We begin a gentle sway as the wings start to fly, but they are capable of lifting only their own weight.

4,000.

Finally, the first marker passes under the airspeed indexer. Our senses are pegged. We've become nervous creatures: shifty-eyed, anticipators of calamity. Now we can't stop this runaway beast if something catastrophic happens. We're committed to flying, no matter what.

3,000.

The staccato sound of the bumps—as much felt as heard—is like rapid cannon fire.

2,000.

The end of the runway approaches in the windscreen. The tall conifers of the dense black German forest loom ahead. I'm able, now, to read the numbers on the last distance-remaining marker.

1,000.

Our rotate speed of 140 knots is coming down to the indexer, still too slow to suit us. The airspeed seems to hesitate slightly at 135, or is it my imagination? If something went badly wrong now in a fighter, I'd brace and pull the ejection handle. But we have to see this ride through.

Finally, the requisite 140 knots appears, and we lift into the air as the red lights at the end of the runway flash underneath our belly. We lumber across the forest cover, gathering precious speed and glance down at the wicked gash in the trees where a C-5 crew gave it all for the liberation of Kuwait. A thrust reverser, which is used to slow a large jet during landing, had inadvertently deployed while the other engines were at maximum power. The resultant asymmetric thrust had caused them to careen to the left and roll into the malfunctioning engine. There were only seconds to analyze the problem. No time to discuss solutions. No ejection handles to reach for.

The broken tree trunks down there and the crater in the earth are silent reminders that it can happen to me, to any of us. When I was a fighter pilot, I had heard all the jokes about the "heavy drivers" and had listened to the condescending remarks and the unflattering stories about those who propped up their feet and drank coffee while they flew. I'm older now and less inclined to confrontation, but the gash in the trees makes me spring-loaded these days, waiting for some swashbuckling fighter driver to pop off about his superiority. Brave airmen died down there, died just as valiantly as the top guns who were catching the missiles and flak over Baghdad.

But the scars are forgotten as quickly as they pass, and we relax a little as our thunderlizzard picks up more of the life-preserving airspeed. We climb out over southern France as the sunlight fades and join our old companion the moon for the long trip across the Mediterranean. The run down across the Med is pretty routine, except that we are spending more time studying the SPINS than we usually do. We don't know what to expect tonight, but we'd rather not have events take us by surprise. Rob and I decide to break out our chemical gear to take with us to the flight-planning office, but not the entire suit. The masks and hoods alone should do. I'm surprised at the effort and time it takes to untie the rubber sack and dig the stuff out.

After a restless respite in the bunk I return to the flight deck as we approach the Red Sea and call Red Crown. I can sense the tension among the crew begin to build as we listen to Navy strike forces checking in and out with the carrier. I can't understand half of what they say. Even their radio terminology is hopelessly mired in traditional buzz phrases and slang. The SPINS ought to contain information to let us decode Navy vernacular. As they've done for years, they are also garbaging up the "Guard" channel.

Guard is frequency 243.0, which is supposed to be monitored by all military flights and held in reserve for emergency transmissions. But the way the Navy frivolously blabs on Guard has always been a sore point with Air Force and Army pilots, who often refer to it as "Navy Common" and religiously protect it from such abuse. More than once I've heard an angry voice, in response to Navy chatter, shout out on the frequency, "GET OFF GUARD, DAMMIT!"

Entering Saudi airspace, we're cleared along a more southerly route than we're used to and proceed without the assistance of air traffic control or ground navigation aids. The stations have been shut down so as not to invite attack. But we have no problem navigating with our two inertial navigation units, as we do over the high seas. Approaching the gulf, we search through the secret air strike frequencies, hoping to monitor the air battle up north, but I guess we're out of radio range. We do, however, hear plenty of activity on the AWACS frequencies, which we're required to monitor. AWACS is the airborne warning and control system, a Boeing 707 with a big rotating radar dish atop. AWACS is busy working with the strike aircraft entering and leaving the target areas and the refueling tracks.

My headset spews the electronic hiss and crackle of the voices of war, and I feel the absurd longing that I knew would come. I'm not satisfied to be on the periphery of this thing; I want to be in it. I want to rip off a stick of Mark-82's over an Iraqi truck park; to squeeze off an AIM-9 and watch it home on a MiG like a lion closing on a weaving gazelle. I ought to be up there.

Years ago I attacked a column of infantry at Fort Carson, Colorado. The Army was throwing a big war game party and had invited the Air Force to show up as the bad guys. I was in a flight of four A-7s approaching the war zone low and fast up through the foothills to avoid detection. We'd planned to split up into two elements of two ships and attack separate targets. As the leader and number two broke off to the north, I popped up behind my element leader and rolled hard to the south toward a large meadow. As I rolled out, with my nose pointing at the meadow in a 500 mph dive, I realized that we had caught the soldiers in a complete surprise.

It was an astonishing sight. Dozens of large vehicles were scattering in all directions, kicking up swirling dust clouds, while hundreds of running figures scurried for cover. It was a "target-rich environment," as the tacticians like to say. We had them cold and had won the game. I was exhilarated. But what if it had been real? How would I carry the baggage of so many deaths? And why the exhilaration? I've always been bothered by it. Yet the same kind of slaughter was being discharged in earnest just over the horizon.

We are approaching Dhahran; strangely, the sky is not as busy as I had anticipated. But I know a few miles northward the air is as frenzied as a shark feed. I hope it stays up there, because the possibility of a midair collision is now our biggest threat. I listen as the pool pilot in the jump seat calls the ALCE and passes on our load information. They brief us that the airfield is under condition yellow, which signifies an advanced state of chemical warfare readiness.

The approach is normal, and the city of Dhahran seems to be as lighted as usual. We touch down at 0415 local time and notice that the civil air terminal is shut down. No airliners are at the gates. We turn down the long taxiway to the military side and are soon aware that this is not the Dhahran of past missions.

It's very different this morning. There's none of the beehive of activity that we're accustomed to. In fact, we're the only aircraft there. The hangar doors are closed. The floodlight coverage is cut back to about a quarter of its usual strength, bathing the flight line in a shadowy ghastliness. Few vehicles move about. I certainly don't expect Iraqi troops to come storming across the field, but still a cool foreboding comes over me. Rob and I don't talk a lot as we walk toward the hangar, but we agree that we need to get our business of offloading and refueling done and leave this place.

While we proceed to the hangar complex to file our flight plan and get an intel update, the rest of the crew works at the aircraft. Dave takes his station on the "long cord" out in front as a safety observer while Larry monitors the fuel panel in the cockpit. Both wear their headsets and are in communication with the refueler back at the right wheel well. Mike is running the noisy electric winch that is used to load and unload trailers and other unpowered rolling stock. Our twenty-five troops wait restlessly for their transportation to arrive. Then, at 0445, the first one comes.

Events take place with lightning speed, and few people know, at first, what is happening. "What was that?" is the first sign of trouble, as Dave's voice cracks on the interphone. But Larry, on the flight deck, sees nothing. An electric streak appears in the sky over Dave's head, shooting south to north. A sonic boom resounds, echoing off the hangars. A maintenance van swings to a stop beside the jet, and men inside yell for the crew to hurry aboard. Dave relays the warning to Larry, who leaps from his seat and yells from the flight deck door back to Mike. Looking up from the winch cable, Mike hears but can't understand Larry's shouted warnings. Then Mike's blood chills when

Larry reappears in the flight deck door wearing his chemical mask, motioning frantically to get off the aircraft.

Mike drops the cable and runs to his chemical bag. It seems an eternity to untie the wrappings. While he fumbles and claws into the bag for his mask, he hears excited shouts from outside, as the soldiers break into a run, and the blood-curdling wail of an attack-warning Klaxon starts up. Mike knows that it would be impossible to don the entire suit in the few seconds he might have left. Finally finding his mask and hood, he bolts for the crew door and into the van with the rest of the crew.

The events of the first missile attack of the war are more subtle for me. As I present the flight plan to the Saudi dispatcher, Rob calls the weather station. Across the room a Saudi with telephone in hand shouts over to the dispatcher in their native language, and I clearly pick out the word "Scud." The dispatcher turns to me with a sort of comical grin on his weathered face and repeats the word.

"Scud."

I play along with this strange attempt at Saudi humor and feign a dive under the planning table. The dispatcher laughs and takes the flight plan, and Rob and I begin the long walk down the hallway to the intel shop. Along the way we meet a number of Marines who are pulling on their masks, but we've seen such drills before, and as transiting aircrew we are not required to participate.

Outside things are not so tranquil. The maintenance van races across to the nearest bunker—nothing more than a trench about four feet deep covered with sandbags on a wooden frame. The guys breathe heavily and with much effort in the cumbersome masks. In his haste Larry has forgotten to snap on the rubber gasket that allows free breathing when not plugged into the aircraft-supplied oxygen system. Under normal circumstances it is a mistake that would immediately have been noticed; the flow of filtered air was minimal, almost to the point of choking. But in his excitement, fueled by the flood of adrenaline, it takes him several minutes to realize that he is slowly suffocating. Mike has the opposite problem. He tries to calm himself down, realizing he's beginning to hyperventilate.

Filing into the bunker, the men are abruptly halted and turned back. It's full. Along with maintenance people, it is filled with another

C-141 crew who arrived after us but parked nearer the bunker. Uttering muffled imprecations, they reverse course and reboard the van, speed down the tarmac to the next hole and dive in. There they hunker for the next half hour, listening to the maintenance radio blaring excited reports about missiles and explosions. The bunker is dark and muddy, and they feel extremely claustrophobic in the heavy gear, but they know that the air could be laced with lethal chemical agents.

The heavy door to the intel shop swings open, and Rob and I are stunned to see the intel staff wearing their chem gear. They motion us in and tell us that the field is indeed under attack, but the shop is fortified and serves as a shelter. We put on our masks and listen as the staff converses on their secure telephones, their speech muffled by the masks. We quickly learn that a Patriot missile has intercepted a Scud, fired from Iraq, at an altitude of 17,000 feet just north of the base. I didn't know the Patriot could do such a thing. I thought it was for shooting down aircraft. I immediately wonder if it was one of the many Patriots I had brought from the States in recent weeks. Reports also come in of Scud impacts east and west of the air base. A few minutes later, we are all astounded when the shop's TV set, tuned to CNN, replays the actual attack that has just taken place over our heads. Fascinated, we watch with the entire world as the Patriot streaks into the dawn and impacts the Scud with a bright flash above the thin cloud layer. Other reports come in of Scud attacks on Israel. A few minutes later, the shop receives a phone patch that the Israelis have launched a retaliatory nuclear strike against Baghdad. I stare through the mask lens and listen with detached horror. The world is coming apart at the seams, and there is nothing I can do about it. Yet I have no feelings of disbelief. Everything that is happening is plausible, even predictable. Pink Floyd was right; this is Armageddon.

As daylight falls on the airfield, the all-clear horn sounds. Rob and I hurry back to the aircraft, arriving before the rest of the crew. The long cord lies outstretched in front of the jet, headset still attached. Various articles of clothing, tools, and personal gear are strewn around, abandoned. The Starlizzard, still powered by the humming external power cart, sits contentedly without human accompaniment. Shortly the rest of the crew arrives in a breathless frenzy of conversation and falls hurriedly to prepping the jet for departure.

Very quickly we make ready for engine start. I'm sitting in the jump seat, programming the navigation computer while Rob and the pool pilot go through a nervous and hurried cockpit preflight. Glancing out the windscreen toward the maintenance trailers, I'm awestruck to see dozens of gas-masked men scurrying toward the bunkers. The fight is on again. I press the interphone and utter the two words, well recognized by all crewdogs, that signify trouble.

Once again the maintenance van brakes in front of us, and the driver beckons furiously for us to join him, which I hastily do. It seems reasonable to get to a relatively safe bunker rather than be strapped to a tremendous target full of jet fuel. But I quickly realize that I am the only member of the crew on the van; the aircraft is starting engines. The idea of being left behind has no appeal, so I abandon the van, which speeds away as I jump off. I race to the crew door and vault up, pulling the ladder up behind me. Larry slams the door down, and the jet lurches forward as I climb up to the flight deck. Vicious lies later circulate for weeks that I pounded on the closed crew door, begging to be taken in.

We depart what is to become known as Scud City with a multitude of sensations. The report of Israel's atomic attack was bogus, but still, Saddam had made it personal with us now. We will never know how close we came to being casualties. We will joke about it for weeks and take dubious pride in having been involved in the first surface-to-surface ballistic missile attack since World War II and in having been witnesses to the first missile-to-missile engagement in history. The name Patriot will take on an entirely new and lasting meaning for us. And we will listen with fascination to the even wilder and more spectacular Scud experiences of other crews in the weeks that follow. I will watch missile engagements from an airborne advantage. Other crews will fly through such battles, watching the rocket plumes flash by their wings in the night, the detonations lighting the skyscapes about them.

But a few days later, we hear sobering news of a C-5 crew from the New York Air Guard that was dispatched to Dhahran to evacuate the children of American residents. The Scuds came as the children were boarding. The crew quickly herded the children into the bunkers, and as they waited in the darkness, a man appeared in the entrance wearing a full complement of chemical gear. He warned them that a chemical agent was present, and casualties were resulting, then hurried away. The crew quickly pulled on their masks and adjusted the fit but then looked around at the children, who had no protection; their eyes were tearful, and a few were sobbing. Some of the kids clung to the airmen in fright.

Then the crew did the most gallant thing I have ever heard of. They removed their masks and gathered the children around them. Their self-sacrifice could in no way save the kids. But these brave men decided that it was not only preferable but also strangely appropriate that they die with the children.

Later, they learned that there was no gas; the Scuds had conventional explosives only. An airman had suffered an epileptic seizure, which resembles the sinister effects of nerve gas, and thus the alert had been issued.

Although above-average courage is expected of a person in uniform, it remains uncanny to me how America has always been blessed with warriors whose integrity and honor exceed those of the general populace. We joke a lot about that closing statement in Michener's *The Bridges at Toko-Ri*. Certainly the admiral would be more gender neutral if he cast his rhetorical plea to the sea winds today. Still, it's really no joke. Where *do* we find such men? I don't know. I just thank God we've always had them in abundance.

FOURTEEN

DAWN PATROL

Looking like dirty brown cirrus clouds, the normally blue skies overhead are corrupted with ominous, oily mare's tails. The sky grows dimmer and greasier to the north, and as we begin our descent into the northern Saudi base at Jubail, we see a long, tarry black line where the horizon ought to be. The Iraqis have set fire to hundreds of oil wells in a despotic act of denial and defiance. Yet I've seen this before. It wasn't on this grand a scale, but it was a desperate struggle under murky skies like these. And it was a different kind of war—one fought right after Viet Nam, for me, and close to home. These smoky skies vividly remind me of one day in that campaign.

The telephone's ring was murderous. My hand fumbled in the dim morning light, trying to find the blasted receiver. I mumbled something and heard the operations dispatcher's pitched voice.

"The Loop's blown up!"

No more talk was necessary. I acknowledged and hung up the phone. It had finally happened. Our territory had been attacked by a vicious and relentless enemy. Attacked at our most vulnerable point. The campaigns of the last few weeks had been skirmishes by comparison.

I rushed to the airfield and dashed into the hangar, switched on the lights, and shoved open the big door. The dawning light spilled into the cavernous structure, bathing the sleeping planes in morning. I trotted over to the winged mongrel, picked it up by the tail handle and heaved it out backward. It was like pulling an unwilling dog out of his house by the hind legs. I could almost feel the wings stretching around behind me, rubbing sleepy windshield eyes.

"Naw, go away. It's too early for this, man," whispered the Cub. I answered it as I strained to drag the main wheels over the hangar door tracks. "Gotta go, Buddy. Today's the big one. The Loop blew last night."

I ran through a quick preflight of N29FC, the 1952 model Piper Super Cub. She was a simple airplane, built of aluminum tubing covered with fabric, doped, and painted a shade of puke green, a 150-horsepower Lycoming under her cowling and an old tube radio with a single frequency mounted in her wing root. "ALA FORESTRY COMM." was painted boldly under her wings.

The familiar sour, pungent odor of old fabric airplanes filled my senses and roused my spirit as I strapped on the Cub and primed the engine. The craft fit me well. It was good to sit centerline again and to have a stick control instead of the wimpy wheel that I had become accustomed to. I flipped the two magneto switches, which clicked with an irreverent loudness in the early silence of the airfield. Then I cracked the throttle and engaged the starter.

The starter motor sang. The prop swung. One revolution. Two. The engine coughed, shuddered, died. But still the prop swung to the starter's strained song.

Then came that explosion of the engine bursting into life, that blessed awakening of this noble creature. My heart soared at the engine's rumble and the sight of the prop blurring, then disappearing. A shudder ran through the airframe from nose to tail, like that of a dog shaking off a douse, as the heavy prop induced its torque.

I nudged the throttle and leaned to the side, peering ahead as the little tail-dragger rolled out. I taxied fast, checking the magnetos and flight controls as I went; there was no time to waste. The battle was raging, and I had a twenty-minute flight to reach it. I checked the final approach for traffic and took the runway, ramming the throttle home and walking the rudder pedals as the Cub surged ahead. Almost immediately, I applied forward pressure on the stick. The tail lifted and the Cub scurried ahead on its two main wheels. One quick glance inside and I saw that the speed was fifty knots. Enough. I eased off the forward pressure, brought the stick back slightly, and we were airborne. And what a glorious word it is: airborne, born of the air, born once again, renewed, refreshed—sweet release.

I held the nose low for a few seconds to let the Cub accelerate, then rolled quickly to the right, banking sharply as we climbed over the forest, coming about to a northwest course. The day had dawned gloriously clear, with a fresh southerly breeze; not a cloud was in sight. But that's what the enemy wanted. It was his kind of day, as yesterday had been and the several days before. And as we climbed above the tall pines, I saw that he had struck with a vengeance.

I was stunned by the magnitude of it. A great, towering mushroom cloud loomed ahead on the horizon. I switched on the radio, and excited voices began to boom through my headset. Our ground forces were being mobilized and sent into the fray. Desperate calls were going out for reinforcements. I announced that I was airborne and en route, but no one seemed to take notice. I announced again, and the dispatcher admonished me to hurry. But the Cub was giving me her all, blazing through the sky at eighty-five knots, her top speed.

I pulled out my charts as we drew closer to the imposing smoke column, but I wondered if my presence could make a difference. Normally, my job was to find each of the little pockets of intruders and call one of our ground teams in to repel it. There was little else I could do. The Cub was unarmed—far too small to carry the heavy ordnance needed to attack this determined foe from the air. But our people were already well aware of the enemy's brutal strike at the place known as the Loop. Our advance ground forces were already engaged. So what was I to do?

As we approached the besieged area, the details of the gigantic cloud began to break out. Brown and black smoke thick enough to crash into boiled, rolled, and churned its way upward, carried northward with the winds. Down sun of the inferno the landscape was eclipsed by darkness. Closer still, the orange brilliance of fierce conflagrations began to show beneath it. What an awesome feeling; the Cub was so small and frail against the nefarious thing ahead. I was no more than a mosquito flying toward a roaring campfire.

Finally we arrived and began to scout the battlefield. It appeared that it happened exactly as one of the old-timers had predicted. "Hap-

Piper Super Cub

pens every three or four years," he had said. The Loop is a great bend in the railroad, winding its way around a canyon nearly to the point of meeting itself again, like a horseshoe bent inward. Sparks spew onto the railside from the trains' hot brakes, as they enter the Loop. Sooner or later, the inevitable happens. The sparks catch in the brush and explode into rampaging fires racing up the ravines, devouring the life-blood of this region—its timber—and threatening the dwellings of the nearby town.

I circumnavigated the fire, trying to determine its extent and to find possible roads or trails through which the trucks could approach it. The big flatbeds carried bulldozers, but the slow dozers were use-less unless they could be deposited at a strategic point downwind and near the fire. I could easily tell the trucks and dozers where best to counterattack, but they had no radios then. I could only communicate with the base station and towers. I watched, frustrated, as the trucks wandered about, the drivers blindly discussing and planning their action.

I was an outsider here, a temporary pilot, flying only for the season, then I would be gone. But the forest rangers down there had lived around these parts all their lives. They knew the land well. And I was a stranger with whom they were guarded, standoffish, and skeptical. I overheard a lookout tower operator once refer to me, in a transmission to the base station, as "that airplane pilot." They really were good people, but from time to time I was the object of their humor, like the time a tower man asked me to check out a smoke sighting. Not know-ing the countryside, I relied on highly detailed maps using the sec-tion-township-range gridwork system, maps that the tower men and drivers also possessed. But this man insisted that I fly over near the place where the old farmer had been found dead.

"Say, what?" I asked incredulously.

"You know," he responded, "the ole black man, the one they found dead in his pickup truck, oh, five, maybe six, years ago. Out that way."

Luckily, most of the time, knowing that I was unfamiliar with the area, they used map coordinates. But today I folded my map and stowed it. Determined to get into this fight, I dove low over the trucks opposite their direction of movement along the old logging road they had chosen. I wanted them to turn around and approach the fire from another angle, and I had picked out a route they could use. My low pass seemed to puzzle them, although I knew it was an accepted signal. The lead driver opened his door and looked up, as I made a second pass, the Cub's wheels flashing only a few feet over the truck's cab. Then they responded and the trucks began to turn around. I spent the next fifteen minutes herding the trucks toward the worst part of the fire, and I could imagine them talking as clearly as if I were in the truck with them: "I hope that tomfool pilot knows what the blazes he's doin'."

Time and again I flew past the advancing face of the inferno, and with the side window slid back I felt the searing heat on my face. And I watched with utter fascination as the fire down below began to "crown"—a frightening spectacle, seeing it jump from treetop to treetop, driven before the wind. On one foray around the leeward side, I climbed high and challenged the smoke column, a supremely reckless deed. But I was loving this time of struggle and combat and started to grow cocky.

I intended only to sideswipe the cloud, to be immersed in it just a few seconds. They were among the most frightening moments of my flying career. At first I felt a bump or two and smelled the burning timber. Then the heat shaft seized the Cub and pitched us violently, as if the raging monster had grabbed us by the throat and was shaking us asunder. I choked from smoke and strained my burning eyes for signs of daylight, hoping that the engine would continue to aspirate. Then, as suddenly as it hit, it spit us out the side of the shaft into clear, calm air.

My watering eyes fluttered for relief, and I filled my lungs with sweet air. Shaking, I radioed the base station that I was recovering for gas at Monroeville, a few miles to the north. I didn't really need gas. There were almost two hours left in the tanks, but I desperately needed a break.

I taxied up to the fuel pumps and shut the engine down, looking back toward the still visible smoke column as I stepped onto the porch. The local gang greeted me and asked about the fire, then allowed as to how they knew the Loop was going to blow up any day now. I grabbed a Coke and strolled to the back room, where my friend Dick Dammon was strumming his guitar as usual, dog sleeping at his side.

Maybe the Chuck Yeager types never need solace, but sometimes the ordinary flier needs to find a confidant upon whom to unload his own nagging inadequacies and shortcomings. I, for one, long for a kindred soul to say (to lie, if need be) that he has been there as well, to say with a soothing chuckle, "Yeah, I know what you mean. I've done that too."

I had come to know Dick quite well in the last several weeks. I enjoyed visiting with him on these stopovers. He worked at night, flying canceled checks in a Cessna Skymaster. He stayed there at the field during the day. They'd given him a cot in the back room. He and I had much in common: we were about the same age, both recently out of the Air Force, and both somewhat outsiders in this rural world—he especially, being a Yankee and all.

But Dick was an enigma. I couldn't quite figure him. Outwardly he seemed to be the model of a person at total peace with himself and the world. All his happiness seemed to require was his guitar, his dog, and his modest flying job. Yet there was a hint of turmoil in his eyes. He didn't talk much about himself, and I knew little of his past, except that he flew C-7 Caribou transports in Viet Nam.

On my normal fire patrol I'd spend more time there, but I had to leave Dick and return to the hunt. Already the base station had telephoned to alert me that more fires were breaking out elsewhere in the district. I fired up the Super Cub and waved to the airport bums.

They wanted to know how quickly I could get airborne. I swung the plane around into the wind, clearing for other air traffic as I turned. I held hard on the brakes, firewalled the throttle, and held the stick as far back as it would go, like a carrier pilot about to catapult. The asphalt runway was about a hundred yards away, but I didn't use it. I released the brakes and bounded across the small parking apron, laboring into the air over the grassy edge not much more than a good stone's throw away. I knew I couldn't have done that if a stiff headwind hadn't slipped me an extra ace, but it was a crowd pleaser. Patting the Cub for its performance and feeling refreshed, I turned eastward. But after a short cruise I saw that something strange was happening.

I was heading for a fire in the distance. It was not very big, but another fire had just started a short distance north of it. As I reached the first smoke, the second one had billowed higher, and now a third baby fire had been born still farther north. I could see that all three fires had broken out along a dirt road barely visible beneath the heavy pine timber. I dropped down as low as I dared, the tires barely clearing the treetops, banking carefully left then right, catching fleeting glimpses of the dirt road. Suddenly I saw what I had suspected.

A yellow Volkswagen bug chugged along slowly, barely moving, the driver obviously concerned about my presence overhead. I passed over and rolled into a steep 360-degree turn, cobbing the power to maintain airspeed above the stall, which at this height, would be fatal. I rolled out and crossed the road about where I had sighted him, but he was gone. Again coming about, I slowed the Cub back and followed the snaking road but to no avail. I then doubled back and caught a glimpse of the bug parked on a side road in a thicket. Again I cobbed the power and swung back around. He knew he'd been discovered, and he fled northward. I chuckled over the reflection that I was in a cat-and-mouse game, but then thought no, this was a cub-and-bug game. I felt immensely alive and totally at one with the Cub.

Certain that I had found an arsonist, I climbed for a higher altitude and radioed the discovery to the base station. I passed along the coordinates of the fires, and the route and description of the escaping bug. The answer came that the Highway Patrol was being notified as well as the large paper corporation that owned the pine tree plantation. I reflected on what one of the rangers had told me of forest arsonists: they are often discontented or terminated employees of the paper companies. I desperately wanted this guy to be caught, but I knew that the charge would never stand up in court, as I had not seen him in the act of torching the woods. But maybe they could match tire prints or something. I finally lost the bug under the heavy timber as it fled northward, and I had to abandon the chase.

The day was finally done and none too soon because I was about wasted, both physically and mentally. I was crossing the lowlands of a river bottom on a long, straight-in approach. The bayous below were clear and glassy calm, their banks laced with Spanish moss hanging in long white curtains from the thick hardwoods. I passed over a boat with two men casting lines and dropped down low, waving my arm out to them. They honored me by returning the wave, which was delightful because I knew then that they had not resented my noisy intrusion. But as I looked back up toward the airfield, the engine—Lycoming Model 0-320-E2A, one each—ceased operation. Quit cold.

The silence was more powerful than the roar of afterburner. Immediately I felt the Cub decelerate. The nose dropped. The prop windmilled. My heart ripped away and clambered up my throat, the torn arteries gripping my clenched teeth, demanding, pleading like an imprisoned sailor, to be released from the brig before the ship went down. I was suddenly transformed into a glider at 300 feet above a heavy woodland. The airfield was still a good mile away. Tremors oscillated wildly up and down my spine as I swung my head with frantic alarm left and right, looking for a clearing or a road, but it was only instinct. I knew there was no such sanctuary out here. I realized then that I was going to have to land in the trees. I had to remember to fly the plane down—to resist the urge to raise the nose and stretch the glide toward the airfield. If I hit the trees in a slight descent, at just above stall speed, I might survive, but a stall would most certainly be fatal.

I had about thirty seconds to run through the engine failure procedure, which was about standard for most light planes. Steeped in fright and foreboding, I figured that it was useless, but at least I'd be doing something rather than just sitting there waiting for the blunt trauma. I looked up at the magneto switches. Both were on. I pushed the mixture control knob in. It was there already. I rechecked the airspeed. Sixty knots. No less. Let's see, I still had oil pressure. I was conscious of a breathless, buzzing feeling. What was left? The fuel selector valve was somewhere down on th——

THE FUEL!!

My hand reached down, trembling, fumbling, groping for the fuel selector; found it; switched it to the opposite tank. Instantly the engine fired up and roared back into life. I laughed wildly at the wonderful noise and yelled at the top of my voice.

"What a stupid, stupid fool you are! Run a tank dry at this altitude! Idiot. Idiot! Idiot!!"

And no one ever so severely berated himself while smiling as happily as did I.

After a restless night I silenced the alarm and rose to prepare for another day of hunting. The dry, clear weather persisted. It would be another busy one. I switched on the TV to catch the morning news while brewing up coffee. The tube came to life with a story in progress of a plane crash last night. I sat down and watched with the concerned curiosity that any pilot would have. Then I froze with shock. A Cessna Skymaster had crashed in the forest north of Evergreen. There was one fatality, cause unknown. Dick was dead.

Although I had my hunches, I never learned why it happened. But it really didn't matter. Whenever a pilot is killed, his death serves to remind us—his friends and peers—of our own mortality. It makes us mindful of that stealthy, indiscriminate hunter that bides its time and waits for any of us to fly near its clutches. Sometimes we're sucked into it without warning, through no fault of our own. More often, the cause is our own carelessness. But if Dick is allowed to be forgotten, then he will have died for nothing, and I'll be closer to the hunter's grasp.

It's the hunter of which Ernest Gann wrote. It's the one Dick saw for an unearthly millisecond.

FIFTEEN

FACE OF THE BEAR

For several minutes Cairo Control has played the devil, trying to establish radio contact with another aircraft. It happens sometimes; the plane is a bit too far away from the control center's antenna, or someone's transmitter or receiver is weak. I'm not paying much attention to Cairo's problem, and I'm jolted when I hear them call us.

"MAC Bravo 5523, Cairo, can you relay to Aeroflot 16214?" Relay? Me? To a Russian? Yeah.

"Roger, Cairo, what's the message?"

"Tell him to contact Athinai on frequency 125.2, please."

I comply with Cairo's request and succeed in informing the Soviet that he is to call Athens Control. The Russian voice is thickly accented and grateful for my assistance. He sounds like a decent guy. Maybe he's the one I met last year. I wonder what that guy did with my wings.

Flying in the Middle East was new to me. With a single exception, I had been no farther east than Incirlik Air Base near Adana, Turkey, when Desert Shield started. But that one flight into the mysterious, forbidden regions beyond NATO's eastern frontier transformed my vision of the world.

It was the eeriest piece of atmosphere I had ever flown through. I developed a case of the creeps, just thinking about where we were. Off to the left was Mt. Ararat, upon which the Ark had supposedly been wrecked. But we only occasionally got glimpses of the historic mountain as we descended below its towering heights through layer after layer of gray stratus cloud. Somewhere off to the right was another huge rock shrouded in cloud. We hoped the Soviet radar was accurate enough to keep us clear of the mountain spires.

We were more than a bit apprehensive and had a right to be. We were descending through heavy cloud into a valley with great mountains all around. Even the valley floor was almost 3,000 feet above sea level. There was no room for error or sloppy flying. And complicating it all was way—unorthodox to us—that the Soviets structure their airspace. Their altitudes are measured in meters, so that we must convert to feet in order to use our altimeters accurately. In addition, they measure atmospheric pressure in millibars, and again we must convert to inches of mercury in order to adjust our altimeters. Topping it all off, they measure flight levels above airport elevation, not above mean sea level, as most of the world does. Climb on board almost any U.S. registered airplane, military or civilian, except for one major airline (not mine) that does it the Soviet way, and you'll see that the altimeter registers the height above sea level of the airport at which you're sitting. Thus we had to correct our altimeters yet again. If you then add in another supremely complicating factor—the easily misunderstood, thick accents of the Soviet radar controllers—you have a recipe for disaster. Two days before, one of the Soviets' own airlifters had cratered somewhere down below while trying to get into Yerevan, killing all aboard.

But there was still more to be concerned about. We were among the first foreign aircraft ever to be allowed in the Soviet Union without an onboard Soviet escort. So we were completely on our own. The big concern was the Iranian border, just a few miles off to the right. We were pretty sure the Soviets didn't intend to splash us if we strayed off course, but we feared that the Iranians would not be as scrupulous.

We finally broke through the lowest layer and began maneuvering for our approach to the airport. The landscape below looked mystifying, like some never-never land from a folktale. The countryside was flat, peppered with villages and snow-covered collective farms, but here and there great inverted cone-shaped mountains abruptly breached the valley floor and rose precipitously into the clouds. Layers of blue smoke from thousands of fireplaces hung like thin veils over the settlements. We strained at the windows to glimpse the earthquake damage but saw none this far south of the epicenter.

We intercepted the ILS localizer course, which worked just like the ones we were familiar with throughout the world, and we soon saw the huge runway ahead. It bore the standard markings to which we were also accustomed. But turning off the runway, familiarity departed like a startled covey of quail. We were confronted by the most imposing control tower we had ever seen, a gigantic mushroom-shaped thing rising high above the airport. We taxied past dozens of Aeroflot airliners parked around the circular terminal and were directed to our parking spot. We were stopped beside a column of huge Soviet planes, and our windscreen came to a halt mere inches from the blade of the biggest, most grotesque helicopter I had ever seen. Even before the engines had spooled down, scores of trucks, all of a strange make, came speeding within feet of our nose, and some of the smaller vehicles even shot beneath our wings. They carried heaping loads of earthquake relief supplies from the long line of Soviet airlifters in front of us.

Soon after we had opened the doors, a couple of solemn men in civilian attire and overcoats climbed aboard and began looking over our cargo, which was experimental portable shelters donated by a U.S. company. Then we learned how unprepared for us the Soviets were. Neither trucks nor a much-needed forklift was available to unload us. We were advised to wait, and wait we did. We sat there for hours, not daring to shut down the auxiliary power unit (APU). It supplied us with electrical power for the lights and radios. We had been ordered to keep one HF radio tuned to the frequency of "Phantom," which was our command post in Europe. We were to check in with Phantom every hour while on the ground. The APU also supplied a small volume of heat, which we directed to the flight deck. It was impossible for the APU's small jet engine to heat the huge cargo bay. Hour after hour we watched as big Soviet jets rolled in one after the other, and it became obvious that they really didn't need us. They had plenty of airlift capacity; it was clear that we were there only in a symbolic sense. Soviet-American relations were warming up under Mikhail Gorbachev's leadership. I figured that we had been offered by our gov-

© Walter Siatruvis 94

ernment as a goodwill gesture, and the offer had been accepted in the same spirit.

After a while Soviet pilots began to appear and asked in broken English if they could come aboard. We welcomed them up to our warm flight deck, where we exchanged handshakes and grins. There followed much pointing at various instruments, handles, and switches, accompanied by grunts, chuckles, and sporadic expressions of mixed English and Russian. Finally, after a mutual display of wallet photos of spouses and kids, they departed, leaving us with invitations to visit their strange-looking jets.

And we did. We walked down the rows of giant jets, stealing glances behind and around us for the mystical men in long coats peering over newspapers, but there seemed to be no such eyes following us. We proceeded to climb ladders into the bellies of the behemoths and stared incredulously at the jungle of instrumented cockpits. I remembered from a briefing years ago that they painted their interiors turquoise, which their psychologists had determined was the best color for reducing pilot stress. And here it was, painted up like the dash of a '57 Chevy. But with a myriad of instruments—more than we had, and all of them seemed to be huge round things with bold, antiquelike numbers painted inside them. Instruments were everywhere they could be installed; they stared at us from every corner of the big flight deck. On the aft bulkheads were switches by the hundreds, which I took to be substitutes for circuit breakers.

Again we performed the ritual: pointing, grunting, nodding, grinning, pretending we knew exactly what our hosts were trying to explain to us about their big Illyushin-76 jet. As we shook hands and departed, I impulsively grabbed and ripped off my Velcro-backed name tag from my flight suit. It had silver USAF command pilot wings embossed on it, with my name and the words "Mississippi Air Guard" underneath. I presented it to the captain of the Illyushin and noticed his startled reaction. He grabbed my hand and pumped it again while saying something that sounded deeply sincere.

I walked away pondering the stunned look on his face when I ripped off the name tag and commented to my old friend, George Fondren, at how astounded the man had been to receive my gift. But George had another idea. "No," he said. He paused to chuckle and shake his head in mock disgust over my naivete. "The guy has just never seen Velcro before."

Back at the Starlizzard, things were still in a quandary, although a platoon of Soviet soldiers was arriving to offload the cargo by hand. The stale ham sandwiches from our flight lunches had been consumed long since, and we began to wonder if we might spend the night in the "Lockheed Hilton." But then the enterprising George, who spreads political goodwill with watermelons and vise-grip handshakes, got a wild idea to wander over to the airport terminal. There we were, in a notorious police state, doing what we could have been arrested for at a large western airport. I was nervous about it, but I followed him across the busy ramp with airliners coming and going and entered the huge building.

We walked through crowded corridors and waiting areas, past concessions and ticket counters, nudging through crowds of civilians and soldiers. I don't think the adventurous George thought anything of it, but I was extremely self-conscious all the while. Here we were in the heart of communism, wearing strange flight suits with American flags on our shoulders. Thousands of heads turned and followed our progress through the terminal as we tried to look as if we had an official destination.

At length we passed a concession stand that had various pastries and cakes displayed. It was illegal to use foreign currency and would be foolish in an open forum like this, but we had no rubles. I sensed another impulse in George and slid away to an empty bench across the corridor. Watching, I saw a well-dressed elderly couple approach him. They began asking him questions in Russian, sensing his interest in the pastries. Soon they began fumbling through their pocketbooks, and he turned and pointed at me, holding up two fingers. Then it was done. He shook their hands and came over handing me the cake, which was uniquely delicious.

Shortly the same couple left their seats and approached us again, offering more money. We wanted to give them some dollars in return but it was too dangerous, many eyes were on us. We could go to jail for that. We didn't want to take the money, but they insisted, and finally we accepted the five-ruble bill. Then George did the only thing we could have done to repay them, although I wondered if it might jeopardize the couple if they accepted. He tore off the Velcroed American flag on his left shoulder and handed it to the lady. I immediately followed suit, handing mine to the gentleman. The two stood there for a minute staring at the flags in their hands, and tears began to roll down their cheeks. Once again we shook their hands and wished them well. As we left they returned to their bench jabbing handkerchiefs at their faces, carefully cradling those little symbols of freedom and hope in their hands.

As we departed, I couldn't help but consider the odds. Out of the billions of human beings on earth, only a relative handful were born American. And yet I, fortunate beyond comprehension, was among them. I had pondered this notion before, but never had it seemed so profoundly clear as that night when our gear finally came up and we banked westward. We were headed home for Christmas, already blessed immeasurably.

SIXTEEN

CREW UNREST

It has been an hour since we shut the Starlifter down here on the Dhahran ramp, and of course the crew bus has not yet appeared. Things have changed dramatically in the last couple of weeks in concert with the cease-fire. They dumped the pool-pilot practice and are now sending us downrange with basic two-pilot crews. The good news is that the twenty-two-hour days that were slaughtering us have now been halved. The bad news is that we lay over here in the desert. More accurately, we go into "stage" here—we wait until an outbound mission is assigned us. It could be twelve hours from now or twelve days.

In the dimming light, some of the crew have moved into the shadows under the gargantuan wings and are sitting among their gear. I notice the cooler lid is hurriedly raised and lowered, and I hear some whooshing sounds. That has to be soft drinks. Surely my crew wouldn't drink beer here, where it is forbidden not only on any Air Force ramp in general but in the teetotaling Kingdom of Saudi Arabia in particular. Tell me it ain't so.

Finally the "bus" arrives, a minivan into which we cram every cubic centimeter with our gear and pieces of ourselves and endure the crude remarks about cozy proximity and sexual orientation. But humor quickly ebbs as limbs begin to tingle from lack of blood. We pass a busy field hospital and rows of captured Iraqi tanks and armored personnel carriers and go through a couple of security checkpoints and onto a four-lane highway laden with military traffic.

After about ten minutes our abode comes into view—the USAF barracks dubbed Eagletown. We pass through a couple of rows of tall fences with concertina wire curling along the top and drive past row after row of long, single-story prefabricated structures, all about the width of a double-wide mobile home. Beside each is a sandbagged air raid shelter.

We check in with the stage manager, who breaks the news that there is a lull in the airlift operations and that consequently we can expect an extended visit. He lethargically warns us that if we have any alcoholic contraband we must deposit it with him, then gives us our keys and room assignments.

My copilot, Mike Connery—a Northwest Airlines pilot in civilian life—and I throw our gear down on the floor in the eight-by-ten-foot room. There is no furniture except stacked bunk beds that are surprisingly comfortable. Already across the hall a thump, a door slam, running boots, and unintelligible yells indicate that my two engineers are perpetrating some sort of horseplay on the wary loadmaster. I pledge not to come to their assistance in the least if some disturbed sleeper from down the hall emerges with a crash axe to exact carnage.

The respite at the Eagletown barracks is not bad. The air conditioning is great, and there is little distraction. Were it not for the clamor of incoming crews, conditions would be perfect for a blissful hibernation, one long overdue.

Mike and I pick through our cold MREs and prepare to turn in when more thumps on the thin walls and a chorus of snickering bring us out to investigate. The two young engineers, Len Alvis and Chuck Lee, are pulling a foolish prank on the load, one Keith Burton. Len and Chuck are thin cigarette-suckers, ever full of pent-up energy and youth, both similar in build and behavior. They've been dubbed the squirrel brothers, namely Fluffy and Scruffy, by the salty load, and they in turn have labeled him the Possum. Keith is an experienced loadmaster, a tough ex-cop who patrolled the most violent precinct in Jackson until he burnt out from police work. He is a man I would not want to get into a fight with. I was riding in back once and watched as his voice boomed and echoed through the public address system above the din of the engines, boldly admonishing some elite and armed Special Forces soldiers to return to their seats.

"YOU BACK THERE! Yeah, YOU. Dammit, I told you to get back in your seats and strap in. NOW, DO IT!"

But I've found another man beneath that tough leather exterior. He once shared with me a long poem he had written about the Starlifter that belied his rugged image and exposed a great sentimentalist underneath.

Mike and I walk to Keith's room and find the squirrel brothers methodically at work, strapping the Possum into his bed. One is holding him down while the other is tightly ratcheting cargo straps over his legs and chest, binding his upper arms against his side. They giggle and guffaw while working, but we notice that the Possum isn't resisting in the least; in fact he's lying back, reading a paperback about World War II Flying Fortresses and listening contentedly to his Walkman. Mike walks away shaking his head over the foolish idea that two flight engineers would try to tie up a loadmaster with the tools of his own trade. We return to our bunks, and a couple of minutes later the hallway bursts with stampeding feet as we see the squirrels streak by with the Possum in close pursuit, straps lassoing.

After a long hibernation, I become restless. There is nothing else to do except walk or run around the perimeter road, or sit on the porch of the hooch and gaze at oil-smoked skyscapes. There is a TV room with video movies, but it is crowded and hot. Later I seize a chance to go off base to downtown Dhahran. The Air Force has begun bus service, and I ride down to the market area as the sun goes down.

The streets are alive with GIs, all clad in desert camo battle uniforms, strolling along in clusters; laughing, toting shopping bags, drinking nonalcoholic beer. Scores of industrious, turban-topped sidewalk vendors hawk selections of watches and electronics, appealing to the GIs in sporadic English. The scene could be a rerun of another war and another place twenty years ago except for the absence of women.

Almost everything sold is imported. The place is oppressively noisy. Busy honks and revs from the streets mix with murmuring crowd noise and an assortment of music. Playing in one shop is the fluty Arabic dance tunes that blend, as I pass to the next, with the electric twangs of Lynard Skynard singing "Sweet Home Alabama."

Suddenly the shops begin to close. All along the street, scrolling metal security doors start to slam shut, as storekeepers usher GIs out. I look at my watch; it is still early. But then I notice that the storekeepers, squeezing padlocks and hurrying away, have left the lights on. It is, of course, prayer time. I'm delighted. Finally I will get to see the real Mideast character.

As I walk to the edge of the street, the prayers begin to roll in from some distant loudspeaker, and I look out to the grassy median between the two streets where a devotee is bowing. But he's isolated. I look up and down the median, and along the sidewalks but see only a few worshipers. Most of the local people stand in groups talking with one another, some smoking cigarettes and chatting with groups of GIs. I'm really surprised. Here in the heart of Islam, very few seem to take their faith seriously. Maybe they're more devout in the other towns. But then maybe they're not so different from us after all.

I go back to Eagletown to find that our crew is nearing the top of the assignment list, and I turn in.

After two and a half days the stage manager finally gives us a mission. But typically, the alert comes after we have been awake about ten hours and I have just turned in for another vain attempt to bank some sleep. It has been an agonizingly long day. The headwinds were fierce, and our trip up from the sands was almost ten hours.

We check in to the transient crew quarters at RAF Upper Heyford, England, and drag our bags up to the rooms. The World War II–vintage building is extremely well kept and nicely decorated. In stark contrast to our facilities at Eagletown, the Upper Heyford officers' quarters feature polished wooden floors with massive doors and high ceilings. The restaurant and pub are all in the same complex, and the pub has been opened to all ranks for the duration of the Persian Gulf operation. We agree to meet with the enlisted guys down in the pub for a round of bitters before turning in.

Mike and I start out the door but turn back and pitch our caps on the beds. He wears a cap bearing the logo of his airline, as do I. We have gotten used to wearing the unauthorized caps. They provide better protection from the sun than the silly flight hats issued us. But the caps are also an outlet for that touch of recalcitrance some of us need in order to avoid feeling like robots. And we were constantly catching hell on account of them. Only a few days before, while walking across a flight line under a relentless Arabian sun, Mike had been hailed by a derisive colonel.

"YOU THERE! YOU WITH THE HAT!"

He put the hat back on as soon as the colonel had blown off steam and departed. Nevertheless, we know better than to wear our hats in high-visibility places such as operations buildings and the like and especially in the club bar.

The pub is crowded with crewdogs. The wall is taking more hits than the dartboard. Flight-suited airmen huddle in corners and around small tables, talking of the usual suite of topics; only the sequence changes, depending on how long the crew has been out and on how tired the men are. A crew fresh from the States, for example, would be discussing the war and the military establishment, most likely, then sports and women. A crew that was tired and had flown many missions without a break at home would generally reverse the order. But the last subject covered was always the same.

The squirrel brothers grab a table, while Mike, Keith, and I squeeze to the bar. A group of a dozen or so crowd together at the center of the bar around a tall guy who is making contorted, impossible movements with raised hands. Mike and I are aghast when we see him. He is wearing *a cap in the bar!* Has the man no decency? He wears the gold leaves of a major on his flight suit. He's been around for a while. Surely he understands the tradition.

> He who enters covered here
> Buys the bar a round of cheer.

Not many traditions have developed over the years in the Air Force. It's certainly not like the centuries-old Navy, which is infested with them. The tradition of the hat in the bar is about the only one we've got, and it's fiercely protected.

The man appears to be the highest-ranking officer in the pub, though I am his equal. Maybe no one else has had the pluck to challenge him. Or perhaps he has already bought the round and thinks he has earned the right to wear the cap. He's lucky; if he had done this at a fighter base, he would have been seized, and the cap forcibly removed. Moreover, fighter pilots would have taken punitive action for a less well known transgression.

We all have a small pocket that holds a survival knife on the inside left thigh of our flight suits, although few people keep one in it. I lost my survival knife years ago. But fighter pilots wear "G-suits" over their flight suits, which have identical knife pockets. Having no need for a knife pocket on the flight suit, they tear them off, in a celebrated ritual, and hang them on a wire over their bar like scalps on a lodgepole. All green fighter drivers and other pilots who wander into a fighter lair will suffer the fate.

We lean against the bar down near the end under the bell and order a pint of bitters. Mike is a veteran of several years' active duty and is as incredulous as I over this inexcusable sacrilege. He walks over and checks the guy out, comes back, and breaks the news that the guy's cap bears the logo of an airline that is a fierce competitor of ours. This revelation intensifies our contempt. Obviously he too is a reservist, like most of us here. But I decide to let matters be. We sip our bitters and try to ignore it.

Then he commits an unpardonable sin. He takes off the cap *and lays it on the bar!!* We reel, with an electric shock running through our veins. Placing a hat on the bar is a brazen and audacious violation of the tradition. I can stand no more. I reach up to the bell, which is reserved for such transgressions, and ring it boldly, continually, for five or ten seconds, while Mike climbs on a stool, points to the offender, and yells.

"Hat on the bar! Hat on the bar! He's buyin'! He's buyin'!"

A momentary hush falls throughout the pub as all faces turn first our way, then his. Then a cheer goes up and the accused disappears in a rushing tide of crewdogs who stake their order at his expense.

As I lean back with a smile of justice and satisfaction, the man resumes his storytelling to his original audience and the dejected crewmen return to their tables. Mike turns to me.

"Can you believe this guy? He's not buying."

The guy is beginning to get on my nerves. He isn't just trouncing the tradition, he's defiling it. Worse yet, he's souring the image that the enlisted men in the pub have of officers. The Possum, Keith Burton, is getting hot and is mumbling some extremely unflattering remarks about the good major.

I've had about enough and am thinking of leaving, but Mike will not let it be. He weasels in among the huddled group, snatches the cap from the bar, and returns to me. I look at the American Airlines logo, tie it to the bell rope hanging overhead, and lean back to wait.

I see the guy's hand reach back for the cap as he continues his yarning to a few still-faithful listeners. Finding it missing, he snaps his head toward me and then looks up at the bell. He is dishonored and now must save face. Shoving people aside, he drives ahead and thrusts his chest at me. But I stay cool and explain that he had not bought the round as per the tradition, a charge that he disputes, which in turn infuriates the Possum.

"You didn't buy my drink!" Keith charges.

The foolish major counters. "You're a liar."

The Possum surges forth, but Mike and I form a barrier. A major confrontation is developing as the guy's crew begins to congregate behind him, but I sense they're only coolly loyal to him. Meanwhile over against the wall, the squirrel brothers sit in a cloud of blue smoke, astutely not interested in participating but urging the Possum on with wild guffaws.

"WEAPONS RELEASED, WEAPONS RELEASED!"

"CLEARED TO KILL, CLEARED TO KILL!"

When the bartender realizes that the mother of all brawls is developing, she pronounces the pub closed and orders everyone toward the doors. The situation having been successfully defused, we proceeded to our rooms, like scolded children being sent to bed early, mumbling along the way about what a jerk that guy was.

I'm glad it didn't come to a fight. I did, however, rather enjoy it. It was a great diversion—a vent for the stress. We would talk and laugh of it for a long time.

But if I ever see that guy again . . .

We touch down at McGuire Air Force Base (better known to us as

Quagmire AFB) after a grueling Atlantic crossing from Upper Heyford, and I again unsuccessfully conclude an argument with the gentleman at the billeting office. He gives me a voucher for our rooms at the Days Inn near the base, and as before, we are to double up. We're not just tired, we're tired of each other. We're not college kids anymore—we don't need roomies, we need rest. But orders are orders.

It seems we are continually frustrated almost everywhere we go in the desert operation, and I think it gets worse the closer we get to the States. It seems we have to do battle with every command post, maintenance officer, crew stage manager, and billeting office that we face. I know they consider us arrogant prima donnas, who expect to be catered to and serviced by all those who toil on the ground to support flying operations. I know of a few pilots who are like that, and they spoil it for the rest of is.

The root of the perception problem is that we fliers are accustomed to an entirely different way of viewing job accomplishment—a way that's often not understood by those whose jobs are more subjective. Either we get our job done, or we don't. There's simply no middle road. We put the ordnance on the target or miss and have to try again from scratch. We get the cargo and passengers to the destination or we don't. There's no gap between success and failure for us to slip comfortably into and bide for a while. If my orders are to get to Tabuk, and I don't see Tabuk out the window when I flip the fuel shutoff switches, my job is not done. However, if I did get there, on time and safely, then I'm categorically successful. And I expect other people whose job it is to fuel, fix, transport, and provide room and board to be equally successful.

Contrast this view of the job with that of a person whose objective is less clearly defined. The billeting situation at McGuire has become emotionally explosive. The base commander made the double-up decision for all crews going off base even when the motels have plenty of extra room. Rules were adopted against that years ago. It's hard to rest when your roommate is restless. His sleep patterns are different from yours. He wants to watch the Saints game while you sleep; you bang around, trying to get your laundry done while he's trying to crash. And besides, we're crammed together enough at the overseas bases and the endless hours in the air. We deserve some relief when we're back here in the land of plenty. So of course we challenged him about the policy. His excuse? In case of a surge operation, he wanted to have extra rooms available. Imagine that: *a surge operation*. What did he think we were in the middle of, for crying out loud? The only way we could have more of a surge was to build more C-141s and train more crews in, say, the next few days or weeks. Furthermore, did he have those extra rooms blocked? No, of course not. The government would have to pay for that. So his extra rooms were constantly subject to being taken by a Shriners' convention or a cheerleader festival or whatever. The motels were certainly not obligated to hold them—we asked them about it. It seemed like a petty matter, but the double-up policy at our major staging base proved to be about the most explosive and morale-shattering incident that befell us. I saw tempers go ballistic with people whom I knew to be mild mannered and tolerant.

At another Stateside base we decided to escape for a while, to get away from the Air Force, even if just for a couple of hours. We needed to get off base, to see some normal folks, to eat some quality food and recuperate from the rat race. We pondered how we would achieve this without having to pay taxi fare. Mike Gandy, my loadmaster, stated that George Fondren would have secured a government vehicle for such an excursion. I knew his statement was a not-so-thinly veiled challenge for me. I walked to the base motor pool and asked for a "U-Drive" vehicle. The U-Drive program had been in effect for a while. The theory was that the Air Force had a complement of staff cars and utility trucks at each base, and someone high up had decided that they might as well be used rather than sit idly, although there had to be a legitimate reason for using them. I walked past a row of at least a dozen such vehicles and entered the motor pool building. When I asked for the use of a staff car, the answer was an emphatic no. "Why not?" I asked.

"Because sir, we can't lend staff cars to flight crews. Crew buses are available to you."

"Yes, but we've already asked if they'd take us off base and they said no. It's Sunday evening; the clubs are closed; we're tired of chow halls; we want a decent meal tonight. So we'd like to check out a vehicle."

"Sorry, sir, but it's against our policy."

"Whose policy?" I asked.

The sergeant shrugged. "Well, ours, sir, the motor pool's."

"Whose, in particular?" I pressed. "What's the name? Show me where it's written, please."

"Well . . ." He took a deep breath and cut eyes toward the key rack as he thought hard and formulated his answer. I knew then that I had him. I smiled. George would have been proud of his old protégé.

"There's several out there; we only need a sedan, and just for tonight. Even a truck will do."

He gave in but saved a measure of face by giving us the smallest, shoddiest station wagon in the pool. As we squeezed into the car, a round of giggling erupted when Jeff Carter quipped that George would have gotten a nicer, bigger vehicle.

Yet most of our sources of frustration came from the operations sector—like the time we were sent to the wrong base. We landed at King Fahd Air Base, just northwest of Dhahran. Our cargo of trucks and trailers, we learned, was destined for Dhahran Air Base. Someone had fumbled the ball. Not us. Our orders clearly read King Fahd. We'd done our job. But the ALCE insisted that we load the vehicles back up and fly them over to Dhahran, which was ten minutes' flying time. I argued that the trucks should be driven the thirty-minute drive to Dhahran, that it would cost thousands of pounds of extra fuel and hours added to our mission time to fly them over. The report came back over the radio that the colonel had made his decision and that he did not appreciate aircrews trying to run his business.

It took an hour to round up the trucks from wherever they had gone and reload them back on the Starlifter. Then we had to wait for a slot to become available over at Dhahran. Finally we flew over and unloaded the trucks—two hours after they could have been driven over. But then, while we were waiting for fuel to go back to Spain, we discovered a bad tire, and Dhahran was out of spares. So the ALCE began a search for a tire. First word came that the nearest spare was at McGuire AFB, New Jersey. We were in for a long wait. We began to download our gear. But then they found one—at King Fahd. Thirty minutes later, it arrived on a truck.

Every war that's been fought is replete with such repugnant displays of obstinacy in the face of threatened pride and ego. And I have come to the conclusion that lieutenant colonels—though I have become one—are the worst offenders.

The lieutenants are cautious apprentices. The captains are the most energetic and resourceful of officers, and the majors are the ones who are the most streetwise and in touch with the lower ranks. But lieutenant colonels are a problem. They are the middle managers, mostly in mundane desk jobs, though the Persian Gulf surge had drawn many of them back to the cockpit. They recognize that their careers are on final approach, and they are panicking. They desperately want to make colonel and are mortally afraid of committing an error that will preclude such advancement. So the favorite tactic of the lieutenant colonel is to avoid mistakes by avoiding decision making. Procrastination, consultation, ultraconservatism, and buck-passing is the light colonel's modus operandi. There are exceptions, of course, but if you see a bottleneck, look closely and you'll probably find an LC nearby. Fortunately, most of the full colonels and general officers have achieved their career goals and have a more realistic outlook. And they are ready to act decisively but only if you can get through to them.

Still, the Gulf airlift fueled widespread frustration among all the ranks, including those who were ground bound. I complained to one wing commander about how his people were fueling the planes. They were in the habit of filling the jets with as much fuel as the zero-fuel weight would allow because it was easy on the drivers and pumpers, shorthanded as they claimed they were. They don't want to wait for me to arrive at the operations center, then calculate a proper fuel load and relay that information to them, as per regulations. But it seems that regulations work one way. I have to abide by the regs, but they don't. They can just top off the tanks at their convenience and get to the next job. But I don't want to carry fuel that I don't need. The extra weight costs extra fuel burned, causes seriously excessive engine wear when the weight requires max power takeoffs, and creates a hazard when something goes wrong. They don't have to worry about these problems, since they're not on board when number three engine blows up on takeoff and takes number four with it.

I filed an operational hazard report. I should have called the wing commander personally. Oh, yes, I should have. George told me, later, that I didn't have the guts to call him. But the fact is I didn't have time. And I was tired. I probably couldn't have gotten through to him anyway. But I would have given that guy both barrels. Shorthanded you say? Not enough fuel trucks either? Yes, yes, I understand, Colonel— the war and all. But what about all those SAC bases that are still just sitting around, waiting for the big Klaxon to go off? Have you asked them to lend you a few fuel trucks and men? Or is that a sign of weakness? Certainly, it's hard to get promoted when you display such dependence on someone else. The big what, sir? Oh yes, the Big Picture. Now I understand. Why is it that I can never visualize that Big Picture? Yet I always thought I was one of those who helped paint that fabled canvas. Cocky, you say? And arrogant? Maybe so. But it comes with the territory.

Yeah, George was wrong about me.

SEVENTEEN

MASTER CAUTION
(Push to Reset)

We've just coasted out over Northern Ireland, and have set course for Newfoundland. This crossing will be an especially long one. We're flying into the teeth of the winter winds. The computer-generated flight plan has several hundred numbers crunched out on it, but the one that I keep glancing at—as if it may change for the better if I glare at it long enough—is the number listed in the space for total en route time: 1115—eleven hours and fifteen minutes from Germany to South Carolina. A normal person could work a full day and another half day's overtime while we're sitting here.

Eight months into the Persian Gulf operation, we have come as close as possible to blending with the Starlifter. To us, it has become a living creature, but to complete the merger we have had to mutate in its direction. We've become more inanimate. We've learned to compartmentalize our minds. We keep the vital doors of awareness open—those that give us access to engines, fuel, and weather, but the door to the clock stays closed. Time drops from our awareness. We are hardened to the clock; the slow sweep of its hands no longer agonizes us. We are time travelers. We strap the jet on. We do our jobs. And wait to emerge hours into the future. The places are not important anymore, except for the one coded KJAN, which is home.

I was home last month, pulling stage manager duty. It's a job being rotated among the squadron's senior pilots that involves spending long hours in the command post, coordinating crew scheduling and aircraft movements. It's no fun, but it keeps you home for a few days.

While I was there, I came to know our new air commander, a fellow by the name of Maxie Phillips. When Colonel Bailey retired, Maxie was asked to leave his job flying RF-4 Phantoms over in Meridian and to join us as Shelly's successor. But Maxie was an outsider, and he was a fighter pilot at that. A few feathers were ruffled because someone from within hadn't been promoted. I didn't know him very well at the time—I didn't really care. I just wanted the Gulf operation to end. After that I doubted I'd be around much longer in the Guard anyway.

Maxie had been a fighter pilot all his adult life. Starting out flying Phantoms when they were first introduced, he became an experienced and skilled warrior and eventually acquired an intense hunger for an even greater challenge. He wanted what they all do, the men of his kind: test pilot school. While stationed in England, he asked General Chuck Yeager to recommend him, and Chuck said he would, but it was a discouraging meeting. It wasn't like years ago, when experience, ability, and eagerness could get you a test pilot job. Now, Chuck explained, you needed tons of specialized education and experience in a variety of aircraft. A few friends in strategic positions didn't hurt either. Maxie put in his separation papers that day.

He returned to his native Mississippi and joined the Air Guard in Meridian. For a few years he flew RF-101 jets, the "One-O-Wonder," as they were called, but then in 1979 the unit switched to Maxie's beloved Phantoms. He was as happy as a weevil in a boll; he was living in Mississippi, he had a full-time job flying low and fast, and the pay was good. But Maxie saw the handwriting on the wall. He knew that the aging Phantom would soon be taken out of service. He didn't know what would replace it, but he suspected it would be large planes. When they offered him the air commander job in our unit, he figured he was in for a great change even if he stayed, so he might as well take the challenge.

When I got to know this man, I realized that the powers at state headquarters who had appointed him had wisdom far beyond my expectations. Maxie was a soft-spoken man with an equally soft style in humor and human relations. He was a deep listener; his door was always open. Somewhere along the line, the Mississippi Air Guard had gone right.

It was a cold day in December when he went over to see them off. The first of Meridian's newly assigned KC-135 jet tankers was already sitting on the ramp. More were on the way. And the last four Phantoms were about to leave for various destinations. Some were bound for the "Bone Yard" in Arizona, others to locations where they would "phly phorever" on a concrete pedestal. Maxie had been invited over to witness the last takeoff. He had expected a ceremony of some sort. Certainly the occasion called for it. There would be a band, a speech, photographs, press coverage, and maybe a gathering of the old heads. Perhaps lots of people and fanfare would help ease his pain.

Pain. What an outlandish notion to the pedantic masses. A lump the size of a cantaloupe in your throat for a piece of noisy steel and fuel. Maxie's emotions would be considered sheer silliness to the crowds who never dedicate themselves to anything other than selfish, mundane pursuits and are content to remain untouched. They'd never understand. A few people could—a few privileged ones. A wildlife biologist watching the last remaining sandhill crane fly away would understand.

The low, dreary gray clouds raced across the tarmac, pushed by the chilled winter winds. They turned up their collars—the small band of pilots, navigators, and mechanics who were there. There was no music, no press, no speeches, no fanfare. Just the wind and the Phantoms starting up the big J-79 engines. There wouldn't even be a four-ship flyby; the weather was too low for that. First a flight of two taxied out and roared away to the west. Then another single ship left, departing to the east. And finally the last lone Phantom started up and taxied to runway one nine.

He watched as it powered up and lit the burners, accelerating away from them, growing smaller, two slender plumes of amber-blue light under the tail from which the earthshaking thunder emitted. Then for a few brief seconds he could see the top profile as the long nose rotated off the runway. For the last time he saw the peculiar jointed wings, angled upward at the outer sections; the ludicrous downward angles of the tail surfaces; the dull gray paint; growing smaller, then

abruptly being swallowed by the grayness. The roar lingered behind like a great invisible tail, leaving the airfield and the wooded countryside, for the last time, awash with its rolling, fading thunder. He stood there a long time looking in the direction of the dying roar. Before it faded completely, it became intermittent, reflected and absorbed by ragged cloud thickets, then it was gone. Only the wind sounded, and it was a bit colder. And as Maxie walked away, nursing the cantaloupe, he realized that the uncelebrated departure was strangely appropriate—just the way he and his band of brothers would have wanted it.

I sink back into the seat and wonder about Maxie—a fighter pilot to the core, cast headlong into the world of the "heavies." Had the aircraft change not come about, his old unit might have been thrown into the fray with Iraq. He's got to be thinking about that. And what must he think of us? I would like to go downrange with him. He needs to be broken in by another ex-fighter driver turned trash hauler. But he has eleven weeks of training to go through first, and God willing, this will be over by then.

Our flying time cumulatives are high, and so we may be able to talk the stage manager at McGuire into sending us home to "burn down." In case that doesn't work, as likely it won't, we are preparing a scheme. In a little while we will establish contact with our own command post back in Jackson and ask the controllers there to bring their influence to bear on McGuire. Sometimes that works even though they are subordinate to McGuire. It depends on how busy our maintenance section is and who is working the command post console at the time.

As we settle in for the oceanic crossing, one of the many radio transmissions from other pilots catches our attention. The voice comes clear through our radio receiver. But something is amiss. I know after the first five words what's happening and look around at the grinning faces of my crew. They've picked up on it as well. The voice is clear, calm, and thoroughly reassuring.

"Good morning, ladies and gentlemen, this is the captain. Welcome aboard flight 1623 to New York's Kennedy Airport. It's a real pleasure having you with us today. Please note that I have turned off the fasten seat belt sign, so go ahead and take a stretch if you feel the need."

It's a speech I've made in similar fashion many times before. But I've never been able to do it as smoothly as this guy. He's been around a while, that's for certain.

"I strongly suggest, however, that you keep your seat belts securely fastened when you are seated in case we encounter any unexpected rough air."

He knows the territory. Most companies advise against using the "T" word. That sounds too technical and scary. "Rough air" is better understood but is an understatement. Turbulence can, and has been, so sudden, unexpected, and violent as to nail people against the ceiling of the plane. Necks and backs have been broken. But the marketing departments say that passengers would rather not hear of such unpleasantness.

I really admire the captain's style; he's very articulate. His voice is deep and soothing. He could narrate a National Geographic broadcast. Too bad the speech is going to waste.

"We'll be flying at an altitude of 33,000 feet today. Our en route time is seven hours and forty-one minutes. We should be touching down at Kennedy at 12:15 P.M. local time."

The poor guy still hasn't realized that he's flipped the wrong switch. He is not on his plane's passenger address system; he is, of course, broadcasting on the air traffic control frequency, which happens to be Scottish Control. We and dozens of other planes are hearing the eloquent address and in fact cannot do business until he finishes. This blocking of the frequency is potentially dangerous, but it would be rare that harm could result from it, especially on a high-altitude frequency such as the one that we're on. He thinks he has a captive audience, and he does: for two hundred miles in all directions.

"Kennedy is currently foggy, but it should have burned off by our arrival time. We can expect partly cloudy skies, a slight breeze from the northwest and an unseasonably pleasant temperature of around sixty five degrees."

His error is not uncommon. The communications panel on most large airplanes is a thick forest of switches and knobs, crowded together and easily confused by a pilot who may have recently changed over from another type of aircraft. Grabbing the wrong switch isn't catastrophic, but it can be humbling. Sooner or later, everyone screws up with the radio and broadcasts on the wrong frequency or, like the captain, goes "out" instead of "in" with his message.

"The weather across the Atlantic should be fairly good today. We're presently over Glasgow, Scotland. Our route from here will take us just south of Iceland and Greenland, across Newfoundland and the Gulf of Saint Lawrence, and down through New England into New York. If the weather cooperates we should get a nice view of the Canadian coastline."

He's really dragging the speech out. It's one of the longest I've heard. He's obviously a people-oriented captain, one who enjoys talking to and interfacing with his passengers. He's the type who stands in the cockpit door and greets them as they disembark. He probably wears a vest beneath his uniform jacket and takes the flight attendants out to dinner occasionally. He's the kind who sends cards back to the first class passengers with a personal greeting. Airline executives like pilots such as he.

He's beginning to wrap it up now. I know what's coming next. Along with every other pilot on the frequency, I start thinking up a wisecrack.

"Relax now, and enjoy your flight. We want it to be as enjoyable and as comfortable as possible. And please, don't hesitate to ask if you have any questions about our flight or if you need anything at all."

He's finally finished. Now the inevitable cracks begin to pour in from civil and military pilots alike, all across the sky.

"Thank you for sharing that with us."

"Can I have a pillow, captain?"

"I need another glass of wine, please."

"Captain, can you warm up the cabin? I'm too cold."

"When did you say we'll be landing?"

The comebacks go on unmercifully for almost as long as the speech lasted.

"I need a blanket, please."

"This chicken is undercooked."

"What city is that over there, captain?"

"I want to go back."

Finally, the clowning is over, and after a few seconds of silence, the same calm, articulate, reassuring voice returns undaunted to the air, sounding as if we were all sitting in a pilot lounge sipping coffee, having known each other for years. "Let him who is without sin cast the first stone."

I think I'd fly with this guy anywhere, anytime.

I stare ahead through the windscreen, chuckling over the captain's blunder. We are sandwiched between two thin layers of cirrus cloud, catching glimpses of blue stratosphere through holes and gaps in the speeding vapors. It reminds me of that astronaut in *2001: A Space Odyssey* when he cruises through endless corridors of light patterns and color. My imagination runs rampant. I'm a being trapped within a being. The jet's windscreens are its eyes, I its soul. I look out and see the world but I'm detached from it. I'm at a console on another planet, controlling this giant probe remotely. When I'm up here, it's easy to—

An orange flashing light catches my attention. Joe Brewer sees it too, and he straightens up as well. It's the master caution light on the forward panel telling us something is amiss. Even as Joe resets the light to cancel it and make it ready for another alert, instinctively, our eyes flash down to the center console quarter panel where one of a bank of sixty lights tells us there is a malfunction in the inertial navigation systems.

The amber warning light flashes its message:

INS 25 DIFF

We know that it means the INS units are in disagreement. They are twenty-five miles apart in their determination of exactly where our present position is. This is critical, because a twenty-five-mile offset could put us halfway into a neighboring track, and as time passes, the condition will doubtless worsen, sending us farther off course. We could easily cross into the flight path of other aircraft flying parallel tracks with us.

In all probability, only one of the units is in gross error, but we don't know which is lying to us and which isn't. If we were committed to high seas navigation, we would have to choose between following one of the two and trying to split the difference and fly a course between the two. We determine that number two is the culprit because it shows

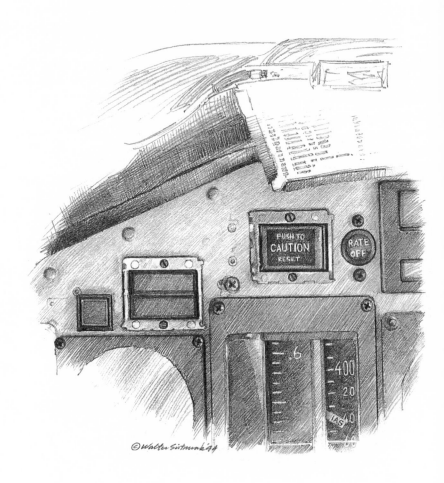

©Walter Sitmunk 94

an excessive ground speed readout. But we can't go on with just one operative unit while we're still in radar contact. So we turn back and request clearance to divert to Mildenhall Air Base in England.

The master caution light spells trouble. It always means inconvenience at best and calamity at worst. But all military and airline pilots live with it. The light is always located up high on the panel where it will catch your eye when it flashes and jolt you out of whatever form of complacency or concentration you're feeling.

Years ago I was pulling off a low-angle dive-bomb delivery when the light came on. I had released a bomb and was pulling four or five Gs, and as the nose came up through the horizon, I noticed it.

MASTER CAUTION

My eyes fell to the annunciator panel and my lungs seized at the sight of the flashing amber warning light.

WING FOLD
WING FOLD
WING FOLD

The locking mechanism on the wing fold hinges was unlocked. The A-7, being originally designed to fly off the Navy's big boats, had a folding wing feature, so that many of the jets could be crammed together.

If the wings folded in flight, what would happen? My mind raced. Would I continue to have control? I thought I remembered that the ailerons operated normally with the wings folded. But would the fixed part of the wings generate enough lift to keep me airborne? And if it did, wouldn't the ailerons now act as additional rudders? How would that affect roll control? And what if only one wing folded? I would corkscrew like a cheap bottle rocket. How would I eject from that at this low altitude? I was only 2,000 feet above the ground.

It took about a nanosecond to interview myself with all those questions, after which I rolled into a right climbing turn and told Lead that I was heading for the emergency strip. I warned the jets to the north, on Guard frequency, to stay high while I flew across two active gunnery ranges in a nervous beeline to the Gila Bend auxiliary field.

The wings never folded. The mechanics found a faulty warning circuit. The master caution light had toyed with me. The jet had winked its eye at me in a practical joke of some morbid sort.

"Got your attention, didn't I, big boy?"

Yeah, that's what it does best—gets your attention. Sometimes I feel like I've got a master caution light inside me. When it flashes, I ought to be looking down deep inside and checking my fault panel. But too often, I don't do that; I just reset it and plow on.

And that's what we're doing—plowing on. On through the post–Desert Storm skies. But the rumors are running like the wind again. Joe Brewer thinks this will be our last trip. I'm not so optimistic.

EIGHTEEN

IN LINDBERGH'S PROP WASH

You fly by the sky on a black night, and on such a night only the sky matters. Sometime near the end of twilight, without realizing when it happens, you find the heavens have drawn your attention subtly from earth, and that instead of glancing from compass down toward ground or sea, your eyes turn upward to the stars.

Charles Lindbergh,
Spirit of St. Louis

Y ou have to cross this vast stretch of frothing nothingness to comprehend what he did. And you can't really grasp it while sitting back in seat 44D on United 913, eating lasagna and watching movies. You have to be up here—in the cockpit.

I don't try to understand why he did it. I know that. What intrigues me is how Lindbergh felt about it. The nearness of death wouldn't bother me so much. But the totality of the loneliness—I don't know how I'd deal with that. At least I've got radios—six of them—to talk with distant voices. And there's the reassurance that there are many other aircraft out here, piloted by people facing the same immense emptiness. And I've got Findley.

Findley is one of my two flight engineers. I look back and see him, sitting sideways to the airplane, in front of his colonies of switches, lights, and dials, their glow reflected in his spectacles. His panel is so enormous and complicated that the very sight of it confounds me.

Technical Sergeant Bill Findley

Findley is an admitted jabberer. He talks constantly to whoever will listen. I guess it's his way of diffusing stress and fending off boredom. Even now he blabs incessantly into his boom mike as he scans his jumbled haunt.

"I just don't know how a man is supposed to make a living farming, these days. The middlemen are taking all the money. I put in eighty acres of beans last year and . . ."

Because of the relative vastness of our cockpit and the noise created by the slipstream, we communicate with one another by headset. With a "boom mike" fixed an inch in front of my lips I can speak with anyone on the crew, fore or aft, in a normal tone of voice. In an electronic sense his ear is only an inch from my lips, and mine likewise from his. But such conversations go largely without eye contact. I have to careen about to see eye to eye with anyone except for the copilot with whom I'm talking or listening. This I do when there's urgency or when I want to emphasize a point. Or when humor is at work.

Normally we push a button to talk and release it to listen, just as we do with the radio. It makes laughing at a joke an awkward thing. You feel like a fool, pushing the talk switch just to laugh, but you don't want to embarrass the humorist with silence. So there's a certain subtle protocol we use to normalize the strange ways that we communicate on the interphone system.

"Hot mike" is the preferred way. We simply pull up two buttons, which makes our boom mikes "hot," or continually open to interphone conversations without our having to press the talk switch. The pilots very rarely use the hot mike because it picks up noises such as breathing on the mikes and the hissing of the slipstream. And the casual conversations between the engineers, who always use it, distract from the task of listening to the radios.

A favorite ploy of mine is to pull up the hot mike "listen" button so that I can eavesdrop on the engineers. Mostly I hear them talking at length about some little problem or curiosity with which the jet has presented them. Sometimes a senior engineer will be lecturing to a newer guy on the finer points of the trade. But occasionally I catch a little gossip.

And they have their own little capers to keep their conversations private. The extra engineer may stand up for a stretch and take a quick gander at the pilots' interphone panels to make sure the hot mike buttons are down. Others, such as the one we call Catfish, are more cunning. While I was once eavesdropping on him, he paused and tested me by asking me when we expected to land. The question was posed on hot mike rather than on interphone. I knew it was a trick because I had my hot mike volume turned lower than the interphone volume. When I ignored the question, he assumed he had privacy and proceeded to discuss some particular shortcomings of another pilot, who happened to be a friend of mine. I listened for a while, then interrupted and chastised him for gossiping and defended my buddy.

But tonight I'm on hot mike with Findley. I hold up my end of the perpetual one-sided conversation by nodding once in a while, grunting now and then, and occasionally posing a question or comment. I depend greatly on Findley's knowledge of the Starlifter's internal workings. He's the jet's doctor, its trainer, its groomer. He's its occasional healer and wizard. He rebukes the jet when it falters and praises it when it performs to his expectations. His is a labor of love, but like most flight engineers, he would never admit it.

The Starlizzard has a complicated nervous system, over which Findley meticulously watches. He sees that ample power from our four engine-driven generators—enough to light the town of Gunnison near his farm—is satisfying the demand of our lights and electronic packages.

He monitors its cardiovascular system as well. The jet has three hearts that pump the blood of hydraulic fluid through hundreds of feet of tangled metal arteries at a pressure of 3,000 pounds per square inch. This pressure drives actuators that provide the raw power to move our flight control surfaces against a wind force of several hurricanes.

He closely watches the jet's respiratory system, which features extremely hot, high-pressured air piped from the compressor stage of the engines and fed through ducts to the air conditioning and pressurization systems.

He's also the jet's nutritionist. The four gluttonous engines drink the putrid fluid stored in our tanks at the rate of a gallon every two seconds. Periodically I hear the clicking sound of Findley orchestrating his clusters of cross-feed valves and boost pump switches—twenty-seven of them—to ensure that the ten wing tanks drain symmetrically and in a specific sequence. I haven't the slightest idea how to do this and depend on him totally. The fuel is heavy; there is seventy tons of it, and the flow sequence is necessary to preserve the wing's balance and structural integrity.

These planes have far exceeded the manufacturer's recommended useful lifespan. Cracks in the shoulders of the wings began to show up several years ago and caused severe restrictions to be placed on some jets. Attempts were made to mend the cracks, but new wings were out of the question. The government had decided not to pay for the storage of the jigs and tooling after production ceased, so the manufacturer just threw them away. Later, we would scoff at General Johnson's response to a congressional committee convened to review the lessons of Desert Storm. When asked about the wing cracks, he replied, "Yes, sir, we took a few chances."

Imagine that. We—*we* took a few chances. Pardon me, but how many times did *you* go downrange in a C-141, General? No, sir. It is Findley and I who take the chances; we and the others of the Cracked Wing Roulette Society.

The watchful Findley continues his prattle: "We tried catfish farming one year but . . ."

We are over Newfoundland. It was here that Lindbergh watched the night settle in over the island's uplands: "Each crevice fills with shades of gray, as though twilight had sent its scouts ahead to keep contact with a beaten sun. The empire of the night is expanding over earth and sea."

I watch the lights sparkle into life along the seacoast and listen to Moncton Center as they issue a routine traffic advisory to a British Airways jet concerning us.

"Speedbird two niner eight, Moncton, you have traffic your one o'clock, ten miles, opposite direction at flight level three three zero, a C-141."

"Roger, Moncton, Speedbird has the traffic in sight. Is he going to the Gulf?"

Moncton Center knows our destination tonight is Germany, but they have no way of knowing our ultimate destination. I hesitate for a second, trying to remember if our itinerary is classified. I don't know. I press the transmit button.

"Roger, sir, we'll end up there eventually."

"Then God be with you."

I appreciate his good wishes but hope we won't need the Lord as badly as he insinuated.

It has been three hours since we departed McGuire for Germany, but we are still over land. I've done this before when passengers have come up asking if that was Ireland down there. I get a kick out of telling them that we haven't even started across the Atlantic yet. Many people simply don't realize that the direct route to northern Europe from the United States is northeastward, up through Canada, which stretches for hundreds of miles toward Europe.

Now it's time for our familiar battle over our clearance with Gander Oceanic Control. Up ahead, as we leave Newfoundland, Gander will funnel us into one of the five tracks leading across to Europe. The tracks, known as the North Atlantic Track System, or NATS, parallel each other sixty miles apart and are redefined each day to take advantage of the high-altitude winds and pressure patterns. The eastbound tracks, labeled "V" through "Z," are active at night and expire at dawn. Then westbound tracks "A" through "E" are activated. Aircraft are fed into the NATS at certain intervals and altitudes. Because air traffic control radar cannot currently reach out more than a couple of hundred miles across the ocean, planes must be separated by lengthy intervals. They must also report their positions by high-frequency, or HF, long-range radio every ten degrees of longitude.

I suspect that Gander doesn't look forward to seeing us coming. We are sixty miles per hour slower than most commercial air traffic, and so the control center must leave a wide gap behind us before allowing one of the faster jets in, or else we will be overrun. This requirement of course makes traffic control harder.

Thus the controllers like to get us out of the way by assigning us an altitude too high for our heavy weight or too low for proper engine efficiency, which would eat into our reserve fuel. Neither is acceptable. The clearance delivery frequency can sometimes sound like haggling over a used car. They make an offer. We refuse. They counter. We compromise. In a while we have an altitude and route that suits us. But others of our kind have had to turn back or divert elsewhere for extra fuel because the clearance was unacceptable.

Tonight Gander has cleared us into track Whiskey at our present altitude of 33,000 feet. But we have agreed to climb to 35,000 feet at forty degrees west longitude, by which time, Findley tells me, we will have burned off enough fuel weight to climb. This will keep Gander happy by allowing faster traffic behind us to overtake and pass underneath us.

We now make final accuracy checks on our two inertial navigation systems before leaving the security of the land-based navigation stations. The INS is a cluster of very sophisticated gyroscopes that remember the point from which they departed and sense direction of movement and acceleration. It feeds the data into a computer, which translates to us carbon-based units such niceties as where we are, how fast we're going, and our estimated arrival times at any point along our route. Human navigators used to do this work. But no more, not on these airplanes. Now the nav seat is only a temporary berth to a dozing loadmaster or an inquisitive passenger.

We pass over St. Johns, Newfoundland, which Lindbergh called the doorway to the Atlantic, and commit ourselves to the oceanic emptiness. Soon we are out of range of radar and normal radio contact and have to rely on the abhorrent HF radio.

Similar to that used by HAM operators, the HF is an extremely long-range radio that achieves its distance by bouncing its signals off an ionized layer of thin air in the upper atmosphere, a feat that our normal land-based, or VHF, radio cannot do. But the HF is painful to listen to. It is filled with shrieking, hissing, squealing, scratching background noises. Through this preposterous soup of racket come staccatolike, half-human Donald Duckish voices from thousands of miles away. Moreover, the HF can be totally unusable during periods of peak solar activity. We hate it with an untold passion and take turns monitoring it.

There is a certain band of HF frequencies that can best be described as "jungle" noises. I once made this observation to a copilot who then related George Fondren's brilliant theory about the origin of the mysterious sounds. It seems that George counsels his younger copilots that the noises are precisely that—jungle sounds: crickets, grasshoppers, frogs, birds, and other chirping and singing creatures. He theorizes that many planes crashed in World War II on deserted jungle islands. And that their radios, with jammed transmit switches, are still operating, picking up the songs of the jungle, and transmitting them worldwide. Fueled by the perpetual power of acids derived from rotting jungle juices, their batteries are constantly being recharged with fresh ions. The theory reeks with a scatological influence of a bovine nature, but I heard that one lieutenant listened with a great deal of attentiveness.

We can relax a little now. Until we coast in at Ireland, we will mostly just monitor the Starlifter's autopilot and navigation devices. Findley is resting now, and Lynn, the carpenter by civil trade, has taken over the engineer's panel. Findley doesn't just lie down on the bunk for a casual nap. He goes to bed. He strips to his shorts and T-shirt, arranges pillows and covers, and settles in for a serious sleep. I should try that.

On a previous flight, shortly after Findley had turned in, we were directed to descend temporarily to a lower altitude, which is a bit unusual. The silencing of the engine noise and the premature descent brought him to the flight deck to investigate. Turning, I saw him standing there in shorts and socks, with the multicolored cockpit lights reflecting in his glasses as he swung his head here and there, searching for trouble.

I thought I'd solicit a little chuckle to break the monotony and shouted back that we had lost an engine and were diverting to Mildenhall Air Base for an emergency landing. I thought that was the end of it, but a few minutes later he reappeared on the flight deck fully dressed. Then he noticed that all engines were running happily. He didn't appreciate the humor but was too much of a gentleman to call me what I deserved to be called.

I guess he gave up sleeping; he sat on the aft bench seat and reached for his box lunch, which I had previously tampered with: I had removed the sandwiches and replaced them with navigation booklets. This was another in a chain of pranks that started before takeoff. He had proudly showed me his new flashlight and boasted profusely of its power and reliability, prompting me covertly to remove the bulb before he began his walk-around inspection in the darkness. We all claimed innocence when he came back aboard, unsmiling, for another bulb. But he knew I was the culprit.

The missing sandwiches tripped Findley's breaker. Still respectfully avoiding indicting his degenerate boss, he unleashed an awesome wrath. "I wish you guys would stop pickin' on me."

I did feel a little bad about it and hoped it wouldn't drive a wedge between us. But a few hours later Findley was back at the engineer's panel, jabbering away at me about federal farm subsidies, and I knew that all was again well.

It was about here, a couple of hundred miles past St. Johns, that Lindbergh wrote: "Here, all around me is the Atlantic—its expanse, its depth, its power, its wild and open water. Is there something unique about this ocean that gives it character above all other seas, or is this my imagination?"

No sir, it's not your imagination. You have never flown over other oceans, as I have. Yes, this one is unique. Many other seas are as cold and gray. Many others are littered with ice and blowing foam. But this one is different because it sits like a restless sentinel between two vastly populated and closely related continents. Its bottom is strewn with the wrecks of storm and war. This ocean doesn't beckon warm and friendly to overfliers as does the Pacific. This one dares you—and bides its time.

Listening to the static and the incessant transmissions of other pilots, I wait my turn and seize the instant as soon as a pause presents itself.

"Gander, Gander, MAC Victor 3512, position."

"MAC Victor 3512, Gander, go ahead."

I speak more clearly and carefully on the HF than I normally do because of the great potential for misunderstanding.

"MAC Victor 3512 checked five zero north, four zero west at zero zero three five. Flight level three three zero. Estimate five two north three zero west at zero one two eight. Five three north, two zero west next. Over."

Gander acknowledges my position report, and as soon as he finishes, a TWA pilot calls for Gander's attention but is inadvertently blocked by an Air Canada pilot. Gander advises Air Canada to stand by, and directs the TWA pilot to proceed while light years in the electronic distance I hear another MAC flight, operating farther south, pleading for a higher altitude from Santa Maria Center.

Such is the business of the HF airways. I relax, glad that the position report went off easily. Sometimes we try for fifteen minutes to get a word in. Happily, the next report is almost an hour away.

The HF is filled with more static than usual tonight, and I think I see why. I dim the instrument lights just a little more and look to the north. At first I see only a long faint brightness stretching along the horizon. But as my eyes adjust I can pick out the subtle colors and geometric patterns of the aurora borealis, the northern lights. The lights seem to hang from the starry heavens in swirling, cascading curtains with bluish green and purple tints.

I look away and then back in a minute, and the patterns have changed shape and tint. I revere the lights. I know that the physicists explain that they are generated by solar energy reacting with atmospheric particles, as it is funneled into the polar magnetic convergence. But they are a majestic display of divine power to me, much too choreographed and beautiful to be simply a freak of nature.

This same northern horizon, so gracefully adorned with aurora in winter, is the domain of the sun in summer. When the north pole is tilted toward the sun, we watch a different production on this grand stage.

In the summer months as we fly east across the north Atlantic, the sun will set behind our left wing. But it doesn't fall vertically; it angles toward the north and disappears like a brilliant submarine diving as it plows ahead. It submerges to a shallow depth, voyaging beyond the North Pole only slightly below the horizon, its cosmic glow hovering above it, holding back the night. And because we fly in the same direction as the turning earth, the sun hurries its journey as if to beat us to Europe and flaunt its victory by casting searing rays into our night-weary eyes. In a few hours it emerges to our left in a dazzling rebirth and climbs across our nose toward its commanding perch.

But this is a spring night, here in the polar latitudes. The sun is deeply buried in the Southern Hemisphere, opposite the planet. Yet our night sky is alive with vitality. The aurora is being upstaged by a newcomer.

A spike of orange light pierces the darkness ahead. With a suddenness far greater than you'd expect of any celestial event, the slender, sharply pointed spire, rises boldly out of the sea and dominates the night. My young copilot, searching his mind desperately for an explanation but becoming impatient with himself, begins to fidget. He turns to me and asks haltingly, "Wha——?" He pauses, looks back, and gestures at it and continues, "What is it?"

In another minute the answer to the question asked with a child-like innocence would become apparent. But I've seen it before and remember that I had the same inadequate feeling.

"It's a moonrise, Steve. Looks to be about a quarter moon. Really pops up there, doesn't it?"

It rises swiftly and hangs in front of us, sheds its orange glow and grows white hot as it climbs from the distorted atmosphere. We are flying directly toward it; it's centered in the windscreen as if it were our target. I've never outgrown my childhood imagination and make no apologies for it. For a minute I forget about the earth and the atmosphere. I'm voyaging through the cosmos in a great starship, and the lunar destination looms ahead—more evidence for George's allegation that I'm an oblivious dreamer. If so, I'm in good company; Lindbergh too felt it: "At times you renounce experience and the mind's heavy logic, it seems that the world has rushed along on its orbit, leaving you alone, flying above a forgotten cloud bank, somewhere in the solitude of interstellar space."

Soon the moon's brilliance drives away the aurora and the dimmer stars and commands our absolute attention. I can see details beginning to break out of the side shadowed from the sun—mountains and clusters of craters. The dark side of the moon is being bathed in the soft light reflected from Antarctica.

The moon is a trusted companion to the night flier. It gives substance to the unseen world beyond the windscreens. It draws his mind out of the confines of his metal cocoon and nourishes his awareness. Without it, blackness encroaches on the windows and isolates the mind. One night long ago when I needed the moon, it wasn't there.

I had taken off in my Yankee from a dark country airport, John Bell Williams Field down near Raymond, with my two-year-old son aboard. There was nothing but forest and pasture around the airfield.

It was a "black hole," as fliers like to say. Shortly after we broke ground, a violent, flapping noise of metal beating against metal erupted near the engine, and the little plane began to vibrate. Shaken, I grabbed the flashlight, shined it forward, and saw that the engine cowling had broken loose and was flapping in the slipstream. But I was reassured by the arc of the propeller in the beam of the flashlight and by the steady rpms on the tachometer. I held the light on the cowling for a few seconds, as the Yankee bored through the night, and pondered whether to turn back to the field or continue to the larger Hawkins Field, a few miles away, which was my destination.

Then I glanced at the vertical velocity indicator. The needle was indicating a 500-feet-per-minute rate of descent. Another quick glance at the altimeter showed our altitude was 500 feet. I remembered that the airfield elevation was 330 feet, and the trees must be 50 to 100 feet high. Instead of being a pilot, I had become a passenger. I had violated the cardinal rule: fly the plane first, then—and only then—work on the problem.

Instinctively, I pulled the yoke back and reversed the terminal dive into a redeeming climb. Scott and I would have become statistics in another few seconds. I learned a valuable lesson that night. But I wish my old companion the moon had been there. If the countryside had been awash with its soft light, maybe I would have been more aware.

My fixation on the moon is suddenly broken by a familiar voice coming through on the HF. Buster Swinney, one of our squadron's aircraft commanders, is giving a position report. Checking the chart, I determine that Buster is within UHF radio range of us. I switch my transmit selector to UHF radio number one, which is tuned to Channel 10, and transmit into the vast oceanic sky.

"Buster, you up on button ten?"

"You bet. Who's this?"

We exchange the usual questions. Where are they headed? From where did we depart? How long have we been out? Who's on your crew? The last question reveals that one of his loadmasters is Duane Hall, a senior master sergeant with about thirty-five years' service. He had a good job in the business world and was thinking of retiring. But then the balloon went up, and now it was too late. He could have retired years ago, but something kept him clinging to the Guard.

Duane's offspring is sitting back in my cargo bay. The Guard is like that, often literally family and not just figuratively. Mike is a clone of his dad. Both are red-skinned, thin-haired, and sometimes boisterous but always jovial and good company. They love to work hard and play hard and are always eager to rap about the things and ideas that keep them going. They're the epitome of southern friendliness.

Mike can't hear the radio transmissions from his station in the cargo bay, but he is hooked into the plane's interphone system with his headset. Hearing those of us on the flight deck banter about the contact with Buster, he shouts into the interphone. "Hey, that's my daddy's crew!"

In an instant Mike is on the flight deck, plugging his headset into a communications station. Within a couple of minutes he is talking with his dad. The conversation is low key and clipped, about family news and such. Mrs. Hall, Mike's mom, isn't taking this well—husband and son both flying under wartime conditions day and night. Too much is at stake for her.

"How's momma?" Mike asks into the radio.

"She's OK," comes the answer. But Mike knows better.

Then, by the moon's brilliance, we spot their jet below and to the left, at the point of a great silver contrail, racing opposite our direction. They are flying a "random route," beneath the NATS. Mike is glued to the side window behind my seat. There is a long pause in the radio conversation while father and son watch one another's craft pass. Then the oceanic night seems lonelier. Being short on words was never a problem with this family, but in the silence I can sense the lump in Mike's throat. I feel it with him.

Maybe it's how Lindbergh felt when St. Johns fell away behind him.

A flicker catches my eye. It originated almost straight ahead, maybe a few degrees left. Straining my eyes, I can make out the silhouette of billowing cloud formations far ahead, their edges painted a soft blue by delicate strokes of moonbeam. There it is again. They light up with a momentary orange glow. The cloud must be home to some colossal giant who just struck a match to light his cigar. Early spring thunderstorms are rare out here, but they can have teeth in them, just as the forecaster back at McGuire cautioned. I tweak the gain knob on the radar and the churning, fiery cells begin to break out on the scope 125 miles ahead, a line of them lying across our course. I recall the forecaster assuring me that the tops would be below our flight level. So maybe we'll be lucky and fly over the chorus line of fire-breathing monsters—thumbing our radome at them as we sail over.

If we have to, we can use the radar to weave our way through gaps between the stronger cells, but if we get any closer than about twenty miles, we could suffer severe turbulence and lightning strikes. Such a development could play the devil with our cracked wings. The result might easily be five wives veiled in black, flanked by sobbing children, which is the most effective vision when it comes to deterring me from doing stupid things.

I cut it a little close once, on a beautiful afternoon over Louisiana. A lone thunderstorm sat dead center on our flight path. It was a beautiful thing, towering upward thousands of feet above us, with almost vertical walls. The air around it was smooth and clear. Far below we could see the base of the storm flaring out near the ground in a sinister blackness. We set the twenty-mile cursor on the radar scope and turned so that the storm would just graze the edge of the yellow cursor. As we passed abeam it, exchanging small talk about how majestic it appeared, it reached for us.

A wicked, gnarled arm of white heat appeared with the suddenness of light speed. It seemed against all logic to be reaching horizontally from the cloud, trying to grab us. It was only there for a millisecond, but its image burned into my retina. I can still see it now, seeming to stretch and strain like a kid on a tree not quite able to reach the rope swing. Maybe, like the kid, it was at play—just wanted to scare us; to give us a playful warning to stay away. It succeeded. The wings of a C-141 never rolled as quickly as they did that day out east of Shreveport.

But the McGuire forecaster was right. It appears we will pass over the squall line, but we are beginning to enter some upper cloud layers. Suddenly the ride turns rough as we encounter some light chop. Lynn remarks that I must have turned off on a dirt road. I reach up and turn on the continuous ignition system, which provides constant electrical spark to the engines' combustion chambers. This will help keep the fires lit if turbulence threatens a flameout. As I reach for the switch, I see that another act has opened in the night's light and energy drama.

A yellow glow is developing on the lower portion of the windscreen. I've seen this phenomenon, called Saint Elmo's fire, several times before. When atmospheric particles, ionized by storm activity, contact an aircraft, something like minilightning develops on or near the plane's surfaces. It's pretty rare; conditions have to be just right for it. Saint Elmo is harmless enough, but the first sight of one of the more intensive displays can be heart stopping.

One night out east of Las Vegas in a Boeing 727, we were descending through a stormy area, weaving this way and that to avoid the intense centers of the cluster of storms. Sheets of rain assaulted us, and lightning flashed left and right, but the air was relatively smooth. Then the glow of Saint Elmo attached itself to our nose. We could clearly see it widening and flaring back as it crept over our windscreens, as if being washed back by the rain and wind. The color seemed to change from green to yellow. Then the strobes came.

Long, bony, stringy, gnarling, fingers of miniature bluish white lightning crept up over our windscreens, disappearing and returning, quivering and jumping as if searching for a handhold but finding the windscreen too smooth, too hot. They wanted in—wanted to find a crack, an opening through which to slither in and sting us; to grab us by the throat; to warn us that we're not supposed to be here; that we'd best leave these parts before the Big Guy finds out. Then the knock came on the flight deck door.

It was a flight attendant wanting to gather our dinner trays so as to stow them before landing. I unlatched the door, and the cockpit was flooded with soft cabin light as she entered. As she reached for the trays I asked her to close the door and look toward the windscreens. In a moment, after her eyes adjusted to the darkness, her face became flushed with fear at the sight of the wicked fingers. But then she judged the sight to be nonthreatening, relaxed, and asked it if that was Saint Elmo's fire. After she left the cockpit the Big Guy came.

A pulsating ball of electricity, or so it appeared, formed in front of our nose, stood there a second and then seemed to rush in like a photon torpedo coming at us from a Klingon cruiser. As it hit, the explosion was sharp and deafening, like an unexpected thunderclap. The jet shuddered and lights flickered, but the generators held on. Stunned, I began to scan the panel for evidence of missing engines and gaping holes, but all was normal. Then the second one hit, but again no damage was done except to our frayed and quivering nerves. As was expected of me, I steadied my voice, swallowed hard, keyed the public address, and explained the static discharges to the passengers, a paragon of confidence and reassurance.

We emerge from the clouds to find a feeble glow of sun ahead. I tilt the radar antenna down and see on the scope the green outline of the Irish coast 100 miles ahead. The sun's brilliance is about to tear into our very souls and torture what little is left of our consciousness. At this point Lindbergh still had eight hours left on his epic journey, yet already we feel the nearness of a bed and a blissful sleep. But the challenge of the crowded European airspace lies ahead, with its attendant rotten weather to boot.

Steve Clark, my copilot, gets a weather update and hands it across. His handwriting has all the characteristics one would expect of a man who has totally lost hope that someone would ever read his scribbling. I look hard, trying to make out the note. It says—no, not so. There's some mistake. If one could make out this chicken-scratching gibberish, it would appear that the weather at the destination is: EDAF 0956 X M 1OVC 1/4R-F 46/46 0000 29.86 R25LRVR1200. I ask him for a clarification and, with an anticipatory smirk, he confirms the vile news. I hand the note back to Findley and Lynn so that they can begin their landing performance calculations.

It appears that we will earn our pay in the final few minutes of this trip. The weather at Frankfurt's Rhein Main airport is well below the normal minimums of 200-feet ceiling and half-mile visibility. The ceiling at Frankfurt this spring morning is obscured by fog. The runway visibility is only 1,200 feet. We will have to fly a rare Category II approach.

We immediately initiate a test of the All Weather Landing System. The AWLS uses the same basic instrumentation we normally use for a precision instrument approach, but it increases the sensitivity of the receivers so as to allow us to go lower while still blinded by cloud. But there is not much room for error. If we don't see the runway when we reach 100 feet above the ground, or if we see it and are not aligned sufficiently to land, we will have to execute a missed approach. Thus the chances are increased that we will not be able to land and will have to divert to an alternate.

Steve's notes also reveal that the weather at Mildenhall Air Base in England is a bit better, confirming that we will have a place to which we can escape. We planned for this eventuality before leaving the states—as we always do—but still, we decide to run through some quick calculations. We all agree that we should have enough fuel to make one approach at Frankfurt and then hightail it to England. But when we get there we will not have much left.

We set our airspeed and altitude markers at the appropriate values, buckle our shoulder harnesses, and run the descent checklist. Passing over Dover we are ordered to begin our descent. On the way down, we review the special procedures of the CAT II approach. Though we practice this a lot, I've only done it once. The others have never seen it. We ensure, that we are all up to speed on what each is to do and say during the critical final minutes and on what our actions will be if certain malfunctions occur.

As we pass through 21,000 feet, the sun suddenly succumbs to the gloom and we plunge into a cheerless abyss of gray. The radio becomes busier as we approach Frankfurt. Our senses heighten as we listen intently to the German controllers for our call sign. The weather has caused an aerial traffic jam. The controllers are barking impatient instructions to a myriad civil and military aircraft. Upon hearing one particular transmission, Steve and I look abruptly at each other.

"What?"

"They're holding at Rudesheim!"

Normally, it was an abomination to get sent to the Rudesheim NDB to hold. The German controllers were strict and demanding. If you hesitated at their commands or gave them any kind of trouble, they sent you there to hold, as punishment. Rudesheim was a penalty box.

Yes, Rudesheim, the quaint little village alongside the Rhine; Rudesheim, where we had sampled the wines and pastries; Rudesheim, where we had often boarded the boat for the scenic Rhine River tour. The name rolled off your lips and tongue as if you were a refined world traveler—a gentleman, a scholar, a master of the German language and culture. Rudesheim was a place of rest and regeneration, but now we would be ordered to hold high above the quiescent village, burning into our reserve, sweating, thinking not of the pleasures below but only nervously awaiting our turn to go "down the chute" to Frankfurt.

Soon, the orders come as expected. We tune in the Rudesheim NDB and proceed direct. Again we calculate. Findley tells me we have a maximum of twenty-five minutes' holding fuel. That should be enough. But if we hold for that amount of time and then miss at Frankfurt, it will put us on the runway at Mildenhall with fumes in the tanks. I decide I will allow no more than fifteen minutes in the holding pattern. If they won't let us down after that, we will break out and head hell-bent to England. Findley appears relieved.

No sooner have we hit the NDB and turned outbound than the fine gentleman at the radar console clears us direct to the Frankfurt VOR. We breathe sighs of relief. Fuel, apparently, will not be a problem for us now. We descend lower. It gets darker. We cross overhead the huge airport, but the swing of our VOR needles is the only evidence that we have done so. Then we are radar-vectored to an intercept heading to the final approach course. We make final preparations. I dial in the localizer course while Steve tunes and identifies the frequency.

I would rather do the CAT II the airline way, letting the copilot fly the approach while I look for the runway. This procedure allows me to make the final decision and then take over the controls for the actual landing. But we will do it the Air Force way. I will take it all the way down, while Steve watches for the ground.

Rolling out on final, we lower the flaps to the approach setting, but here at Frankfurt we must not lower the landing gear until we have passed over the outer marker. Doing so would require more engine power, which would trip the noise sensors planted down there among the suburbs. The Air Force pays the city of Frankfurt a big fine if we trip one, and I get to go to the kick-butt room. Like most noise abatement procedures, this one preempts good safety practice. It complicates our approach by forcing abrupt pitch and airspeed changes later on and lower than we would prefer in such weather.

Soon we hear the tone in our headsets that signifies the passage of the marker, and I order the gear down. It falls into the slipstream with a roar and clunks heavily into place. We set the flaps to the landing position and stabilize our airspeed. As the needle on the radar altimeter steadily unwinds toward zero, I fight to suppress the urge to glance out the windscreen. My eyes zip like a busy hummingbird from one instrument to another. Altitude, descent rate, airspeed, fuel flow, heading, course deflection, glide slope deflection, AWLS fault panel—all are brief stops along the hurried course of my concentration. My eyes move so quickly that if one instrument reads amiss, I may not realize it until I'm one or two more stops along the scan.

"Approaching decision height."

Steve's call alerts me that we are at 200 feet, almost the length of the airplane, above the earth. I steal a glance, but see only murk. Back to the panel.

"LAND!"

This is one of only two things he is permitted to say at this point. The other is "go around."

I look up. We are already well over the runway. I can't even see the edges, only the centerline stripes and the twin rows of lights embedded in the runway, unscrolling toward me from the gloom. Hundreds of black tire marks directly in front of me seem to explode in the windscreen. Where has my depth perception gone? No time to judge height. No time to check and roll. No time, no time. God, I'm tired.

With a jolt we hit. We roll. Steve pulls up the spoiler lever. I pull the throttles into reverse. The little lights embedded in the runway thump underneath our tires as we slow. A crackling voice in our headsets tells us to turn left at the next available turnoff and contact Mil Ramp.

We taxi past the rows of airlifters sitting on the wet ramp under dreary veils of fog and turn into our assigned parking spot. The marshaler crosses his wands, and I break to a stop, flip the fuel shutoff switches, and collapse back into the seat. The crew door down below is shoved open and the spooling down of the engines again floods the flight deck, tranquilizing us. Another Atlantic crossing ends.

Desert Storm is ending as well, to the cheers of thousands, like Lindbergh's arrival in Paris. And rightly so. But I suspect the Persian Gulf airlift will conclude with lethargic sighs and muffled moans, like those coming from my crewmates.

As fliers, we are conditioned to think ahead, but we have learned

lately not to reckon beyond the engine shutdown checklist. God only knows where we'll be headed tomorrow, if anywhere, and He ain't saying just now. So we've stopped guessing about the future. That takes too much energy. But just maybe, as Steve predicts, we are on our last mission.

He could be right. Lately, optimism has started to flourish. Desert Storm was a resounding victory. Celebrations and parades are being planned back home, and the mother of all parties will soon commence.

It has taken the courage and sacrifice of one generation of warriors to exonerate another. Those who fought in Viet Nam deserve a share of the Desert Storm victory. Their legacy, perverted by an inept government and an uncaring populace, has been redeemed and at last laid to rest. This one was for them.

The past year has taught us much about ourselves. We have developed the patience, endurance, and perseverance of blue-water sailors, and the Starlifter has become our square-rigger. We stow the stores, batten the hatches, set the throttles, and run before the wind. We consign our spirits to the song of the slipstream and dwell in the contentment of the moment, waiting, waiting, for that blessed roar of the landing gear to signal our final delivery—our delivery home.

But even now, I sense the pull, the call, the longing. Even while home is yet a distant gleam in the windscreen, I feel it—as I knew I would. I'll be back this way. Back to this skyscape. Back to this sanctuary. Back to gaze at them again, to behold the billowing topgallants. Back to leave trails of glory among them.

EPILOGUE

The 727 slips along with a whisper under the long expanse of burning blue stretching ahead toward the Rockies. There's a knock at the flight deck door, and a pretty lass named Michelle comes up, passes us coffee and soft drinks, and sits down in the forward observer's seat. She crosses her legs and, with a strong sigh, pushes a fallen strand of golden hair back to its place.

"Are the natives restless?" the captain asks with a chuckle.

"Very," she responds. "There's this one guy back there who, like"— she pauses, in the peculiar way of her generation, to relate with mimicry instead of language—"you know, stares at me."

"I can't imagine why," I retort, winking at the captain.

"Oh, he gives me the creeps." She shudders.

She promises to bring up our meals as soon as she takes care of first class, then departs with a cheery smile, making our day complete before it even ends.

This, my first airline trip after the Storm, is replete with contrasts. Michelle is one. She compels me to reflect on guys with names like Wormy, Mad Dog, Killer, and Bucky. Not because they look like her— dear God, no—but because, like her, they're indispensable to the other end of the jet.

The notion keeps hitting me time and again. Was the last year a dream? And if so, was it a good one or a nightmare? It passed so slowly, yet now it seems fleeting. The tribulations we suffered don't seem all that distressing now. I don't regret it. My military flying career began as one war ended, and spanned twenty years to the close of another one. I'll be content to let it end there.

I know I'll miss the camaraderie; there's not much of that in this job. To fly with someone is to share, but to fly and serve with someone is to bond with them.

I'm glad to be back to these "friendly skies." Yet I'll always be glancing backward, always checking six. But for memories, not bandits. And when I do, I'll see not places, nor planes, but faces. More important than flight itself are the faces of flight. And they reside in me in abundance.

GLOSSARY

AC   Aircraft commander.

AFB   Air Force base.

AHARS An emergency backup system for attitude and heading.

AIM-9 Heat-seeking air-to-air missile.

Aircraft commander The pilot responsible for the plane, its crew, and its mission. Same as "captain" in the airlines.

Airlift control element A unit that controls and coordinates airlift operations in a deployed area.

ALCE   Airlift control element.

Alert time The time at which a crew is alerted for a mission, after it has received a legal rest period.

Altimeter The instrument that indicates aircraft altitude, pronounced "al-tim -eter."

AOR   Area of responsibility.

APU   Auxiliary power unit.

Area of responsibility The operational area for which a major commander is responsible. In the Persian Gulf War, Central Command's AOR spread from east Africa to the Indian subcontinent.

AWACS Airborne Warning and Control System.

AWLS All Weather Landing System.

Call sign A name, number, or combination of the two, assigned by higher headquarters, by which aircraft identify themselves via radio. During routine home base training, call signs may be permanent. They vary for operational missions.

CDS Container delivery system.

CINCMAC Commander-in-chief, Military Airlift Command.

Command post A continuously manned facility that controls and coordinates air operations.

Conn The verb form of contrail, i.e., to leave a contrail.

Copilot Pilot qualified for right seat operations only.

CP Command post or Copilot.

CRAF Civil Reserve Air Fleet.

Cursor A marker that can be set to a desired range on the radar scope.

DZ Drop zone.

ETIC Estimated time in commission.

FAA Federal Aviation Administration.

FAR Federal air regulations.

Federal air regulations The rules established by the FAA to which all pilots must adhere.

Federal Aviation Administration The branch of government that regulates and controls flight in the United States.

First pilot Pilot qualified to fly in either the left or right seat but not as aircraft commander.

Flameout The complete loss of thrust in a jet engine.

FP First pilot.

G Symbol for gravitational force. A pilot is "pulling Gs" when he is pushed down into his seat by centrifugal force as a result of a flight path that is circular, either horizontally or vertically, as water is forced to the bottom of a bucket when the bucket is swung overhead.

Glideslope The angle at which an aircraft descends toward a landing on an ILS approach. Usually about 3 degrees.

GMT Greenwich mean time.

G-suit A garment worn on the legs and abdomen by fighter pilots that inflates with air pressure to keep blood from pooling in the lower extremities during high "G" flight.

Guard bum Air Guard crew member who has no regular civilian job and who derives most of his income flying more missions than are required.

Head-up display A transparent screen over the instrument panel in some planes that displays vital information to the pilot as he looks out ahead of the aircraft.

HF High-frequency radio.

High-frequency radio A long range transmitter/receiver used in oceanic operations.

HUD Head-up display.

IFR Instrument flight rules.

ILS Instrument landing system.

Instrument flight rules Rules for flying in low visibility weather. This type of flying is closely monitored by radar or other controlling facilities.

Instrument landing system A system that sends electronic signals up from the runway, allowing pilots to align with the runway and to descend toward it in inclement weather.

Intell Intelligence, the people responsible for gathering and distributing classified information.

Interphone A closed-circuit communication system for crew members aboard an aircraft through the use of headsets equipped with boom microphones.

IP Instructor pilot.

JP-4 Type of jet fuel used by most Air Force aircraft.

KTO Kuwait theater of operations.

LC Lieutenant colonel.

Loadmaster Crew member responsible for passenger safety, supervision of loading and offloading cargo, and computing weight and balance.

Localizer The course that aligns an aircraft with the runway on an ILS approach.

MAC Military Airlift Command.

Mark-82 Commonly used 500-pound general-purpose bomb.

Mic Slang for microphone. (Pronounced "mike.")

Mike mike Slang for millimeter.

Military Airlift Command Formerly the organization responsible for all airlift operations, now called Air Mobility Command.

NATO North Atlantic Treaty Organization.

NATS North Atlantic Track System.

NDB Nondirectional beacon, a simple navigation station that an aircraft can home in on or can fly away from on a desired straight line course.

Nomex An olive green fire resistant material from which flight suits and gloves are made.

Pitot-static System that supplies atmospheric pressure information to altimeters, airspeed indicators, and other instruments. (Pronounced "peeto-static.")

Prop wash Wind blast generated by an aircraft's propeller.

Radar vectors Instructions issued by a radar facility directing an aircraft to fly a certain compass heading.

Radome The nose of an aircraft, which houses a radar antenna.

RAF Royal Air Force, the air force of Her Majesty, the Queen of England.

Reporting points Points identified by latitude and longitude over which aircraft not in radar contact must report their time and altitude of passage to the controlling agency.

ROTC Reserve Officer Training Corps, the curriculum through which college students earn commissions as officers in the various U.S. military services.

RSU Runway supervisory unit.

SAC Strategic Air Command.

SAR Search-and-rescue operations.

SKE Station Keeping Equipment.

Slipstream The rush of air around an aircraft in flight.

Special instructions Guidance, issued to aircrews, with regard to a specific combat operation.

SPINS Special instructions.

Stall A condition in which the airflow over a wing becomes turbulent rather than smooth, causing a sudden loss of lifting power.

Stan/Eval Standardization/Evaluation, the office responsible for monitoring proficiency and job knowledge through periodic written tests and check flights, which is historically loathed by crew members.

Static discharge Explosivelike blast experienced when an electrical charge builds up on an aircraft and suddenly discharges into the surrounding air mass. Usually occurs in or near thunderstorms.

Tango Uniform International Phonetic Code for "tits up," i.e., broken, or out of commission.

TDY Temporary duty.

TJ Torrejon Air Base, Spain.

TRT Takeoff-rated thrust.

Turboprop A jet engine that spins a propeller.

UHF Ultra-high frequency, a frequency band used in most military aircraft communications.

UPT Undergraduate pilot training.

USAF United States Air Force.

UTA Unit training assembly, the weekend period of duty required once per month of guardsmen and reservists. Commonly referred to as "drill."

VFR   Visual flight rules, rules applied to aircraft flying in relatively good weather and not under positive control by a radar or a tracking facility.

VHF   Very high frequency, a frequency band used in most civil aircraft communications.

VOR   Very high frequency omnidirectional range, a reference to both onboard receivers and ground navigation facilities that allow aircraft to fly specific courses between stations.

Wake turbulence Disturbed flow of air left behind after an aircraft wing passes through. Can be violent and long lasting behind large aircraft.

Walk-around inspection External inspection performed by crew members before flight and between flights.

Zero fuel weight (ZFW) The weight of the aircraft plus its passengers and cargo, exclusive of fuel. The maximum fuel load is calculated by subtracting the ZFW from the maximum allowable takeoff weight.

ABOUT THE AUTHOR

Alan Cockrell is a commercial airline pilot. He spent twenty years in the Air Force, the Reserve, and the Air Guard. During the Persian Gulf War he logged almost 1,000 hours as a C-141 aircraft commander. He resides in Huntsville, Alabama.